Pregnancy in a High-Tech Age

Pregnancy

in a
High-Tech
Age

Paradoxes of
Choice

Robin Gregg

New York University Press
New York and London

NEW YORK UNIVERSITY PRESS
New York and London

Library of Congress Cataloging-in-Publication Data
Gregg, Robin, 1953–
Pregnancy in a high-tech age : paradoxes of choice / Robin Gregg.
p.   cm.
Includes bibliographical references and index.
ISBN 0-8147-3067-1   ISBN 0-8147-3075-2 (pkb.)
1. Pregnancy—Decision making.   2. Pregnancy—Psychological
aspects.   3. Prenatal diagnosis—Decision making   4. Choice
(Psychology)   5. Social control.   I. Title.
RG556.G74 1995
618.2'4—dc2094   -39520
                    CIP

New York University Press books are printed on acid-free paper,
and their binding materials are chosen for strength and durability.

Manufactured in the United States of America

10 9 8 7 6 5 4 3 2 1

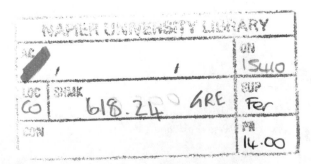

Contents

PREFACE   VII

ONE   Introduction   1

TWO   American Politics, Feminism, and the   9
       Rhetoric of Choice

THREE Choosing Pregnancy   29

FOUR   Choosing a Health Provider   40

FIVE   The Meaning of Chosen Pregnancy   54

SIX   Risky Choices: Decisions about Prenatal   85
       Diagnosis

SEVEN Pregnancy and Choice in a High-Tech   129
       Age

APPENDIX A   The Women in the Study   149

APPENDIX B   A Methodological Note   155

              Notes   161

              Selected Bibliography   183

              Index   199

Preface

Medical research, medical practice, policy analysis, and academic research in general have long been conducted from the vantage point of men, with women left out or disregarded entirely; implicitly included in the category of "men" and therefore assumed to be the same as men; or, more recently, with women and our perspectives "added in" at some later point. This book is part of a burgeoning literature—in the social sciences, bioethics, law, the popular press—about human reproduction, women's procreative choices, and related concerns (e.g., genetics; maternal/fetal conflict). Some of the medical literature—medical textbooks and official policy statements and recommendations by the American College of Obstetrics and Gynecology, for example—acknowledges that prenatal tests involve both risks and benefits, but women's subjective and varying perceptions of those risks and benefits are generally not addressed. Popular literature written for "lay" readers also tends to neglect differences among women, with some notable exceptions, such as Robin J. R. Blatt's *Prenatal Tests* (1988); Barbara Katz Rothman's *The Tentative Pregnancy* (1986), and the Boston Women's Healthbook Collective, *The New Our Bodies Ourselves* (1992), that incorporate an awareness of women's diversity.

The stories told to me by thirty-one New England women illuminate the complexity of their experiences of pregnancy and choice, and demonstrate differences among women that are often glossed over within medical and popular literature. This book is based on the stories and standpoints of a small group of women. They share both commonalities and differences. All of them are white, middle-class, and have male husbands or partners. All have chosen to become biological as well as social mothers. Why should we be interested in these women's stories? I share with a growing group of feminist researchers and theorists the belief that making women's stories the central focus of research and starting place for theorizing helps us see the world differently and more accurately. Outside of the feminist literature on procreative technologies (and even to some extent within some feminist theories, as I argue in this book) the complex and paradoxical aspects of pregnancy and procreative technologies for women in general, and specific groups of women in particular, are rarely acknowledged.

This book is part of a large feminist literature about women's experiences, and an example of an approach promoted and demonstrated in the work of numerous feminist scholars during the last twenty years (and in the writings of some nineteenth-century social scientists such as Jane Addams, Harriet Martineau, and Ida B. Wells; for more on these and other nineteenth-century foremothers, see Shulamit Reinharz, *Feminist Methods in Social Research,* 1992). Called by various names—women's standpoint(s) research, research for women, feminist research—the approach begins with the stories of "ordinary" women. Practitioners of this approach (and allied approaches, such as rediscovering and communicating the stories of exemplary or exceptional women of the past) seek to challenge the male bias inherent in much previous scholarship; help give voice to women, as members of underrepresented populations; expose the gendered character of social reality; create new models of working and theorizing; and develop policies, practices, and theories that promote women's interests and are based on women's actual experiences.

Given the importance and validity of research and writing that makes women and their experiences central, why should we be interested in these particular women? After all, they comprise a largely homogeneous group, at least in terms of widely recognized social categories such as race, class, and (perhaps) sexual orientation. Their families and places of origin, work experiences, and ethnicities are diverse: their backgrounds are Catholic, Jewish, Protestant, Anglo-Saxon, German, Italian, Irish, Anglo-Canadian, French-Canadian, Russian, Scottish, Scandinavian, Eastern European, Portuguese. Their points of view, too, are different from one another. These New England women's perceptions and stories demonstrate that women experience and understand pregnancy and choice in a multiplicity of ways that cannot easily be categorized. Their stories illustrate the existence of diversity within presumed homogeneity.

Individually, these women's stories are fragments and, as a group, quilt pieces in a much larger patchwork. Listening to the voices of ordinary women (as well as women more widely recognized for their accomplishments) and analyzing the nuances, contradictions, and ambiguities in their stories helps us see and understand the full range of women's experiences. These women are worth listening to, even as we remember that my analysis of their stories cannot be extended to other groups of women without further research. My intent in illuminating some of the ways women perceive and make choices about pregnancy is not meant to suggest that differences among women make all generalizations or policy-making impossible. Rather, I wish to suggest that we take such differences into account when we develop theory, construct policies, and devise practice protocols.

I have quoted the women directly as much as possible, to present their views in their own voices. This book is not an example of conversation or discourse analysis, and I did not use a coding system to note pauses, silences, or tones of voice. In the quotes in the book three dots (. . .) indicate places where portions of a woman's quote have been omitted. I truncated some of the longer quotes to eliminate redundancies, highlight the essence of what a woman said, and avoid having the reader wade repeatedly through long quotes. In doing so, I have tried to remain true to the original sense of what each woman said, to preserve the content as well as the meaning(s)—to her—of her comments.

Regarding my argument that these women perceived themselves as intentional actors in their own lives and must be recognized as such, I am reminded of Mary Catherine Bateson's compelling portraits of women's lives and choices in her book *Composing a Life* (1989, repr. 1990). Bateson's intermingled portrayal of her own story and the stories of four of her friends provides a picture of women's lives as "works in progress." That picture of women's lives is consistent with my conclusion that women's choices are both illusory and real. As "expert witnesses" of their own lives, women's interpretations of those lives must be honored and respected. Valorizing women means attending to their perspectives, whether or not those perspectives conform to our theoretical, political, or personal predilections. I suggest that we do this not with the aim of ignoring our intellects or our politics, but instead, as a way to inform and ground our intellectual and political endeavors.

That I can offer these women's stories and my analysis is possible because of the generosity and support of many people, too many to thank individually. Those who really made my research possible, of course, are the thirty-one women I interviewed, whose words are included in this book. They shared their time, stories, and insights, and believed my questions were worth asking and answering. I am most grateful to all of them. To preserve their anonymity, I will refrain from mentioning them each by name. I hope they recognize themselves in these pages, appreciate the times I captured their perceptions, and forgive me for the times I did not.

I wish to thank many other people who shaped my thinking and sustained me over the years. The members of my study group, originally a dissertation support group, gave me love and inspiration during the last eight years. For their intellectual, political, and emotional support, their sisterhood and their laughter (and their flowers, books, and chocolate), I offer my appreciation and love to Carol Hardy-Fanta, Jennifer Jackman, Maggie Martin, and Beth Miller.

The members of my doctoral dissertation committee provided encouragement, constructive criticism, and innumerable insights during the planning, research, and writing phases that culminated in the dissertation from which this book is adapted. For their questions and their suggestions—as well as their ongoing support—I thank Louise Levesque-Lopman, Shulamit Reinharz, Deborah A. Stone, and Irving K. Zola. They and a large, wonderful group of feminist foremothers, sisters, and kindred spirits—some of whom I know only through their writings—have served as intellectual mentors.

I am grateful to Patricia Herlihy, Esther Griswold, and Eileen Rawnsley for helping to evaluate my original interview guide at an early stage of my research; Susan Bell and an anonymous reviewer for their suggestions about transforming the dissertation into a book; Jo Glorie for her superb editorial expertise; and Despina Papazoglou Gimbel, Jennifer Hammer, Niko Pfund, and Kathe Sweeney for their enthusiasm and assistance.

Many friends and colleagues have followed the progress of this project with keen interest, and helped me believe that the book actually would come to fruition. My thanks especially to Mitzi Bales, Patricia A. Geller, Andrea Gilbert, Susan S. Helton, Helen Bequaert

(Becky) Holmes, Regina Kenen, Nina Shandloff, and Dorothy C. Wertz.

Finally, in an era of much rhetoric about "the family," I wish to express gratitude to mine. Billy D. Horton, my husband, is a questioner of everything. He has shared his critical analysis of social reality and his commitment to social justice, providing me with intellectual and political companionship for nearly twenty years. Without his emotional and material support, this book would not have been possible. My parents, Andrew Philip Gregg and Jeane Goldstein Gregg, also questioners, have given me unwavering affection and approval. Their opinions and actions continue to inspire me, and their presence in my life continues to sustain me in innumerable ways. My brother, Kenneth Donald Gregg, shares his sensitivity, good sense, and humor, able always to prompt laughter from his oldest sister. My sister, Nina Gregg, provides me with friendship and intellectual food for thought. She offered a listening ear at many crucial moments during my writing, and acted as a volunteer research assistant, sending pertinent news clippings and bibliographic citations. Douglas A. Gamble, Clerissa Ellen Goad Horton, James Edgar Horton, the rest of the Horton family, and Monet M. Monaghan provide me with care and affirmation. It is with much love and many thanks that I dedicate this book to my family.

Introduction

When I first met Sarah Worthington,[1] on a morning in early December, she was in her kitchen. I had traveled on winding country roads, by fields and farm stands still laden with late autumn pumpkins and apple cider, to reach her Victorian-era home just outside a small New England village. The radio in the kitchen was tuned to a station playing classical music. She offered me a cup of tea and a slice of just-baked cake. We moved into another room to begin the interview. We sat in comfortable chairs and, between sips of tea and tastes of cake, I asked her to talk about her current pregnancy. Her four-year-old son played happily in an adjacent room, occasionally wandering over to his mother to ask her a question. The morning sunshine of early winter streamed through the windows, and we talked. In subsequent weeks and months, I drove through more New England countryside, villages, and towns to talk with other women at their homes or offices. I drove on snowy roads and then the muddy ones of early spring. The changing rural scenery I enjoyed on my drives and the pastoral settings of many of the women's homes provided a contrasting backdrop to their stories of visits to doctors' offices, prenatal diagnosis centers, and hospitals, where they experienced a variety of high-technology procedures.

The pregnancy stories of the thirty-one New England women I interviewed contained descriptions of multiple prenatal visits and tests. Most of the women told me about pregnancies that were scheduled, measured, and monitored. These women used and were offered many tests before and during their pregnancies. Some tests, such as ovulation predictor kits or do-it-yourself pregnancy tests, were self-administered at home, whereas others, such as infertility tests, blood tests, and prenatal diagnostic tests, took place in doctors' offices, hospitals, or laboratories. All but one of the women were offered one or more high-tech procedures by their doctors, and most of them experienced some form of prenatal diagnostic technology. Sarah Worthington, for example, experienced a variety of high-tech procedures during her current pregnancy: ultrasound, chorionic villi sampling, and maternal serum alphafetoprotein screening.[2]

Pregnancy in the late twentieth century is pregnancy in a high-tech age. Pregnant women—those with access to prenatal care, that is—in the United States and other industrialized countries experience more medical innovations and procreative interventions than ever before.[3] Pregnancy has increasingly become redefined as a process requiring medical and technological intervention, even before a woman becomes pregnant. Fertility testing, techniques of "assisted conception" (e.g., in vitro fertilization, embryo transplant), tests to confirm pregnancy, prenatal screening and diagnosis, fetal monitoring, induced labor, and cesarean sections have become normal, if not expected, components of contemporary childbearing. But the development and use of technologies such as in vitro fertilization and prenatal diagnosis have led to a paradox. The technologies enhance both the range of choices for women and the possibility of greater social control of those choices. This book is about the ways women experience pregnancy and choice in this paradoxical context.

Procreative Technologies: A Paradox of Choice and Social Control

Procreative technologies can be liberating for women by extending reproductive choice. Three of the women I interviewed, Blossom Hunneycutt, Nancy Wilson, and Barbara Smith, became pregnant and gave birth after successful infertility treatments, for example. Women with fertility problems may welcome medical interventions such as the use of fertility drugs or treatments. Though some women eventually may have become pregnant without the treatments—Barbara Smith suggested that her baby might have been the result of her move from a city to rural New England, rather than an outcome of all the tests and procedures she experienced, for example—others might never have been able to conceive or carry a pregnancy to term without medical intervention. Some women welcome conceptive techniques of "assisted reproduction," such as in vitro fertilization or embryo implantation, which enable them to attempt to bear children. In vitro fertilization (IVF) and gamete intra-fallopian transfer (GIFT) are costly, invasive procedures with low success rates. Nevertheless, the existence of these and related technologies offers infertile women the possibility of procreative choice. Nancy Wilson told me she probably would have attempted in vitro fertilization had she not become pregnant when she did, and other women were clearly grateful for the technologies available to them, whether or not they chose to use a particular test.[4] The women I interviewed did not use conceptive technologies such as IVF and GIFT, though; thus, this book does not address them.

Some women view prenatal diagnostic procedures such as amniocentesis and chorionic villi sampling as technologies that enable choice. Women who are carriers for genetic conditions may wish to consider the information offered by prenatal diagnosis as they make decisions about attempting pregnancy or carrying a pregnancy to term. Women at higher risk of bearing a child with Down syndrome because they are over the age of thirty-five may welcome the reassurance provided by a negative prenatal diagnosis. As Sarah Worthington said, "Let's put it this way. I'm forty years old, and without the diagnostic tests that are available I wouldn't have risked a pregnancy." In these instances the technologies may provide women with the possibility of choices that can yield them greater procreative control.

On the other hand, procreative technologies may provide new avenues for medical and social intrusion into women's procreative processes, their bodies, and their lives. For some women the technologies may represent unwelcome interventions, and may force them to make burdensome, agonizing choices. Such decisions include the choice to use expensive, risky techniques to attempt medically assisted conception (e.g., in vitro fertilization) or to discontinue the attempt following repeated failures, or the decision to terminate or continue a wanted pregnancy following a positive or ambiguous prenatal diagnosis.

Once a medical technique becomes routinized, the element of choice regarding its use can become obscured or overlooked. Standard medical protocols can lead to a priori assumptions on the part of

doctors and their patients about the necessity for particular procedures. When Barbara Sanders first visited her doctor's office after
learning she was pregnant, for example, the receptionist asked her to
schedule an amniocentesis—*before* meeting the doctor or having an
initial prenatal visit. When doctors assume that certain tests are a
routine part of care, they may schedule those tests without informing
the patient or asking her to make a decision. As additional technologies become routine features of prenatal care, women may lose the
freedom to choose not to use them or the information they provide.
When pregnant women assume that certain tests will be part of their
prenatal care (e.g., amniocentesis for pregnant women who are
thirty-five years old or older), they may not realize they can choose
whether or not to have them. And when alphafetoprotein screening
takes place routinely as part of the laboratory analysis of a pregnant
woman's blood, for example, she may not even know that the test
has been conducted.

The "genetics revolution" may well contribute to the routinization
of further medical interventions in pregnancy. New genetic information—about genetic "markers" that signal the predisposition to particular genetic conditions, for example—is now available as a result
of international human genome research. As additional genetic information is discovered and disseminated, and as additional forms of
prenatal diagnosis are developed, patients, physicians, genetic counselors, and policy-makers increasingly will be faced with sensitive
ethical and political choices about pregnancy and technology: How
will the new genetic information be used and who decides? Which
prenatal tests, if any, should be offered routinely to pregnant women?
Should any tests be mandated, and if so, for which women and which
conditions? Who should pay for such testing? Will a woman or her
children be penalized if the woman chooses not to have a particular
prenatal test? Who controls the new genetic information? Is there
such a thing as genetic privacy? How can genetic discrimination
be prevented? Should doctors withhold particular kinds of genetic
information from patients, family members, or third parties such as
insurance companies or employers?

Procreative technologies and genomic research already have engendered much controversy. Feminists, bioethicists, social scientists,
and health providers have raised questions about genetic privacy, the
danger of genetic discrimination, the stigmatization of people with

disabilities, and the increased medicalization and social control of women's procreative processes.

How do women experience pregnancy and make pregnancy-related choices in this context? The women I interviewed provided no unanimous answer to this question. Their experiences were individual and particular; women's experiences of pregnancy and their pregnancy-related choices cannot be summarized in monolithic or universal terms. But there were commonalities among the women's stories, and this book highlights two of them. First, in making choices before and during pregnancy, these women considered many things: their past choices, their current personal and social circumstances, their definitions of risk, and their potential future choices. This complicated process of making choices was demonstrated in the women's decision-making about becoming pregnant, choosing a doctor, and deciding about prenatal tests, as described in chapters 3, 4, and 6. They made choices by considering relational and contextual factors. The processes they used to make decisions, their "ways of choosing," were complex and their choices were intertwined with one another.

The second commonality among the women in the study was that their experiences of pregnancy and their choices during pregnancy were characterized by ambiguity and contradictions. For them, pregnancy entailed feelings of uncertainty and ambivalence. Their choices were paradoxical: simultaneously real and illusory.

These two findings are interconnected. The women I interviewed used complicated decision processes to make choices in an effort to control their procreative destinies. When control proved elusive, they made additional choices. The women attempted to transform situations in which they experienced little or no control by making additional choices and taking additional actions. This ongoing quest for control was illustrated in many ways: choosing to become pregnant, but when unsuccessful, making choices to feel empowered in that situation, such as choosing to try infertility treatments or choosing to let nature take its course; deciding to have a home birth, seeking a health provider to assist with that birth, failing to do so, then making new choices about childbirth in a context of limited options; responding to unanticipated problems during pregnancy, such as miscarriage, by making particular choices about subsequent pregnancies.

That the women made choices over and over again, carefully

considering multiple factors, in an effort to exert control to the greatest extent possible is not a surprise. After all, most people use this kind of decision-making in many aspects of their lives. We adapt to changes in our personal circumstances and social environment in part by making additional choices, as a way to take charge of our lives.

The advent of high-technology pregnancy, like the advent of high-technology medicine in general, carries with it an assumption about control. The idea that using procreative technologies will result in predictable outcomes—becoming pregnant, carrying to term a healthy pregnancy, experiencing a safe childbirth, and giving birth to a healthy baby—is an often unstated assumption communicated (inadvertently or not) to women by their health providers, friends, family members, and the popular media. This assumption of control contains within it the seeds of potential disappointment. When women have experiences that demonstrate the limits of their procreative choices (as well as the limits of technology), the illusory aspects of that control—the ways control is, ultimately, unattainable, despite rhetoric, promises, or hopes to the contrary—become very real.

The Paradox of Procreative Control: Illusory, Yet Real

"I see this pregnancy as an obstacle course," said Sarah Worthington, early in our first interview. I had asked her, as I did with all of the women: "Tell me the story of your pregnancy." After a few moments of reflection, she described her decision to attempt to become pregnant, her first pregnancy, the birth of her first baby, and the deliberation that led to this, her second pregnancy. Like most of the other women in the study, she felt she had choices, and she worked consciously to make those choices, in an effort to exert control over her procreative processes. She did not play "reproductive roulette."[5] She also decided she wanted a woman physician, and she found and chose a medical practice with a woman physician.

Sarah Worthington wanted to maintain control of her body, her pregnancy, and her life. She had given birth to her first child four years before, when she was thirty-six. During that pregnancy, she chose to have amniocentesis for prenatal diagnosis. This time, she chose to have chorionic villi sampling. She planned to terminate the pregnancy in the case of a positive diagnosis:

I . . . know what our resources are . . . certain kinds of handicaps . . . we couldn't deal with . . . I don't think an abortion is an easy choice . . . to have to say goodbye to a handicapped child . . . Given the odds of Down syndrome . . . it seems to me silly, if not stupid, not to use whatever testing we have . . . I go through the testing to find out what it has to tell me.

The test results were negative, but she was still anxious about the pregnancy, because she was older this time and knew more about the risks associated with pregnancy and motherhood, and because she was experiencing some specific health problems: "I know that I shouldn't worry, but I do worry . . . my obstetrician told me I should bank some of my own blood, because . . . post-partum, I can hemorrhage. So, I'm sitting there thinking, this could really turn into a disaster . . . I'm not in a home-free zone by any means." Sarah Worthington's worries during this, the beginning of her second trimester, foreshadowed what she would experience following the birth of her baby.

Sarah Worthington had chosen to get as much information as possible during her pregnancy. She would not have chosen to become pregnant at age forty without the option of prenatal diagnosis. None of the tests she had—chorionic villi sampling; the maternal serum alphafetoprotein test; ultrasound—indicated that anything was wrong with her baby. But when he was born, he had numerous birth defects. His physical and neurological problems were so severe that, despite intensive, extensive treatment in a leading children's hospital, her son died on his sixteenth day of life.[6]

Sarah Worthington believed she had choices that would enable her to achieve a high degree of procreative control. She had tried to assert that control, to do all she could to guarantee a healthy pregnancy and healthy baby. In a telephone conversation a year after the death of her son, she told me of her shock, anger, and disappointment. She was enraged that she had done all she could—monitored her eating, took vitamins, avoided exposure to harmful chemicals at work and at home, chose a doctor whom she respected and trusted, and had prenatal tests designed to assess fetal health. But ultimately Sarah Worthington could not control her pregnancy, despite the choices she made in an attempt to do so. The medical expertise and technological interventions she chose did not predict or prevent her baby's problems or, ultimately, his death. She felt betrayed.

What can be learned from Sarah Worthington's story? Were other women able to attain some sense of control as a result of their prenatal choices? As it turned out, pregnancy was "an obstacle course" or "a gamble" for most of the women I interviewed. They made choices to eliminate or minimize the risks and pressures of pregnancy. In doing so, they attempted to take control of biological as well as social processes, their bodies and their social environments. But, like Sarah Worthington, they often found that true procreative control was elusive, if not illusory.

The idea that procreative choice may be more illusory than real is a theme within one strand of feminist thinking. Radical feminist and socialist feminist critiques of procreative technologies and developments in women's health care in general emphasize the dangers to women posed by the medicalization and "technologizing" of women's bodies and procreative processes. In contrast to liberal feminists, who generally maintain that access to procreative technologies increases women's choices, radical and socialist feminists suggest that these "choices" are socially constructed and constrained by patriarchal power. The women I interviewed experienced choice as both illusory and real. They depicted themselves as active agents, not passive victims of medicine or technology. But they also talked about the personal and social forces that constrained their procreative choices. The women's stories pose challenges to radical, socialist, and liberal feminist depictions of procreative choice, even as those same stories support certain aspects of the feminist analyses. I discuss these feminist perspectives in more detail in chapter 2.

American Politics, Feminism, and the Rhetoric of Choice

Choice is a central concept in American culture and politics. Its enduring salience is reflected everywhere: in television advertisements, the rhetoric of "choice" is used to sell everything from insurance policies to antacids to cars to lipsticks; in popular newsstand magazines, readers are urged to "choose the diet (or hairstyle or career or lover or skin care product) that is best for you." In public policy discussions, the importance of choice is proclaimed by journalists, academicians, and politicians who discuss issues such as school vouchers or the merits of Health Maintenance Organizations (HMOs), "managed competition," or a single-payer health-care system, with respect to maximizing consumer choice (i.e., choice of a school, doctor, or hospital). In electoral campaigns, candidates proclaim themselves "the people's choice" or "the choice for change."

The prevalence of the language of choice in popular culture and everyday discourse is not surprising, given the central place of the idea of choice in American politics. The rhetoric of choice is rooted in a long political tradition. Choice is a fundamental concept in Western liberal political theory and one of the dominant values of American political ideology in particular: "[T]he concept of choice, the desire for choice, and the experience of choice pervade modern life and reconstitute modern law to fit the culture of choice."[1] In the American political culture, rights, freedom, and individual choice are inextricably linked: the right to privacy, freedom of religion, freedom of expression, and other liberties guaranteed by law all entail the freedom to make individual choices.

The American emphasis on freedom of choice dates back to John Stuart Mill, who felt that "deliberation and the exercise of choice are the essence of what it means to be human and that therefore government should interfere with individual choice as little as possible."[2] John Stuart Mill's rejection of governmental paternalism, based on earlier British and European political traditions, is the basis of much of Western political thought regarding freedom of choice and individual autonomy. Mill's definition of liberty is freedom from undue governmental constraints, exemplified in American politics in the libertarian notion of minimal governmental interference in people's lives; it is a negative concept of liberty. This concept of liberty is proclaimed on every New Hampshire automobile license plate: "Live Free or Die." An example of personal choice in the context of this kind of liberty is a woman's choice to carry her pregnancy to term or have an abortion, where abortion is legal, not prohibited by law. This interpretation of liberty differs from a positive definition of liberty, one entailing the social provision of opportunities and resources which enable individuals to have, and exercise, choices.[3] In a situation reflecting a positive definition of liberty, a woman's choice to carry her pregnancy to term or have an abortion would not be constrained by law—abortion would be legal, in other words; in addition, though, society would ensure that she have the necessary resources to exercise her choice. She would have access to accurate and timely information about pregnancy and abortion; access to a facility where legal, safe abortions are provided; money or health insurance to pay for the procedure; transportation to and from the abortion clinic or health center; and the freedom to enter and exit the abortion clinic unimpeded if she chose to terminate her pregnancy. Society would also provide a woman with access to resources that would enable her to become a mother if she chose to carry her pregnancy to term, such as access to timely and affordable prenatal care; safe and accessible childbirth options; information about disability and the resources available to people with disabilities; child-care services and other social supports for child-raising.

In many cases, choices are not prohibited by law, but some choices require more than the absence of prohibition for their actualization. For example, as of this writing, pregnant women in the United States may choose legally to terminate their pregnancies, a result of the Supreme Court decision in the case of *Roe v. Wade* (1973); and pregnant women and their partners may decide to have a home birth, because home childbirth is not illegal. But abortion must be truly accessible for pregnant women to exercise the choice of pregnancy termination, as noted above; and health providers must support and insurance companies pay for home births to make childbirth at home a viable, accessible choice for pregnant women and their partners.

American liberalism entails a complicated and sometimes curious mix of the two types of liberty, with ramifications for choice in both theory and practice. The notions of choice that emerged from American liberal theory and its antecedents continue to motivate contemporary life; the complicated reality and the omnipresent rhetoric of choice continue to influence our choices and our interpretation of their meaning(s).

The importance of the idea and language of choice in contemporary American society is paralleled in contemporary American feminism, where women's choices about procreation, in particular, have received much attention. The right to choose is an essential value and a key organizing theme for feminist health activists and the women's health movement. The movement to protect a woman's right to a legal, safe abortion is called the "pro-choice" movement by its adherents, for example. Over the last twenty years or so, feminists have generated theory about women's procreative choices, and worked to preserve and enhance those choices. Feminists have been the strongest critics of mainstream, or "malestream," medical perspectives on women's procreative experiences and choices, and the strongest advocates for woman-centered theory and practice. Feminist perspectives on procreation and procreative technologies take varied forms; no monolithic feminist analysis exists. Making sense of the multiple, varied, and changing forms of feminism is no easy task, but many writers describe contemporary feminist theory by focusing on three major perspectives: liberal feminism; radical feminism, and socialist and/or Marxist feminism,[4] and I, too, have chosen to use this categorization in this chapter to convey some of the major features of feminist perspectives on procreative technologies and procreative choice.

Feminist Perspectives on Procreation and Choice

Liberal Feminism and Procreative Choice

The liberal feminist perspective suggests that women are, and should be, free to choose from a variety of procreative technologies and options. Liberal feminism, like the liberal political philosophy from which it developed, emphasizes individual rights and choices: individuals must have the right to pursue their own self-interest(s) in order to achieve equality, liberty, and happiness. Generally, the liberal feminist perspective suggests that procreative and reproductive technologies represent potential choices for women. There are different strands within liberal feminist thought, however. Some liberal feminists embrace a libertarian, or "classical" liberalism, based on the idea that individual choice is enhanced when it is least constrained by government. This form of liberal feminism is rooted in the ideas of Mary Wollstonecraft, John Stuart Mill, and Harriet Taylor.[5]

Many contemporary American liberal feminists depart from a strict libertarianism though, recognizing instead that women are prevented from pursuing their self-interests even in situations where those pursuits are permitted by law and not constrained explicitly by public policy. Women cannot exercise their choice(s) fully, due to sexist attitudes and practices—individual as well as societal—and the inequality of women and men. These "egalitarian" or "welfare" liberal feminists recognize that inequality between women and men is caused and perpetuated by sex role socialization in childhood, institutional sexism and discrimination, and the inequitable distribution of economic and social resources.[6] Only when those processes are changed will women's choices be equal to the choices available to men. This distinction between classical and welfare liberal feminism reflects the distinction between negative and positive forms of liberty. Libertarian feminists define liberty as the ability to make choices free from governmental barriers, wheras egalitarian or welfare feminists define liberty as the freedom to make, and the resources to actually exercise, choices.

To the liberal feminist, procreative and other medical technologies are neither inherently bad nor inherently good. Amniocentesis and other prenatal technologies are options, nothing more and nothing less. Prenatal tests such as amniocentesis, for example, offer pregnant women the option of getting information about their developing baby. Individual women can decide whether they wish to have this information and can decide whether to exercise further choices on the basis of that information. Liberal feminists differ in the degree to which they recognize the social barriers that constrain women's choices. Many liberal feminists advocate reforms in the ways procreative technologies are developed and distributed. Women should be involved in developing, using, evaluating, and distributing these technologies. Information about and access to the technologies should be available to all women: lesbian and heterosexual women, rural women, urban women, single women, married women, women with disabilities, women of all ages, social classes, races, religions, and ethnic groups, and all women should be free to choose whether or not to use them. Income, geography, and other barriers which prevent some women from having access to the tests should be removed.[7] But even when liberal feminists acknowledge women's unequal access to procreative technologies, they still suggest that once equal access to procreative technologies is assured, all women will have procreative freedom of choice. And this freedom of choice is a good thing, from the liberal feminist perspective.

Not all feminists who maintain the position that women are, and should be, free to choose whether or not to use procreative technologies would call themselves liberal feminists. I include in this category those feminists who suggest that procreative technologies can and do benefit individual women and argue that women should have the right to take advantage of those benefits, and those who reject the radical feminist idea that women's procreative choices are completely illusory.[8] From a liberal feminist perspective, defined as such, women like Sarah Worthington are free to make their own procreative choices. They have multiple options available to them, and need merely to consider those options carefully, weigh the ramifications of each potential choice, and then choose the best option(s). In this view, Sarah Worthington and other women are free to choose whether to become pregnant (or to attempt to do so), to choose a health provider, to choose whether or not to have prenatal tests, and so on. The presence of procreative and prenatal technologies—gamete intra-fallopian transfer (GIFT), in vitro fertilization (IVF), the maternal serum alphafetoprotein (AFP) test, ultrasound, amniocentesis, chorionic villi sampling—gives women and their partners choices, and they may freely decide whether or not to exercise those choices.

In its emphasis on the importance of the individual decision-maker, her right to make choices based on her understanding of her own best interest(s), and the neutrality of the choices themselves, the liberal feminist perspective is consistent with the rational choice model of classical microeconomic theory, with its emphasis on individual preferences, costs, risks, and benefits. The rational choice model of decision-making, derived from the logic of mathematics, has influenced theory and research in economics, political science, policy analysis, cognitive psychology, sociology, communications, law, consumer studies, public health, and organizational theory. Rational decision models include: cost/benefit; risks/benefits; risks analysis; and choice, preference, or utility models. Rational choice models involve the quantification of decision-related variables and outcomes to explain, predict, and proscribe individual as well as organizational choices and behavior. Their proponents use the models to turn risks or uncertainties into statistical probabilities which can be predicted and weighted to come to a "rational" decision.[9]

Rational decision models involve choosing among alternatives to select the best solution, or the best means of achieving a particular goal. Focusing on the *outcomes* or consequences of decisions, these models are less concerned with decision *processes,* the ways people understand and make choices. In decision analysis, one form of a rational choice model, outcomes are evaluated by calculating their probability or likelihood of occurrence and their "subjective expected utility" (SEU), and "plugging" the resulting figures into a decision tree. For the accurate use of such a model, all courses of action, all probabilities, and all outcomes must be considered.[10] This is one reason rational decision models have been widely criticized: it is difficult, if not impossible, to know all possible outcomes or all possible influences on those outcomes.[11]

Few people accept a totally "pure" rational model, but social science literature is full of variations of the model. Rational choice models are used to assess the social and environmental risks of industrial technologies, to evaluate the consequences of health and safety regulations, and to make determinations about the value of offering mass population screening for conditions such as sickle cell anemia and cystic fibrosis. The health behavior model, a variation of a rational decision model, is used to examine patients' perceptions of risks, costs, and benefits to understand behaviors such as patient compliance with medical treatment and decisions about genetic screening. The model suggests that people's feelings of susceptibility to disease, their perceptions of the disease's severity, and their ideas about the benefits and barriers involved influence their health behavior.[12] Early versions of the model incorporated "modifying factors" such as demographics, psychosocial, and structural variables, and later formulations incorporate social learning theory and perceptions of self-efficacy.[13]

Even proponents of the rational decision model acknowledge that it may not capture actual human decision processes. Herbert Simon's notion of "bounded rationality" is one of the most well-known adaptations of the rational choice model. He suggests a behavioral model of decision-making in which people essentially compromise, or "satisfice," by simplifying complex choices and setting attainable, satisfactory goals instead of seeking to optimize or maximize utility.[14] Even this modified view of rational choice, though, assumes that people use a conscious process of decision-making that involves consideration of the costs and benefits of a range of choices.

Two critiques of the rational choice model are most relevant to an analysis of women's ways of making choices about pregnancy, prenatal tests, and other procreative technologies. These critiques also may be used to assess the limitations of liberal feminist perspectives on women's procreative choices. First, the rational choice model is overly individualistic. The model assumes a single decision maker, "who has the psychological capacity and legal authority to make a coherent, single decision."[15] The model ignores the social nature of attitude formation and the fact that "humans' experience of their environment is mediated by conceptual categories which are fabricated in social intercourse."[16] The model neglects the social construction of individual decision processes and outcomes, and excludes the ways individuals are influenced by their social location, their relationships, and by "moral or political feedback." In the pure rational model, the individual decision-maker is isolated, and "the rational agent of theory is deculterated."[17] Just as many microcconomists and other rational choice theorists pay inadequate, if any, attention to the impediments that constrain individuals' ability to transform their preferences into rational choices, liberal feminists sometimes underemphasize, if not overlook entirely, those social forces that impede or coerce particular choices and construct and maintain the very notion of choice itself.

The second major criticism of the rational choice model is that its purported objectivity obfuscates its political uses and their consequences. For one thing, choosing to use the model is, in itself, a political or strategic choice because of the assumptions about human behavior that the model entails.[18] The model ignores the impacts of configurations of power, or "relations of ruling,"[19] on the processes of goal setting and choosing alternatives, and also disregards the political consequences of making particular choices.

The rational choice model is often presented by its advocates in a way that is not self-critical. Problems that might arise during the practical application of the model—such as a lack of adequate or accurate information for rational decision-making—are minimized and characterized as "market failures" by proponents of free market liberalism, for example. Similarly, liberal feminists stress the importance of "informed choice" in decision-making, assuming that women who have enough information about their procreative options and the potential consequences of those options will be able to make choices in their own best interest. The notion is that information is power. Unfortunately, though, the liberal feminist perspective does not adequately address the political character of the production and distribution of information itself, or effectively analyze the interests served by the differential distribution of particular kinds of ostensibly neutral information.

The rational choice model also ignores the politics of the choices themselves; the "menu" of particular options from which to choose is in itself influenced by politics and power. In addition, the model's reliance on sophisticated mathematical calculations places it in the hands of experts and out of the hands of ordinary people.

The individualistic orientation, claims of objectivity, and reliance on expertise which characterize the rational choice model of decision-making reflect features of contemporary American culture which have been criticized by feminists. Yet liberal feminism implicitly accepts a rational choice model, by focusing on the importance of individual women's choices and overlooking the inherently political nature of competing definitions of choice. Liberal feminism also tends to forget the potential implications of women's individual choices, for other women, the community, and society at large. The individualistic, uncritical response of many liberal feminists to procreative technologies and their implicit acceptance of a rational choice model of decision-making contrasts dramatically with the perspectives of radical feminism. Many radical feminists reject the notion that procreative technologies provide women with choices, and strongly criticize the development and use of these technologies, suggesting they have many negative implications for women and society.

Radical Feminism and Prenatal "Choice"

The dominant radical feminist perspective on procreative technologies and choice suggests that "choice" is illusory, because women's procreative (and other) choices are constructed and constrained by male domination and patriarchal power. Radical feminism addresses the impacts of gender and biology on women and their choices, and some radical feminists also address the interrelated impacts of race, class, and culture. From this perspective, the rhetoric of choice obscures the power imbalances that result from gender and other forms of inequality and "assumes a society without differential distribution of power and authority."[20] In this view, women who feel they have choices have internalized the dominant cultural ideology and are experiencing a form of false consciousness.

The radical feminist critique of procreative technologies is lodged in a larger critique of the ways medicine and technology have been used for the social control of women. Concerns about the social and medical control of women by men and malestream institutions are based in part on the fact that as women's procreative processes have become highly medicalized, interventions often have become routinized, without adequate consideration of their long-range negative effects on women or their children.

Radical feminists emphasize the social construction of women's "choices," and radical feminist critics of technology examine interactions between technology and the social environment. The existence of technologies may in fact lead to the "choice" to use them. Rather than being developed to meet particular human needs, some technologies may be discovered or developed first, before they have specific uses. Once a technology becomes scientifically possible, people seek to find ways to use it: "solutions seek the problems they might be able to solve." Demands for technologies are determined, at least in part, by their availability.[21]

Some technologies are developed for particular uses, and then applied in additional ways. Sonography, for instance, was developed initially for military use and now is widely used for prenatal screening and diagnosis. After medical uses are developed for particular technologies, medical students and doctors are taught about them. Doctors then "offer" the technologies, such as ultrasound and other prenatal screening and diagnostic techniques, to their patients. Even when the technologies are presented to women as choices by their doctors, though, these offerings sometimes are made and perceived as implicit, if not explicit, recommendations. Women then ask for the procedures, doctors continue to offer and perform them, and the ensuing consumer "demand" for their use contributes to the development of a medical standard of care. Doctors then conform to the standard of care, bolstered by peer pressure, professional guide-lines, and the specter of legal liability, and women patients continue to expect and request the tests.[22]

Procreative "choice," in this context, is influenced, if not deter-mined, by social expectations and feelings of responsibility. Doctors feel bound to offer patients the available technologies, and patients feel compelled to use them. Acting as if the technologies do not exist is no longer possible; the existence of the technologies provides a powerful impetus for their use: "From now on, doing nothing will be evidence of negligence, lack of concern, pig-headedness or inepti-tude."[23] From this perspective, choice is a misnomer. Furthermore, what passes for choice may not result in procreative control for women.

Robyn Rowland suggests that recent procreative technologies do not provide women with real choices or greater control, since it is not women who control their development and use. She distinguishes between reproductive choice and reproductive control: "Within the area of abortion, we claimed 'the right to choose,' but I argue that we mean the 'right to control' our own bodies. We have then to ask whether the new reproductive technologies give women greater con-trol over our lives."[24] For real choice to exist, women must determine the menu, as well as the context, of choices.

Many radical feminists view procreative technologies as dangerous tools of oppression, not techniques which empower women. Unlike liberal feminists, for whom reproductive and procreative technologies are ethically neutral (i.e., it is in their use or their distribution that they become good or bad), some radical feminists claim the technol-ogies themselves are problematic, controlling women rather than leading to women's empowerment.

Radical feminists point to the power of science and technology in America, and assess the deterministic elements found in some technologies. Technologies have "valences," biases or charges that are "analogous to that of atoms that have lost or gained electrons through ionization." Technological systems and individual technol-ogies have "a tendency to interact in similar situations in identifiable and predictable ways."[25] Without positing a strict technological de-terminism, these feminists describe the ways technological "fixes" have become the norm in America and other Western societies, and illuminate some of the problems caused by technology, which addi-tional technologies then are often developed to solve.[26]

Feminist abolitionists[27] such as Maria Mies, and members of the Feminist International Network of Resistance to Reproductive and Genetic Engineering (FINRRAGE),[28] have called for an end to any further development of genetic engineering and procreative technologies. Maria Mies notes that the commodification of women's bodies caused by procreative technologies is consistent with "the logic of the natural sciences," which is based on "exploitation and domination over nature, exploitation and subjection of women, exploitation and oppression of other peoples."[29] Procreative technologies take women's reproductive processes out of their hands and place those processes in the hands of medical and scientific experts, many of whom are male. This expropriation of women's bodies and procreative processes has a long history, including the displacement of female healers and midwives by male midwives and doctors, the replacement of social childbirth at home by routine hospital births, and the routine use of fetal monitors.[30] This legacy provides evidence for contemporary radical feminists who see procreative technologies as additional tools for the social control of women.

Contemporary radical feminist critiques of the increased emphasis and reliance on prenatal technologies by doctors are in the tradition of earlier feminist analyses of childbirth, in their emphasis on the social control functions of medical technologies and the ways the medical establishment has taken procreative processes out of women's hands.[31] Feminists' concerns about the social control implications of procreative technologies and their warnings that the uses of these technologies may harm women—whether or not they view the potential uses of the technologies as positive—are grounded in reality. The ability of women to maintain control of our procreative processes has been threatened in the past by (male) medical and corporate power. Women's experiences with the IUD and DES are two well-known examples. More recently, feminists have expressed concerns about the use of in vitro fertilization and other conceptive technologies, the routine provision of Norplant to teen women attending Baltimore public schools, and the possible uses of information gained as result of the human genome project, among other developments potentially threatening to women.[32]

Radical feminism, like liberal feminism, may be divided into "subperspectives" though, and some radical feminists have welcomed technologies such as in vitro fertilization, seeing them as tools for women's liberation. This perspective on procreative technologies is exemplified by the work of Shulamith Firestone, who claimed that such technologies offer women the prospect of liberation from the constraints of biology. To Firestone, procreative technologies are potentially liberating for women; her view entails a pro-technology form of radical feminism.[33] Radical feminists who support Firestone's perspective point to the ways procreative technologies have helped women overcome the limits of biology; lesbian women have used alternative insemination to become pregnant, for example.

Firestone's position seems inconsistent with the critique of procreative technologies and women's procreative choices in other radical feminist writings, but she, like other radical feminists, recognizes and cautions that "male supremacy and partriarchal institutions will continue to determine the role that technological advancements play in oppressing women" in the absence of major changes in ideology and social structures.[34] Firestone's perspective is quite different from another form of radical feminism, which celebrates women's biological, "natural" abilities—most notably, the ability to procreate. These radical feminists take the "positive essentialist" view that women's "natural" procreative abilities and the biological ability to become a mother are sources of potential power and pride for women. Firestone's perspective can be called negative essentialism, in contrast, as she sees those same biological abilities as barriers to women's liberation.

The valorization of female biology by some radical feminists is connected with the idea that male "womb envy" is the reason for patriarchal attempts to control women's procreative processes.[35] These feminists oppose developments in procreative technologies because those developments interfere with women's procreative processes and experiences and allow men to take control of those processes.[36]

Differences among varieties of radical feminism with respect to the analysis of women's choices about procreative technologies stem in part from very different perspectives on mothering and sexuality. These differences are reflected in the lack of a monolithic feminist position on topics such as surrogate motherhood and pornography. There is a large and growing body of feminist literature on sexuality, childbearing, motherhood, childcare, and women's work and family roles, full consideration of which is beyond the scope of this book.

Radical feminists emphasize the complex relationship among individuals and society, paying particular attention to the ways women are oppressed by male-dominated institutions, male-based standards and policies, and a male-oriented culture—in short, by patriarchy. Some radical feminists would suggest that Sarah Worthington and the other women who chose to use amniocentesis or chorionic villi sampling for prenatal diagnosis were attempting to liberate themselves from the constraints of biology. By choosing to obtain information about their fetus(es), women who have prenatal diagnosis are attempting to take charge of their pregnancies, and thus their lives. But in a context where those technologies are developed and controlled by men, those attempts will meet with failure, and women cannot fully liberate themselves in a social context of male domination.

According to the dominant radical feminist perspective, Sarah Worthington and other women in this book are deluded when they feel they are making choices in their own best interest by using procreative technologies. They are rejecting their own, natural procreative processes—and therefore relinquishing a potential source of strength, pride, and identity—in favor of male-determined and male-controlled technological alternatives and interventions. From a radical feminist perspective, by choosing to use prenatal diagnosis, for example, Sarah Worthington and other women in the book have "bought into" a male, technocratic, model of pregnancy, consciously or not. Socialist feminists, too, are critical of procreative technologies and their impacts on women, but their analysis adds a dimension to the radical feminist perspective, by addressing the role of capitalism in preventing women from having true procreative choices.

Socialist Feminism and Prenatal Choice

The socialist feminist perspective combines the radical feminist critique of patriarchy with the socialist critique of capitalism's negative impacts on women. Socialist feminists suggest that intersecting forms of domination account for the inequality between women and men: the social relations of both production and reproduction support domination and exploitation, and the existence of that inequality prevents women from having real procreative choice.[37]

Socialist feminism may be compared with its sister form of feminism, Marxist feminism: "Whereas socialist feminists believe that gender and class play an approximately equal role in any explanation of women's oppression, Marxist feminists believe that class ultimately better accounts for women's status and function(s)."[38] Some theorists further distinguish between two varieties of socialist feminism: dual systems theory and unified systems theory. Dual systems theorists suggest that women are oppressed in separate spheres: class and gender, and unified systems theorists see class and gender oppression as inextricably connected and interdependent.[39] My description of socialist feminism is most consistent with the latter variety.

Socialist feminists object to procreative technologies for three major reasons. For one thing, the technologies have been developed and implemented by men. Second, they have been developed and implemented under capitalism, for profit, and, as a result, they contribute to the commodification of procreation. And finally, procreative technologies "contribute to women's alienation, by separating women from the products of their reproductive labor."[40]

That reproductive technologies have been developed and are used by men does not guarantee they will be used against women's interests. However, in the context of capitalist and patriarchal structures of domination, it is likely that such technologies will be used in ways that replicate existing societal power imbalances. Until existing configurations of power are transformed, it is likely that malestream medical developments will continue to reinforce women's oppression rather than serve women's interests.

Some socialist feminists argue that the use of these technologies in the context of a profit-driven capitalist economy contributes to the commodification of reproduction, in which babies become products and "children become luxury items . . . subjected to both quality control and quantity control."[41] The potential profitability of reproductive technologies has been well-documented.[42] An article in the *Boston Globe* described the competition among companies seeking a share of the $1 billion sales market for real-time ultrasound (a form of ultrasound that produces moving images,) for example.[43]

Procreative and other medical technologies are marketed by their manufacturers to physicians as well as patients, with a potential for exploitation of both groups: "Commercial laboratories need high volumes of tests in order to make their operations profitable, and many are competing in the market for physicians' and hospitals' business by offering special tests, or savings-by-volume."[44] Some laboratories routinely send announcements about new or improved tests to physicians, encouraging them to suggest the tests to their patients. Even when the particular techniques have not been evaluated or recommended by an appropriate professional medical organization (e.g., American College of Obstetricians and Gynecologists— ACOG,) such advertising can contribute to the development of a new standard of care. These marketing techniques sometimes involve additional inducements for doctors. In the case of new technologies for fetal monitoring, for instance, one manufacturer of devices for the home monitoring of fetuses recruited obstetricians to contribute $1,000 to become shareholders in its company. The doctors would then receive 15 percent of the payment for services prescribed by the physician shareholders.[45] Aside from the obvious conflict of interest such practices entail, they also demonstrate the way profit-based health care can create a demand for technologies that may or may not be needed, and may or may not be in the best interest of patients.

Socialist feminists have identified additional problems associated with the marketing and use of prenatal diagnosis, in particular. Though prenatal diagnosis is presented to women by doctors as choice-enhancing, its use places subtle constraints and pressures on women in terms of the "choice" to continue a pregnancy after a positive test result. Because prenatal diagnosis is concerned with the "products" of procreation—"healthy" babies—its use can minimize the processes of procreation (conception, pregnancy, and childbirth) and women's central role in them.

An emphasis on the "products" of procreation adds a "quality control" dimension to pregnancy. In this way the use of prenatal diagnosis can transform women into "fetal containers" and babies into products. Doctors and prospective parents use prenatal tests to screen for risk factors and diagnose specific fetal conditions. In the case of a positive prenatal diagnosis, the birth of a baby with particular genetic and other detectable conditions may be prevented through pregnancy termination. In other words, the tests are used to control who is, and who is not, born; they are used for eugenics. Perhaps one source of evidence for the feminist concern about the potential eugenic implications of prenatal diagnosis may be found in the fact that many geneticists in the United States, Canada, and the United Kingdom recently agreed that "the improvement of the general health and vigor of the population," one goal of eugenics, is important, and the majority of geneticists in those countries agreed that "the prevention of disease or abnormality" is an important goal of genetic counseling.[46] The eugenic implications of prenatal testing are one focus of feminist critiques: scientists and doctors are "developing the means to decide which lives are worth living and who should not inhabit the world."[47]

Feminists and others who raise questions about the use of prenatal diagnosis for individual child-bearing choices and mass population "quality control" base their concerns on historical precedent. The use of restrictive immigration and marriage laws and compulsory sterilization practices in the United States, Britain, and Germany has been well documented. In the United States, women of color, women on welfare, and women with mental retardation have been sterilized without their knowledge. As recently as a decade ago, statutes permitting the compulsory sterilization of people with mental retardation or mental illness still existed in fifteen states, and four states still authorized mandatory sterilization for people with epilepsy.[48] Feminists and others warn that new developments in procreative and genetic technologies may be a "backdoor to eugenics," even if they are not intended explicitly as state-controlled, population quality-control measures.[49]

The "perfection ideology" which leads to and reinforces policies and practices of human "quality control" is also a focus of the contemporary disability rights movement.[50] Prenatal screening and other attempts to guarantee "perfect babies" can stem from and enhance fears of disability, and perpetuate the stigma attached to people with disabilities. For women actually to have a choice, as Marsha Saxton has noted, the choice to have a disabled child must be included.[51] Most feminist disability rights activists vehemently support women's right to choose abortion, though there are exceptions. Alison Davis, a founder of the British group Disabled Women for Life, embraces an anti-abortion stance, for example.[52]

The perspective of most feminist disability rights activists and disability studies scholars entails an emphasis on the social context in which a woman's (and her partner's) choice to terminate a pregnancy occurs. In a society where individual disabilities are exacerbated and sustained because essential social supports are not available to people with disabilities, a woman's "choice" to terminate her pregnancy on the basis of a positive prenatal diagnosis is socially constructed. In such a context, even though her "choice" may not be the result of overt coercion, it may be the outcome of subtle pressures and social circumstances.

The third problem with reproductive technologies, from the perspective of socialist feminism, is the way they can alienate women from their own reproductive labor, fetuses, and babies. By promoting the medical treatment of two separate patients, technologies such as ultrasound help to create separate and potentially conflicting interests for women and their fetuses. When this happens, women's wishes may be overlooked or dismissed by doctors and others (e.g., the courts) when those wishes are deemed potentially dangerous to the fetus.[53]

Physicians now treat the woman, the "expectant mother," as well as the fetus during the course of pregnancy. With the development and use of prenatal technologies, doctors have access to more information about the fetus. Ultrasound, for example, has been described as a "window on the womb."[54] Fetology, a growing medical specialty, actually focuses on only one party during the pregnancy process: the fetus, with the woman's role relegated to that of a host for the growing fetus: "Far from being an inert passenger in a pregnant mother, the foetus is very much in command of the pregnancy. It is the foetus who guarantees the endocrine success of pregnancy and induces all manner of changes in maternal physiology to make a suitable host."[55] A focus on the fetus is a focus on the product, not the process of pregnancy. When the process is de-emphasized, the woman's role is, too.

With the recent emphasis on fetology, the pregnant woman has become two patients: herself and her fetus. When doctors consider pregnant women and their fetuses as different patients, with potentially different interests, determining whose interests come first in the case of medical interventions can become a difficult decision. When fetal interests come first, the woman becomes the "fetal container," no longer a person.[56]

There is ample evidence that an emphasis on the fetus can thwart pregnant women's autonomy. Pregnant women who are users of alcohol or illicit drugs have been sentenced to "preventive detention" in the name of fetal rights. Women have been charged with prenatal child abuse or neglect, despite the fact that, as Katha Pollitt notes, "by law the fetus is not a child."[57] Women have been arrested after giving birth to infants who test positive for drugs, and sentenced to drug treatment and birth control.[58]

Women in America have been forced by the courts to have cesarean sections in the ostensible interest of fetal well-being, and punitive policies have been applied to pregnant women accused of "prenatal child abuse" when their behavior has been deemed inappropriate or dangerous to the fetus. Two of the most widely cited examples of such cases are the stories of Angela Carder, in Washington, D.C., and Pamela Rae Stewart, in California. Carder, who was dying, was forced to undergo a cesarean section, though neither she nor her family members had consented to the procedure. She and the baby both died following the surgery. Stewart was accused of prenatal child abuse for not following medical advice while pregnant. She was ultimately acquitted.[59]

From a socialist feminist perspective, Sarah Worthington's and other women's procreative "choices" are linked to the social, political, and economic contexts in which they live. Sarah Worthington's decision to use prenatal diagnosis is socially constructed, an outcome of multiple social pressures and influences, not a real choice. She is a product of her culture, and, as such, cannot escape the power of a market-based society in which every action becomes a consumer choice. In a situation where the technologies are available to her, she is forced to make choices about them; furthermore, the technologies "make certain choices less profitable or downright impossible."[60]

As a wage earner in an individualistic, capitalist society, Sarah Worthington has to balance her ability to earn a living with her ability to meet the needs of a potentially "less-than-perfect" baby as well as the needs of her four-year-old. Her attempt to maximize her chances of having a healthy baby by using prenatal diagnosis is merely an example of the power of market capitalism, in which everything has become commodified, everything has a price, and everything is measured rationally, in terms of costs and benefits. And Sarah Worthington's feeling that she probably would choose to terminate her pregnancy in the case of a positive prenatal diagnosis is an example of the power of a perfectionist ideology that is an outgrowth of capitalism.

How Do Women Make Procreative Choices?

In liberal feminism and other largely noncritical perspectives on procreative technologies, choice and control often become conflated. The message is that women are free to make choices to use or refrain from using procreative technologies, and that the technologies, once chosen, will enhance women's personal, individual procreative control. But radical and socialist feminists make a distinction between choice and control, and question the reality of both. In assessing procreative technologies, radical and socialist feminists ask questions such as: "Who are the developers, the promoters, the 'experts'? Who benefits—which sex, which class, which race? How much does it cost, and who is going to pay?"[61]

Unlike liberal feminists, radical and socialist feminists examine the implications of the technologies and individual women's choices to use them in the context of larger questions. Radical feminists examine the social control of women and the role of technology in patriarchal society. Socialist feminists are concerned with the related impacts of patriarchy and capitalism on technology, and the social construction of an ideology of perfection. Radical and socialist feminists show how social forces construct choice—and how those forces promote the concept of choice itself.

To radical and socialist feminists, true procreative choice is a myth bolstered by the rhetoric of choice and the ideology it supports. Choice is a social construction that makes people feel free, even in a context of oppression, and supports the status quo: capitalism and patriarchy. These feminists counter the assumptions of their liberal sisters by showing how a capitalist society based on liberal principles transforms true control into the rhetoric of choice, and substitutes individual solutions for social ones.

The feminist analyses of procreative technology and choice raise important questions that deserve further consideration and elaboration, and a rapidly growing body of feminist scholarship continues to engage these and related issues. My brief description of feminist perspectives here cannot possibly do them justice. To capture that rich literature, to fully explicate the nuances, commonalities, and contradictions within various feminisms (including feminist perspectives I have not mentioned here),[62] and describe the ways diverse feminist perspectives overlap, influence each other, change, and grow, would require a very long book or several books, and that endeavor is not the purpose of this volume. Despite the existence of a rich feminist theoretical literature about women, procreation, and choice, though, there has been relatively little empirical research about the ways women actually perceive and make choices about procreative technologies.[63] Such studies can contribute to the development of a grounded feminist theory, by providing an understanding of women's procreative choices, from the standpoint of women speaking in their own voices.

My intent in describing some of the most well-articulated feminist perspectives on procreative technologies and choice is to illustrate the diversity of feminist thinking on these topics. It is a rare feminist who conforms completely to the principles of any one approach, and the particular feminists I have mentioned may not claim the labels I have used to describe their positions. I provide this discussion as a context for the consideration of women's actual experiences and procreative choices. One of the primary ways women try to take procreative control is in choosing whether, or when to attempt to become pregnant. That choice is the topic of the next chapter.

Choosing Pregnancy

Tell Me the Story of Your Pregnancy

When I asked Sarah Worthington to tell me the story of her pregnancy, she said, "this pregnancy was a long time in coming, psycho-
logically, not physically." She then talked about her experiences over
the last four years, as an "older first time mother," and mentioned
the joys and stresses that made her think "very long and hard" about
having a second child. She told me that during her twenties she did
not want children, and then suddenly, at age thirty, she "couldn't get
this idea out of my head."

Sarah Worthington became pregnant and gave birth to her first
child at age thirty-six. She started thinking about having another
baby when her first child was two years old. The desire for a second
child was "just a hankering," she said. She suggested that this hankering was a result of "biology plus emotions," because she "wasn't
intellectually, at all, ready to have another kid," with "a two-and-a-
half-year-old running around," and a job. But "the urge was there
before this one was conceived." Two years later, Sarah Worthington's son was four, and "I realized that if we let this slip a little bit
more, all hope of a sibling relationship would be gone . . . if I'd go
five, six, seven years, it would be like two only children."

Sarah Worthington and her husband had talked about eventually
creating a different life-style for themselves, perhaps in a more rural
setting than their current location on the outskirts of a small New
England village, perhaps even in a different country from the United

States. Thoughts of these possibilities influenced her thinking about becoming pregnant again:

In the back of my mind there's always . . . are we going to go and live in a different way, and what kind of family structure should we have to do that . . . I thought it would be a lot easier on two kids, than on one . . . you know, because we do actually want to create some kind of alternative lifestyle for ourselves. It would be an experience they could at least share . . . the retrospective analysis about it at some point in their lives.

In addition, "the timing seemed right," so she "threw away the birth control and I got pregnant, really on the first try."

In her response to my question Sarah Worthington mirrored the responses I heard from other women and would hear again from additional women during our conversations. When I asked women to tell me the story of their pregnancy, they talked about explicit as well as implicit choices. Explicit choices included the decision to attempt to become pregnant, the selection of a particular doctor or midwife, the decision to use prenatal tests, and the choice to learn the sex of the fetus, among others. Implicit choices often flowed from the explicit ones, and included the choice to give birth in a hospital after choosing a doctor who would not attend home births, to accept a fetus (or baby) without discovering its potential genetically related anomalies after refraining from prenatal diagnosis, and the choice to be surprised about the baby's sex instead of learning its sex from ultrasound or amniocentesis, for instance. These choices are examples of women's attempts to take charge of, or control, their own procreative processes, and thus, their lives.

For most of the women (twenty-four of the thirty-one), the first explicit procreative choices they made were about contraception and conception prior to the present pregnancy. Twenty-eight of the thirty-one women who talked with me chose deliberately to attempt to become pregnant now, but three of these were surprised when they actually became pregnant, two said that the pregnancy happened earlier than they had expected, and one woman had been trying to conceive and hoped she was pregnant at the time of our interview. The three women who had not planned this specific pregnancy deliberately chose to continue the pregnancy after conception. Thus, all of these women's pregnancies were wanted pregnancies.

All of the women talked about their pregnancies and choices in ways that reflected a kind of agency, a capacity to act deliberately.

The women I interviewed were not "taking chances" with respect to conception and contraception; they were not playing "reproductive roulette."[1] Of the three women who told me their pregnancy was an "accident" or a "surprise" (Betty Mell, Sarah Abraham, Anna Simas), all had decided to carry any future pregnancy to term before conceiving this pregnancy.

Choices Have Contexts

The women I interviewed were at a point in their lives where they had decided to become mothers and/or were mothering young children. The experiences of pregnancy comprised only a part of each woman's total procreative and mothering experiences, and those experiences, in turn, comprised only part of her total life experience.

When I asked women to tell me the story of their pregnancy, they started talking about feelings and choices that predated the pregnancy. The women who had experienced earlier pregnancies compared them to the present pregnancy, and all of the women talked about the decision to become pregnant in the context of other, earlier decisions. Such choices included the decision to get married and decisions about employment, school, or moving to a particular geographic locale.[2] Jill Anderson was the sole exception, in that she initially responded to my question by telling me about the time of conception. She talked about the time when she became pregnant, "a special, sort of three days that we had." As the interview continued, however, she, too, situated her pregnancy in context, describing her earlier decision to have a child, connected with positive experiences she had when helping to raise a younger sibling, and her plans with her husband to try to become pregnant. The women's experiences and the ways they talked about them transcended the narrow focus of my initial question, and reminded me about the importance of contexts—personal, social, temporal, and situational—in studying and understanding women's procreative experiences and choices, and human choices and behavior in general.

One Pregnancy Differs from Another

The women who had been pregnant before told the story of their current pregnancy in the context of their other pregnancies, and described current choices in the context of other choices. Eighteen women told me about earlier pregnancies that resulted in miscarriage or in the birth of a child. When women told me about earlier pregnancies that ended with elective abortion, they described those experiences later in the interview, with the exception of one woman, Anna Simas, who described her pregnancy in the context of all of her earlier pregnancies.

Even for the same woman, one pregnancy story—and one pregnancy experience—was different from another. During Rachel Howard's first pregnancy, for example, she had few typical pregnancy symptoms. Comparing her earlier pregnancy to this one she said, "I had no idea what it was like." This time she experienced morning sickness, backache, and fatigue. For Jane Lowe, though, this pregnancy was easier than her last one: "With the last pregnancy . . . I worried . . . this pregnancy I just have . . . the faith that I did it, I had a healthy baby once so I'll probably have another one . . . it feels very familiar . . . my body has been in maternal mode for a long time now." Roxanne Thomas said that this pregnancy was not as much fun as her first pregnancy: "It's not so much the romantic, oh honey . . . we should share our life with another human being. It's . . . let's have a sibling for the other one, and can we afford it. There's more practical questions involved . . . than just, oh, wow! You've been through it once before and you know that it's not that easy." Sara Ashley, on the other hand, did not remember much from her earlier experience: "I'd forgotten how it feels to feel so clumsy, and large (laughter)." To her, this second pregnancy "seemed like being pregnant for the first time all over again."

These descriptions of present and past pregnancies illustrate the diversity of women's experiences. The stories also contained commonalities, though. One of the similarities in the women's stories was in their descriptions of the planning that accompanied their choice to attempt pregnancy.

Attempting Procreative Control: Pregnancy Begins before Conception

One of the most fundamental ways women make choices about their procreative processes is by attempting to control conception to avoid or achieve pregnancy. Women planned their pregnancies in the context of other choices: decisions about marriage, career, and having more than one child. Pregnancy—or at least the women's plans for their pregnancies and their visions of themselves as pregnant women-to-be—began long before conception for these women.

Scheduled Choices

One form of planning concerned a woman's life circumstances. Laura Aston waited "until I was part way into [psychology] internship to start to try to get pregnant," and Penny Adams scheduled her pregnancy by waiting until she and her husband both had jobs before attempting to become pregnant: "We said, okay, we're comfortable enough, and we feel secure enough, and we know we're going to be together, and we know we're going to live here, and we feel steady . . . we're ready. So, we said, okay, now it's time, and . . . went off the pill."

Age was another factor that contributed to women's decision to try to become pregnant. In Lauren Fagan's case, age and circumstances made the time right: "The pregnancy started before I became pregnant . . . my husband is fourteen years older . . . we . . . decided to get married last October . . . related to having a child . . . we'll get married, and settled, and then we'll be in a position to have this child." Evelyn Michaels decided to attempt pregnancy "because of my age, I'm thirty-five . . . I wanted to do it as soon as possible." Sara Swanson expressed a similar concern, but she and her husband wanted to have some time together as a married couple before becoming parents: "I just turned thirty, and my husband's thirty-four . . . [but] we wanted to give ourselves some time just being married before we had kids, so we decided to wait a little while." The third reason women gave me for planning their pregnancies at a particular time was an earlier decision about having more than one child. Carol McAllister and her husband knew "when we had our first child that we would like to have a sibling for him . . . because we both have siblings." Rachel Howard and her husband "always knew we wanted more than one child." Jane Lowe also knew that she wanted to have more than one child. When their first child was seven months old, Jane Lowe and her husband talked about their feelings about attempting pregnancy again:

We had to decide, okay, what do we want to do. Do we want to start using birth control . . . space these guys out, or . . . just go for it . . . have them close together . . . being aware of the fact that things would have to be put off if we have another baby right away . . . we weighed all the pros and cons . . . and decided we wanted to really have a baby close in age to her.

These women chose pregnancy. They considered their life circumstances and decided to become pregnant. But when women choose to attempt to become pregnant they do not always become pregnant, and becoming pregnant does not always lead to the birth of a baby.

The Myth of Procreative Choice

Women and men have taken measures to control fertility for generations.[3] Much has been written about reproductive choice and the ostensible achievement of procreative control since the development of birth control, and especially since the advent of the birth control pill.[4] Despite the threats to procreative freedom posed by anti-choice activists, state legislatures, and the courts, the notion that women can choose when to bear children is one that is widely accepted. As noted in the last chapter, feminists differ in their analyses of the potential control actually provided to women by procreative technologies. But despite their lack of consensus about the impacts of these technologies on women and society, feminists and women's health activists have had considerable success in promoting equal access to safe procreative and other health services for all women.[5]

The women I interviewed attempted to take charge of their lives by making conscious decisions about becoming pregnant. But complete reproductive choice is a myth, despite the gains of the women's health movement in the ongoing struggle to advance women's control as individuals and women's influence as a group on reproductive and other health-care services and policies.

Women's control over whether to have a child is restricted for many reasons. Women can attempt to control procreation to some extent, by choosing celibacy, using contraception, or using conceptive techniques. But not all women have access to contraceptive or conceptive technologies. Barriers include age, disability, education, geography, income, marital status, sexual orientation, and race, factors that affect women's access to procreative technologies and health-care services in general. Women exposed to workplace or environmental toxins known to impede fertility also face barriers to procreative choice.[6]

Even when women use conceptive and contraceptive methods,

techniques and technologies may fail. Unplanned pregnancies occur and longed-for pregnancies never happen.

The women's experiences forced them to confront the limits of procreative choice. These experiences included: "surprise" pregnancies that occurred even when using birth control; unanticipated difficulties in becoming pregnant; and unexpected problems, including miscarriage, that arose during pregnancy.

Anna Simas and Barbara Sanders had experiences with earlier pregnancies that demonstrated the myth of procreative control, and each responded by implicitly planning her current pregnancy. Anna Simas had two unplanned pregnancies before conceiving her current pregnancy. The two earlier pregnancies had occurred in spite of the fact that she and her partner had been using contraception. After becoming pregnant the first time, Anna Simas had chosen to have an abortion. The second time she became pregnant, she had a miscarriage while she was deciding what to do. So Anna Simas experienced a lack of control over her procreative processes in two ways.

Anna Simas' current pregnancy also was a surprise, but following her earlier experiences she had decided to carry any subsequent pregnancy to term: "Well, it's a surprise, and I had had a miscarriage last year, and an abortion, and I said, no more, never again, and so the decision was made beforehand to go ahead with the pregnancy if anything ever happened." Anna Simas responded to her experiences by attempting to control the uncontrollable. She made a decision to "choose" this pregnancy if it "happened," without really choosing explicitly to become pregnant, thus implicitly planning her current pregnancy.

Barbara Sanders also experienced an earlier unplanned pregnancy that ended in a miscarriage. In response to my question, "Tell me the story of your pregnancy," Barbara Sanders said:

Now where do I begin. About two years before this pregnancy I had a miscarriage. And that pregnancy was a total accident, but by the time I had the miscarriage we were sort of disappointed about it. And I guess at about that time we decided . . . that we would just stop using any birth control and see what happened . . . And I guess we tried for a little over a year, and nothing happened, and that was fine. And then when we least expected it, I got pregnant.

For both Barbara Sanders and Anna Simas, the current pregnancy began with an earlier experience and an earlier decision. They each made a conscious choice, in advance, about their current pregnancy.

Unlike Anna Simas and Barbara Sanders, some women find they cannot get pregnant when they decide they want to have a baby. Nancy Wilson and her husband went through infertility testing and treatment. She was on the verge of attempting in vitro fertilization when she became pregnant with her first child. She was expecting her second child when I interviewed her for the first time.

Infertility can be a major life crisis, and its frequency belies the myth of procreative choice.[7] Recent public controversies about (so-called) surrogate motherhood, adoption, and in vitro fertilization reflect the growing interest—expressed by members of the media, health-care providers, and policy-makers, as well as by potential parents—in possible procreative alternatives for people with infertility. Popular magazines and television programs have exploited the topic, conducting interviews with "desperate" women and their partners, and rejoicing at the conception and birth of "miracle babies." Popular media presentations and the dissemination of scientific research findings and developments in the technologies of conception both create and demonstrate the social and individual quest for procreative control in the face of procreative uncertainty.[8]

Different women respond to infertility in different ways, as illustrated by the women I interviewed. Not all infertile women seek to enhance their fertility by choosing medical testing or treatment. Marie Bickerson was trying to become pregnant when I first met her, for example. She was experiencing "secondary infertility" two years after giving birth to her first child. It took her and her husband a year to conceive her first pregnancy. During that time, she realized "this isn't something I can choose anymore, it's something that may not happen." Marie Bickerson knew that choosing to become pregnant and becoming pregnant are two different things. She was aware of the limits of procreative "choice":

I had had a child before, which apparently is a good sign, it's not true infertility . . . there's something to work with there. But I remember sitting there and thinking, that's something that I can't control. I mean, you know, you can color your gray hair, you can get back in shape.

Marie Bickerson and her husband chose to respond to their possible infertility by "not trying to force things, not trying to take control." Despite the fact that she had decided to accept some medical intervention (she was taking clomiphene, a widely used fertility drug that prompts ovulation), Marie Bickerson was simultaneously attempting to accept the limits of procreative choice. She was consciously trying to recapture some degree of procreative control, recognizing that complete procreative control is impossible.

Just as experiences of infertility challenge women's and men's feelings of control, pregnancies that end involuntarily and perhaps for no clear reason also contradict the myth of procreative control. An unanticipated, involuntary pregnancy termination, through spontaneous miscarriage or fetal death, can challenge a woman's belief that her procreative choices will result in the chosen outcome(s). A woman's involuntary pregnancy loss involves multiple losses: the loss of the pregnancy itself and the pregnant identity, the loss of the baby, the loss of anticipated motherhood, and the loss of a belief in the myth of procreative choice. Laura Aston and Barbara Smith both experienced miscarriages during earlier pregnancies, and both were shocked when their miscarriages occurred. Not only had they not worried about miscarriage, it had never been mentioned to them as a possibility by their doctors.

Laura Aston had a miscarriage with her first pregnancy. She had never considered the possibility of miscarriage and it did not come up in her discussions with her obstetrician. Referring to the education classes provided by her doctor's group practice, she said:

Miscarriages did not come up . . . He talked about amniocentesis, he talked about chorionic villi sampling, he talked about cesarean births, everything. And he didn't say, there's eleven of you in this room, and several of you are not going to have babies, he didn't say that. Now, I would probably have been upset if he had said that at the time . . . it's just interesting that it didn't come up.

It took Laura Aston and her husband five months to conceive her first pregnancy, "which seemed an eternity" because everyone else in her husband's family "sneezes and they get pregnant." Once pregnant, she worried about the possibility of having an ectopic pregnancy, but not about having a miscarriage: "It never occurred to me that I would have a miscarriage, no one in my family has ever had . . . all those kids, with no problems." Even when Laura Aston had ultrasound and the technician made a note on her chart, a question mark about viability of pregnancy, she thought it was just too early in the pregnancy to tell anything definitive. When attempting to become pregnant for the second time, Laura Aston's previous miscarriage influenced her feelings. When she did conceive, again five

months after she and her husband started trying, the previous miscarriage influenced her response to the pregnancy. This time, she said,
"I was pregnant, but that didn't necessarily mean that there was going
to be a baby." Becoming pregnant was no longer an indication of
procreative control.

Barbara Smith experienced multiple miscarriages before the birth
of her first child. She underwent extensive testing and treatment and
eventually conceived and carried a pregnancy to term. Like Laura
Aston, Barbara Smith also told me that there had been no mention of
miscarriage by her health providers:

I had six miscarriages, all in the first trimester . . . I had every test under the
sun . . . No one ever told me that I might miscarry . . . It was out of the
blue . . . The worst part is going twelve weeks and feeling ill the whole time
only to find out . . . my body had rejected the fetus at eight weeks . . . I
could have been spared four weeks of discomfort. [RG: But it never came
up, is what you're saying?] Not the first three times. [RG: The first three
times?] Yes . . . but the specialist that I ended up seeing won't even see new
patients until they've had three miscarriages.

Barbara Smith eventually conceived again, carried her pregnancy to
term, gave birth to a daughter, and was expecting her second child
when I interviewed her.

Miscarriage can be a terrible surprise, particularly for women like
Barbara Smith and Laura Aston who never thought that it was a
possibility. Losing a pregnancy can be a shock because women tend
to believe they can "control everything and because women are under
the care of physicians who are thought to be scientists and thus able
to control nature."[9] As Shulamit Reinharz wrote about one woman,
attempting to become pregnant again following repeated miscarriages: "Getting pregnant was redefined as risk-taking, working
within a range of odds, dealing with uncertainty. Gone was the idea
that pregnancy would yield a child; gone was the sense of decision
making. Now she 'took chances'; pregnancy had become a gamble."[10] For many of the women I interviewed, choosing to become
pregnant was a toss of the dice. Jane Foster referred to her pregnancy
as a "gamble" and Sarah Worthington called her pregnancy "an obstacle course," for example. These women discovered and acknowledged the limits of their procreative choices at different times and in
different ways. Though they planned their pregnancies carefully,
considering other aspects of their lives, they had experiences—un-

planned pregnancies, infertility, miscarriages—that challenged their sense of procreative control. Once pregnant, they made other choices, and these also felt chancy to some extent. But all of the women continued to make deliberate choices, acting as conscious agents of their own lives. One way these women attempted to take charge of their pregnancies—and their procreative destinies—was by making a deliberate, considered choice of a health provider. That choice is the topic of the next chapter.

Choosing a Health Provider

Among the early choices made by the women after becoming pregnant was the selection of a health provider. All of the women had access to prenatal care, had at least some health insurance, and consciously chose particular health providers, making them members of a relatively privileged group.

Many other pregnant women in the United States do not have the opportunity to choose a doctor. Some women have very limited options, due to geography, age, and/or socioeconomic status. Other women do not see doctors until late in their pregnancies, if at all. In Alabama, for example, twenty-nine counties had no doctors who delivered babies in 1990, and rural women often had to travel fifty miles to a hospital emergency room to find a physician willing to attend their births.[1] In New Hampshire, women's health-care advocates have struggled to find obstetricians and gynecologists who will accept Medicaid patients, and in 1993 parts of the state were designated underserved areas in terms of access to primary health-care.[2] Clearly there are many women who do not have the privilege of choosing a health provider, and many who have no health provider at all; the right to health-care is not yet a reality in the United States, despite rhetoric to the contrary.

Interestingly, though, despite the fact that all of the women were receiving prenatal care, they also faced constraints in their choice of a health provider. Even these privileged women found that their choices were somewhat limited. Twenty-nine of the women live in small towns and rural communities in New England. These women had few health providers and few medical practices to choose from. The one woman who lives in Boston and the one who lives in a Boston suburb, on the other hand, had a vast array of health centers, hospitals, private practitioners, and group practices from which to select a health provider. In comparison with poor inner-city and poor rural women, and women with no health insurance, though, all of the women I interviewed clearly had some choice.

Sarah Worthington selected her health provider because she wanted a woman doctor. She was one of twelve women who said they preferred a woman health-care provider.[3] Though women doctors experience the same training and professional socialization, and at least some of them are likely to demonstrate the same professional behaviors as their male colleagues, these women felt—or hoped—that a woman would be more attentive to their needs. Eleven of those twelve women were going to a woman doctor or midwife for health-care during this pregnancy. Sarah Worthington described her choice of an obstetrician: "I'd been looking around for one [a woman] . . . her training impressed me . . . she's very honest and she doesn't use the . . . doctor on a pedestal routine. She shares information, wants you to have information." Despite being pleased that she was able to find a female obstetrician whom she liked and respected, Sarah Worthington worried about her choice:

I don't know if my pregnancy in any shape or form is going to become a quote/unquote "high-risk" pregnancy, and if it does I'm concerned about delivering at [hospital] . . . if anything problematical does occur . . . I'm just knocking on wood that that doesn't happen . . . she doesn't have . . . delivery privileges at [a highly regarded Boston hospital]. But she's got my emotional confidence. So, I feel lucky.

Betty Mell also sought and found a female obstetrician. She expressed her reasons for choosing a woman:

I had gone to male gynecologists . . . I really prefer . . . a woman . . . I just think, women are better . . . they're a little easier going, more willing to listen to you and not foo-foo everything you say. I get tired of the, you know, "don't worry about it, don't worry about it" if it's something that's worrying me. So I like that about women, you know.

Another reason women gave for choosing a particular health-care provider was a preference for a family practitioner instead of a specialist. Rachel Howard switched to a family practitioner when she became pregnant with her first child, though she had used a local obstetrics practice for her routine care in the past. She sought a health provider whose approach matched her own philosophy of care—her feelings about health, illness, and treatment. She made an appointment to meet a team of family practitioners and "liked them very much." She compared their practice to the one she had used in the past: "They were mildly indifferent to my concerns. I was always a healthy person, so it was like they were rushing me in and out . . . because I didn't have any problems." She had observed the members of the obstetrics team when she assisted a friend of hers during childbirth, working as a labor coach: "They just seemed very unfeeling, in and out of the room without really even saying hello." She was "looking for a more comfortable, personal feeling with the doctors."

Roxanne Thomas also expressed a preference for a family practitioner. She described why she was happy with her choice, a wife-and-husband family practice team: "I like the fact they have three small children . . . they know . . . how you have to arrange your schedules and everything. They're real down to earth . . . very gentle, and they pretty much will let you handle things . . . if you are totally uninvasive . . . if you don't want ultrasounds."

She compared her current health providers with the group practice she used during her last pregnancy:

I was happy with them as doctors, but I wasn't happy with the office . . . It felt like we were all cattle. We were all herded in . . . They're also not women . . . When I walk into the office [now] . . . they all know who I am: "Hi, how are you, how are you feeling?" It makes me feel special. And they don't . . . lecture me . . . don't prejudge . . . they even share something about themselves . . . the other doctors never did that, and it makes you feel closer to them . . . they're not so detached . . . like he or she is down there, and I'm up here, and we're separate, you know.

Rachel Howard and Roxanne Thomas chose their health providers on the basis of a philosophy of care, and they each found doctors they liked and respected. Some of the women chose their health providers by "choosing" a doctor affiliated with their health maintenance organization or doctors with whom they or their family members were already associated as patients.

Barbara Smith's choice of a doctor was circumscribed by the provisions of her health maintenance organization:

Those are the only ones that are in the area that are in the health plan that we now subscribe to . . . we quite liked the hospital, and the small, homey atmosphere . . . since I don't expect . . . problems with delivery, I wasn't worried about having all the scientific technology ready and available.

Luckily, Barbara Smith was pleased with her choice, so her limited options did not seem like constraints to her.

Some of the women considered or initially hoped to find a midwife or nurse-midwife to attend their births. The word "midwife" sometimes served as a synonym or code word for a home birth. Jane Lowe associated midwives with home birth, as did Carol McAllister, for example, despite the fact that the midwife who attended her first birth did so in a hospital. As it turned out, though, both of them chose doctors: Jane Lowe chose an obstetrics and gynecology group practice, and Carol McAllister a family practitioner.

Carol McAllister eventually decided to use the medical practice where her son and husband were patients, but she made the choice by considering other factors as well. She described how she chose a health provider last time, when she was pregnant with her first child:

We had just returned from being overseas for a year, and we'd seen a lot of women and children in simple, basic, primitive rural conditions, who had children . . . squatting in the hut, or in the field . . . so I had a real trust of innate mothering instinct . . . I really wanted a health-care provider who would deal with pregnancy as a healthy thing, and not, "well let's make sure everything is computerized and labeled and high-tech."

By asking people in her area for recommendations, Carol McAllister found a midwife who was in practice with five physicians. She described her delivery of her first child, at a hospital, with the midwife in attendance:

Everything was available, high-tech wise, but . . . her care was to me as a healthy individual giving birth . . . I didn't need any intervention, other than a lot of care. It was wonderful. She was professional, and very personal. She treated me like . . . an adult, a human being who was giving birth, and not as a check-off on . . . the day's agenda.

During this pregnancy, Carol McAllister considered her previous birth experience, her preference for a woman health provider, and her feelings about the family practitioner who had treated her son and husband:

I like the idea of a woman . . . a gut reaction, an understanding that, even the most sensitive man probably doesn't have about what it feels like. I like the care that she's given to [son] . . . we're already associated with her as a family, it would be a great way for me to get to know her better, and for her to get to know me . . . and then also she would be the pediatrician, we just really believe in the whole idea of family practice.

Though she gave birth to her first baby in a hospital, when she became pregnant again Carol McAllister considered a home birth. To pursue that possibility, she would have to find a different health provider, as the family practitioner she chose does not attend home births. She eventually decided to have the second child in a hospital:

If I had been convinced that I wanted a home birth, I wouldn't have chosen to go with her . . . there's just a little, teeny part of me concerned about having a second baby who . . . has a need of intervention of some sort, and the last thing I would be comfortable with would be a change in the last week or two, to another health-care provider . . . So it's that little question mark—"what if?" that made me decide.

Carol McAllister's decision was based on a complicated mix of factors, and she took time to think about her feelings and options before making a choice.

Louise Frey also took time to think about her choice. She visited two or three different hospitals and talked with several health providers. She chose a female midwife who was in a practice with a male obstetrician. She had been "turned off" by medical practices that automatically put a thirty-five-year-old pregnant woman in a high-risk category: "The people that I ruled out instantly . . . told me . . . We'll start out with the ultrasound, and then we'll schedule the amniocentesis, and we'll do this and we'll do that . . . I didn't want assumptions made about me . . . because of my age." When she talked with the receptionist at the medical practice she eventually selected, Louise Frey asked if women thirty-five and over were "put on a different little track." The receptionist replied that a woman aged forty or over "would be aware of the statistical information about Down syndrome and other kinds of genetic disorders, and it would be up to her to consider that," but they do not consider women who are "thirty-five, or thirty-six or thirty-seven, the people who need to be thinking about those things." The receptionist also told her about her own pregnancy: "When I was twenty-eight," she said, "twelve years ago, I remember being treated like a high-risk woman." Louise

Frey thought to herself, "yes, thank you for saying all that," and set up an appointment with the midwife.

Like Louise Frey, Meg Fryer had a clear idea of the kind of pregnancy and birth she wanted, and she chose her health provider accordingly. Both of Meg Fryer's first two children were born at home and she wanted to have a home birth this time, too. The obstetrician who attended the home births of her other children had a "giant practice" and was not always available, so she decided to look elsewhere. She described her attempt to find a doctor who would participate in a home birth: "None of the doctors in town at all were sympathetic . . . their attitudes were primitive . . . the thought of going to them was . . . out of the question."

Meg Fryer and her husband then went to see a midwife and asked about her medical and childbirth methods:

We're very into natural medicine. We don't like a lot of intervention, we also don't like a lot of drugs prescribed . . . She knew about our doctor, who's something of a homeopath . . . an MD . . . into alternative medicine . . . she is comfortable with that . . . she does home births . . . so all the components were there, and it was just the logical choice.

Meg Fryer was fortunate: she found a midwife who was willing to attend a home birth, was comfortable with her and her husband's approach to pregnancy and childbirth, and lived within an hour's drive of their home.

Sarah Worthington, Betty Mell, Rachel Howard, Roxanne Thomas, Carol McAllister, Louise Frey, and Meg Fryer, among others, had explicit expectations they sought to fulfill in their selection of a health provider. Women also expressed implicit reasons as they talked about their choices. Women who preferred women health providers and/or family practitioners talked about appreciating information, time, attention, care, options, and being treated like adults or "human beings" by their health providers.

Seven of the thirty-one women chose their health provider by default, at least to some extent. These women each rejected the same-area health facility, which I will call the Town Clinic.[4] Five of the seven "chose" an alternative regional medical practice instead, and two of the seven chose medical practices located in other, more distant communities. In an area without an abundance of health-care providers, choosing not to use one medical practice can lead to the nearly automatic "choice" of another medical practice.

Jane Foster did not like the Town Clinic because "it was very conservative . . . it was really just a feeling, on one meeting, with one doctor." Jane Lowe and her husband also decided not to go to the Town Clinic: "We went there to meet a doctor and we weren't really impressed. We weren't really unimpressed, but we weren't impressed." Both Jane Foster and Jane Lowe had heard good things about the other regional medical facility, which I will call Mountain Clinic, and both decided ultimately to "choose" the doctors there. Jane Lowe described her experience at the Mountain Clinic: "We just really liked him [doctor], right away, and just felt really comfortable with their whole philosophy, and their laid backness, and um, so, we decided to go with them." Roxanne Thomas also rejected the Town Clinic and chose the practice at the Mountain Clinic: "Based on the experience of friends [Mountain Clinic] allows the babies in the room practically the whole time . . . I've heard good things about it. And the alternatives being [Town Clinic], which I just haven't heard any good things about, it's very hostile." Like Jane Foster, Jane Lowe, and Anna Simas, Jill Anderson said she did not want to go to the Town Clinic:

I have a handful of really wonderful women friends . . . and all of them had chosen, in a more thoughtful fashion, the [Mountain Clinic] over the [Town Clinic] . . . there seems to be, about the [Town Clinic] . . . an understanding, that it's not that terrific . . . women are very dissatisfied, and there are a couple of doctors who have the reputation of having a very . . . sexist approach and bedside manner.

She called the Mountain Clinic for an appointment on that basis, and said she "felt very comfortable going with them."

Interestingly, as Jill Anderson continued to talk, she expressed the same ambivalence about the Mountain Clinic that I heard from women who had chosen other health providers after having had experiences there:

My initial experience with them was a little disappointing . . . I remember saying . . . I don't have the same "wow, these guys are wonderful," kind of response that everyone else seems to . . . I felt a little rushed . . . the practice just felt busy. And I didn't feel . . . individually attended to, in the way I would have liked.

In addition, the practice "felt male, it felt very male." She had chosen women as health-care providers in the past, but this group practice had no female doctors. Jill Anderson's choice of the Mountain Clinic meant she had her first male doctor in sixteen years, a contradiction for her, given her feeling that with "pregnancy, and birthing . . . the support that I needed and wanted for it was female, needed to be mostly female."

Jill Anderson's experience illustrates a dilemma faced by many, if not all, of the women. When it came to choosing a doctor or other health provider, they spent time and energy to find the right person, and they rejected doctors who did not meet their needs. They considered the health providers' philosophy of care, reputation, and location, as well as their own previous experiences and those of their friends. Yet none of the women was completely satisfied with her ultimate choice. Roxanne Thomas and Rachel Howard both had used the Mountain Clinic for their last pregnancies and births. They felt that the Mountain Clinic was too rushed, that there was not enough time or attention given to patients. They both were able to identify more pleasing alternatives, and both switched to another practice for the present pregnancy. On the other hand, both Jill Anderson and Jane Lowe also expressed dissatisfaction with the Mountain Clinic, but each continued to go there for prenatal care, and each had her baby there. Jane Lowe, who felt she was not given enough time or attention from her doctor during her first pregnancy, continued to use the Mountain Clinic during this pregnancy, in part because she saw no better alternative.

Sara Swanson also ended up with a doctor due to a combination of choice and circumstances. She sought advice from friends and colleagues and made telephone calls to get a sense of the practitioners in her area. She decided to consider a family practitioner, because she liked the "holistic" approach she associated with family practice. She also wanted a woman health provider, and she was pleased when she found a woman family practitioner in her area whose practice included obstetrics: "I interviewed her . . . she did her own deliveries unless she was on vacation, and that sounded perfect . . . it all sounded great." When she went into the family practitioner's office to have a pregnancy test, though, the nurse said the doctor she had chosen had "decided last week that she wasn't doing obstetrics" anymore. So Sara Swanson resumed her search for a doctor. She remembered how she felt at that point: "it was a little bit of a shaky start. You know, I had done all of my homework . . . and it didn't work out." She tried to take charge of her choice of a doctor, but discovered that her ability to choose was out of her control.

These women did not describe many options with respect to choosing a health-care provider. They chose doctors, midwives, and particular group practices in part because they were the only ones in the area or the only ones affiliated with their health maintenance organization. All of the women exercised some choice in this matter, but all faced some constraints as well. The choice of a doctor was a combination of real choice and circumscribed circumstances.

Most women expressed some degree of satisfaction with their ultimate choice of a health provider, but retrospective rationalization may play a role here. Some women may have convinced themselves that their choice was a good one, despite misgivings. Many women described a satisfaction tempered with ambivalence. When choices are, or feel, limited, women may need to talk about even ambivalent choices in positive ways. In this way women may be able to reduce their feelings of doubt or resolve the cognitive dissonance they may be experiencing, to live with themselves and their decisions.

None of the women felt they had made the best possible choice; all were choosing the best option available, given geographic and other constraints. I suspect that their tendency to justify their choices to themselves and others, including me, is a sign that these women feel a sense of responsibility for the consequences of those choices and yet feel somewhat powerless, too. Feelings of maternal responsibility and projections of guilt about potentially "wrong" decisions, including but not limited to the choice of a health provider, were common elements in the stories these women told.

Women's prenatal choices, including the choice of a health provider and the choice of a birthplace, often are scrutinized or judged by friends, family members, and strangers. Meg Fryer and Carol McAllister described the censure they faced (Meg Fryer) and anticipated (Carol McAllister) from family members regarding the potential choice of a home birth, for example.[5] Radical and socialist feminist analyses address the impacts of concrete barriers, such as the inequities inherent in the current American health-care system; and ideological influences, such as sexism, racism, and homophobia, on women's procreative choices. When women internalize these influences, psychological impediments to a truly "free" choice of a health provider may also play a role. Yet within the constraints they faced, these women still tried to find a health provider whom they trusted or who seemed consistent with their needs or philosophy of care.

High-Tech versus Low-Tech Medicine Is Subjective

Another theme that ran through women's descriptions of their choice of a health provider was that of high-tech versus low-tech medicine. Anna Simas wanted a health practitioner and/or hospital that offered all of the state-of-the-art medical technology, for example. Dorothy Lee wanted a doctor who would be willing to prescribe medication during pregnancy and labor, also wanted a female health provider, and ultimately chose a midwife associated with a major medical center. Meg Fryer and Carol McAllister, on the other hand, wanted a health provider who treated pregnancy as a natural process and minimized interventions.

When describing how they chose a particular health provider, many of the women talked about "low-tech" and "high-tech" medical practices, and low-intervention or high-intervention styles and philosophies of care. Women looked for health providers who seemed to reflect their own values regarding the medicalization of pregnancy and childbirth.

During the early interviews, my initial hunch was that "high-tech" and "low-tech" were two ends of a continuum, and I felt that most women would fall somewhere toward one end or the other. I assumed that some women would want to have all of the available tests, and others would want to avoid as many interventions as possible. Some women would be "high-tech women" and others would be "low-tech women," I thought. As I listened to the interview tapes and reviewed the transcripts, I discovered that different women have very different perceptions of the meaning of high-tech or low-tech health-care. One woman's low-tech medical practice is another woman's high-tech practice. This was illustrated quite clearly in the women's varying descriptions of one particular medical group.

When I asked Barbara Smith if she was going to the same health provider that she went to during her first pregnancy, she said: "No, totally the opposite. The previous one, I had . . . all the technology in the world, specialists right and left. I had my first trimester specialists . . . I had all the specialists . . . any kind of test or question of anything was taken care of . . . I had the best medical care technology could offer." Choices were "more left up to you" in the current practice, in comparison with the previous one, where "they assumed, in most cases, that we'd have every test going . . . they just expected that you would avail yourself of all the technology." The implication is that her current health-care provider is a low-technology and low-pressure one.

Anna Simas selected her doctor by looking for an interventionist style of practice: "I'm thirty-seven and I want my hand held every inch of the way and I want to be watched over and monitored." She chose an obstetrics and gynecology group practice, "and boy they've monitored me and tested me." The implication is that Anna Simas's doctors belong to a "high-tech" medical practice that routinely conducts extensive monitoring and testing of patients.

Jane Foster told me about the doctors she ultimately chose during this pregnancy: "They're very low key in this office . . . maybe they're a little too much that way . . . I think their idea is basically . . . leave it [pregnancy] alone. But there are so many things, I think mostly nutrition, that I think they should talk about a little bit." She described her doctors' practice as low-key and low-tech. Their philosophical approach seems to entail a belief that pregnancy is a natural process that "works." They are not highly interventionist, and patients are not highly monitored or tested.

Jill Anderson described her initial contact with the obstetrics/gynecology practice she chose:

The first thing that she [the receptionist] said was, we're not seeing any new patients until May. And I said, well, I think I'm pregnant, and she said . . . for obstetrical care they would take you sooner. She said in that case, what's your age? I don't know if I'd even given her my name yet, I guess maybe I had, but it had to be maybe the second, or third sentence out of her mouth, how old are you? And then, well, for women of that age, you know, over thirty-five, we recommend the amniocentesis procedure.

Jill Anderson's doctors are apparently high-tech, at least with respect to prenatal diagnosis. Rather than a low-pressure approach, her doctors seem to favor a directive style: patients are told which tests to have and tests are prescribed routinely.

Laura Aston told me about her doctor's group practice, which she felt reflected her philosophy of health-care:

It's a good, sort of general attitude of, you should change your life as little as possible. Pregnancy's not an illness . . . They said that you needed your sleep, and shouldn't drink coffee because of that . . . and they encouraged moderate exercise . . . They do a battery of tests . . . a lot of blood tests, screening for syphilis, and they'll do HIV screening if you ask them to.

Laura Aston's doctors seem to be somewhat holistic, and generally low-technology. Though they do conduct "a battery of tests," they only use ultrasound "if you want it."

Barbara Sanders described an experience she had with her health provider:

Right after I found out I was pregnant I thought I should make an appointment for my first prenatal visit . . . I talked to the nurse and she said, have you thought about ultrasound or amniocentesis, and I thought, my God, how can she be asking me these questions already, I just found out that I'm pregnant. And I was really offended by that.

Barbara Sanders's doctors were high-tech and high-pressure, and seemed to think that prenatal diagnosis was so routine that it could be handled by the nurse at the time of a woman's first prenatal visit, if not before.

All of these women—Barbara Smith, Anna Simas, Jane Foster, Jill Anderson, Laura Aston, and Barbara Sanders—were describing the same medical practice, a three-person obstetrics/gynecology team. What struck me about this discovery is what it says about the choice of a health provider. When women seem to be making the same choice of a doctor, they may actually be choosing very different things. When women seem to be making different health-care choices, they actually may be choosing the same health provider or medical practice. Of course, by articulating their wishes, the women also may have shaped—to some extent—the degree to which their doctors took—or suggested—a high-tech or low-tech approach.

These women's experiences provide contradictory evidence regarding the question of choice. A paradox of choice is that making choices does not eliminate the dilemmas of control, because women's choices do not always have the desired outcome(s).

When women discovered that full procreative choice was a myth and became aware that some of their choices entailed uncertainty, they responded by trying to exert control in other ways. One way was to deliberately relinquish control, as in Marie Bickerson's decision to "let go" with respect to her possible infertility (as described in chapter 3). Other women chose high-tech, interventionist doctors, or low-tech, noninterventionist ones, to avoid making particular choices. By choosing a doctor who stated she only performed amniocentesis on women who planned to terminate the pregnancy in the case of a positive diagnosis, Betty Mell never faced the decision of what to do following a possible positive test result; instead, she refrained from having the test altogether. By choosing a family practitioner who would not attend home births, Carol McAllister never had to face the possible criticism of her choice from family members, or her own fears about having a baby at home.

Though the myth of procreative control was shattered for some women when they experienced infertility, miscarriages, or other unanticipated problems, all of the women found that some of their choices resulted in a desired outcome. All described experiences that confirmed the idea that women can take control—at least to some extent—of their own procreative processes. All of the women eventually became pregnant, and all carried at least one pregnancy to term, for example.

The women's experiences both reflect and contradict the liberal feminist perspective on procreative choice and the rational choice model described in chapter 2. These women felt they had options and consciously set out to learn about them. They attempted to get as much available information as they wanted or needed, and made thoughtful choices on that basis. But two things impeded their ability to attain procreative control. For one thing, the choices themselves were limited. The women faced constraints when searching for a suitable health provider, for example. That they faced such limitations is consistent with both radical and socialist feminist perspectives on procreation and choice. The male, medical control of women's procreative processes described by radical feminists was reflected in the difficulty women had in finding a doctor or midwife who would attend a home birth. The socialist feminist analysis of the inability of laissez-faire, market capitalism to provide appropriate, equitable, or desirable health services was reflected in the relative scarcity and homogeneity of health providers in rural and small-town New England, and the virtual monopoly over gynecological and obstetrical care held by two regional medical centers in an area where several of the women live. In addition, the women who experienced infertility, miscarriages, and other pregnancy losses discovered the ways biology (and other, inexplicable influences) can thwart a woman's ability to realize her procreative choices.

So far, the women's stories present a mixed message regarding the various feminist perspectives on procreative choice. The women were able to make choices and take control in some ways, but not in others. But even when women's attempts to become pregnant were successful, the experience of pregnancy varied among the women and changed over time for individual women. The experience of chosen pregnancy is the topic of the next chapter.

The Meaning of Chosen Pregnancy

To understand the choices pregnant women make, it is necessary to understand the ways they experience pregnancy. These women experienced pregnancy in multiple and disparate ways, demonstrating that the meaning(s) of pregnancy differs for different women, and, equally important, at different moments in each woman's individual pregnancy. Pregnancy, like other major life events, is not a monolithic experience. Women's representations of their own pregnancies reflect the diversity of their pregnancies, their perceptions, and their lives.

Confirming Pregnancy

When a woman thinks she is pregnant—perhaps noticing swollen breasts, a missed period, nausea—she often decides to confirm her intuition by having a pregnancy test. In a high-tech age, women with the necessary resources (money, health insurance) have access to over-the-counter home-pregnancy-test kits as well as pregnancy tests at doctors' offices and laboratories to confirm that they are indeed pregnant. Pregnancy tests sometimes validate what women already know. In response to the question, "how did you know you were pregnant and when did you know?" Jane Lowe remembered that she missed a period, but felt this was not surprising, as she still was breast-feeding her daughter, and she "figured that it was just going to be irregular for a while." At the same time, though, she said, "part of me, my intuition was saying, I bet you're pregnant." Unlike her first pregnancy, when she "knew physically, almost the day I conceived, that I was pregnant," this time she did not feel anything physical. Nevertheless, she had "a funny feeling that I might be," so "without even telling my husband" she went to the pharmacy and "got one of those home tests." As she prepared the test and waited for the results she thought, "well, this is kind of a farce . . . it's probably not going to be positive, but I'll just do it . . . out of curiosity." After waiting the appropriate amount of time before checking the test results, she "pulled the little pregnancy stick out, and it was blue." Jane Lowe was holding her daughter in her arms at the time, "and I just looked at it, and I was shocked." She felt "this real combination of incredible joy and also sadness for [daughter] and my relationship . . . like I had been betraying her a little bit. And she was just so, innocent . . . it was going to be a big change, and it's like, you have no choice, [daughter], you know, it's no longer just going to be you and me." While her feelings were mixed, Jane Lowe felt primarily a sense of "total, overjoyedness." In recounting the experience, she laughed, remembering how her husband "just couldn't believe it. It just happened so quickly."

The discovery or confirmation of pregnancy was primarily an enjoyable, exciting time for these women, most of whom chose deliberately to become pregnant. Roxanne Thomas also used a home pregnancy kit to confirm her pregnancy. She said that learning the news in this way "was . . . an emotional type thing for me." She went to a friend's house with the test kit. The friend "had to help me," as Roxanne Thomas "was a nervous wreck." When the test was positive, they "jumped around and cried, and then I went over to where my husband works and told him."

Jill Anderson's experience with a home pregnancy test was similar to Roxanne Thomas's experience in the sense of euphoria that she felt when the test result was positive. She got up in the dark, early in the morning, to do the test. She waited in the bathroom for the result to appear: "It was one of those little cubes that shows a plus or minus." When the plus sign appeared, she felt "sort of a euphoric . . . still very cautious . . . But . . . a real flush, yes, of excitement . . . and not quite belief . . . you have to wait for it to appear, and you can't quite get it into focus." She saved the test kit, saying "it's still on my bureau. In my jewelry box."

The pregnancy test result was a welcome confirmation for women who had chosen pregnancy and an enjoyable and exciting part of the early days of pregnancy. Jane Lowe, Roxanne Thomas, and Jill Anderson had chosen to become pregnant, and they hoped the test would show they were indeed pregnant. A positive pregnancy test tells a woman who wants to be pregnant that her choice has resulted in the desired outcome, whether or not she "knows" she is pregnant or "feels pregnant" before that confirmation.

Before the advent of home pregnancy tests, women depended on doctors and laboratory tests to confirm their pregnancies. Before the advent of laboratory pregnancy tests, women learned of their pregnancies by observing and feeling the changes in their own bodies. All pregnancy tests, whether administered by the woman herself, by doctors, or by laboratory technicians, play a mediating role between a pregnant woman and her sense of her own body. Even in cases when women "knew" they were pregnant, they looked to the test for confirmation. Many of the women held their own bodily sensations and their own awareness of a missed period or other signs of pregnancy in abeyance until they received corroboration from the test(s); they waited for external evidence, or proof, before trusting their own feelings and observations.

A positive pregnancy test result can give women permission to acknowledge the pregnancy to themselves and/or to other people, but not all of the women believed the results from home tests. Louise Frey wanted to be pregnant, and she was almost afraid to believe the test result for fear that the test was not accurate. She "did a home pregnancy test that I had bought in the spring." When it came out positive, she thought, "it can't be true. It's been in the linen closet all through July, it's been a real scorcher, and it says on the back, do not store above eighty degrees." She did not believe the test results, in part because of an earlier experience, when she felt certain she was pregnant and then learned she was not. So, though she wanted to be pregnant, and though the test indicated she was pregnant, she did not believe it. She thought, "well this says this, but, I'd better go get a pregnancy test today. I better ask somebody else." She stopped into a family planning clinic later that day, had another test done, and "it was positive, and I thought, well, that's two. Should I get one more, should I get a blood test just to be sure?" She asked the staff members of the clinic about having yet another pregnancy test, "just to be sure":

They said, no, you're pregnant, we'll celebrate with you, this is so exciting! And I said, well, I don't know, I'll wait about two weeks, and if I don't get my period, then I'll know I'm pregnant. So I waited again . . . until about the tenth of August, to really acknowledge that my period wasn't going to come late.

Louise Frey's earlier experience, when she thought she was pregnant but had not yet conceived, made her reluctant to accept the positive test result when she actually became pregnant. Even though her pregnancy test was positive, she waited to tell people, because she had "this intuitive feeling that I was having these very early miscarriages." She "went from one extreme to the other, thinking that I must be pregnant right now, to thinking, it can't be happening."

Louise Frey was not alone in her skepticism regarding the pregnancy test result. Other women repeated the home pregnancy test or waited for a doctor's confirmation before believing their own symptoms, feelings, or the initial test result. Jane Lowe suspected she was pregnant and went to get a laboratory test the day after she got a positive result on the home test: "I went and had a blood test. I still could not believe it, I just thought I did the test wrong or something . . . they told me it was positive. I was still amazed."

Penny Adams received a positive result from a pregnancy test at her husband's medical office. She decided to get the results from a second test before calling to tell family members about the pregnancy, "so that I could be sure." She and her husband drove to his office, he showed her how to do the test, and she "did it myself, he went out to get the mail, I did the test." For Penny Adams, this experience of doing the test herself, and receiving a second, positive test result, was "real satisfying. I was afraid that I was going to tell people, and then it wasn't going to be real."

Women who felt they were pregnant sometimes questioned a negative test result. Sara Swanson was perplexed and disappointed when she got a negative result the first time she used a home pregnancy test. She was "still convinced . . . that I was pregnant," so she and her husband waited two days before doing another home test, this time getting a positive result. For Sara Swanson, this experience of attempting to confirm her pregnancy was puzzling. When she and her husband "got the first negative one, I was very confused and disappointed, because I just felt that there was something different." As it turned out, she was right, and the second test confirmed her feelings.

Anna Simas had a similar experience. Her first home test result was negative. She was perplexed by the test result, because she felt she was pregnant: "I kind of started feeling like fainting, or flaky or something, and I just said, this is not right, I'd better test again." When she conducted a second home test, "sure enough. It was only four or five days later, but—bingo." She went to her doctor's office the following day for a laboratory test, "and—double bingo."

In addition to indicating that a woman is pregnant, a positive pregnancy test symbolizes a successful choice, a woman's choice to take control of her procreative destiny by choosing pregnancy. For Penny Adams and her husband, pregnancy was an explicit goal, perceived and described as such; they "attained pregnancy." For other women this phenomenon was implicit: they worked to attain, or accomplish pregnancy or the state of being pregnant, by keeping basal body temperature charts and scheduling sexual intercourse, going off the pill, pursuing infertility tests and treatments. The point here is that being happy about pregnancy, in cases where pregnancy is both desired and actively pursued, is also happiness about the success of the pursuit itself and confirmation of one's agency: "The pregnant woman experiences herself as a source and participant in a creative process."[1] The happiness celebrates the transformation of a choice, or an attempt at control, into a reality.[2]

"Going Public"—Choosing When to Share the News

Laura Aston chose not to tell people she was trying to get pregnant, but told people about her first pregnancy as soon as she knew she was pregnant: "once I'm pregnant . . . that's a public event . . . a public thing, and I can tell people." The first time she became pregnant, she and her husband "told people after the blood test . . . our families, and friends . . . when we ran into somebody we'd tell them."

Laura Aston's first pregnancy ended in a miscarriage, as noted in chapter 3. When she became pregnant again, with her current pregnancy, she and her husband were less eager to share the news: "The second time, we called up our family . . . and told our family, but we didn't make a special effort to contact other people." They chose to do "less advertising I guess," to be "less aggressively public" about the second pregnancy. Their awareness of the risk of miscarriage made going public feel somewhat risky.

Like Laura Aston, Barbara Sanders responded to her current pregnancy in the light of a previous experience of pregnancy loss through a miscarriage. When Barbara Sanders became pregnant again, she had "a feeling of disbelief for a little while," both accepting and questioning the current pregnancy: "I believed it because I was having symptoms, but . . . for the first several months we really didn't believe . . . that this was happening." She experienced no extremely "high or low emotions . . . it was just . . . we'll see what happens." She worried about having another miscarriage: "There was also a nagging doubt in my mind . . . so even though I knew I was pregnant, until I passed the three-month mark I was very hesitant to tell people about it . . . very hesitant to believe that it was happening." Like Laura Aston, Barbara Sanders felt that going public about her pregnancy when she perceived herself as only "a little bit pregnant" was risky.

The risks associated with going public are not limited to women's feelings about protecting themselves; they also wanted to avoid the risk of disappointing other people. Laura Aston disagreed with a colleague of hers who felt that it was important to avoid telling people about experiences that might bring them pain. Unlike her colleague, who felt that "it's just too painful for people if things go wrong," Laura Aston felt that it was important to tell people: "my perspective is well, jeez, if I don't tell people, and I have a miscarriage, what's going to happen?" Laura answered her own question, suggesting that people would "see Laura going around, acting strange for a couple of months and then she has this horrible depression, you know, how are they going to understand, and how am I going to have anybody to talk to?" She felt that telling people would allow her to get support in the case of another miscarriage.

There are two different paradoxical risks involved in going public: the risk of telling people about a pregnancy that might end with a miscarriage, thus risking their disappointment or sorrow and, on the other hand, the risk of not telling people and being left to suffer a possible miscarriage alone. Women can deal with both risks by taking action that serves as a form of prevention or control, by choosing to keep the pregnancy private or sharing the news. "Going public" or telling people about the pregnancy is a form of emotional "insurance," one way to deal with risk. It is a way for a woman to protect herself by allowing her to get support, later, if needed, following a miscarriage.

Women who never had experienced miscarriages also considered the relationship between the risk of pregnancy loss and their feelings about going public. Penny Adams articulated these contradictory perspectives as she speculated about her needs and responses following a possible miscarriage: "If I don't tell people, and I have a miscarriage, then I grieve alone. If I tell people, and have a miscarriage, it might hurt when they ask me, but I think it might be helpful to have people who know." Like Laura Aston, Penny Adams felt that telling people would provide a form of emotional support. Both women felt they would rather risk telling people than risk being isolated in their sorrow. Penny Adams's feelings about a situation that might happen mirrored Laura Aston's feelings about an actual experience.

Meg Fryer also speculated about how she would feel about going public in the event of a miscarriage. She compared her parents' and her own attitudes about "going public" about pregnancy in general, saying that her parents are "concerned about the improprieties." Meg Fryer has always shared the news when she becomes pregnant: "I'm not embarrassed . . . I don't mind telling people." If she had a miscarriage, "I don't feel that I would have to apologize." About her mother's attitude about going public Meg Fryer said: "she didn't even go out when she was pregnant . . . To publicize being pregnant, was something that you did in private, like sex."

Women who had previous miscarriages—Barbara Sanders, Laura Aston, Barbara Smith—did not always make the same decision about revealing a new pregnancy to others; neither did women who had not experienced miscarriages—Jill Anderson, Meg Fryer. This suggests that a previous experience of miscarriage is only one of many possible influences on women's feelings about sharing the news.

The feelings expressed by some women about waiting to tell people about their pregnancies were echoed in the feelings expressed by Nancy Wilson, Evelyn Michaels, and other women who chose to keep potential abortion decisions private, decisions they might make following a positive prenatal diagnosis. These feelings prompted some women to keep secret their choice to have prenatal diagnostic tests such as amniocentesis, as we will see in chapter 6.

Images of Pregnancy

Following the confirmation of pregnancy, women settled in to the experience. Their descriptions of this experience contained varied images, both positive and negative. One extremely positive image of pregnancy is that it is the most exciting time, if not the culmination, of a woman's life. Marie Bickerson described pregnancy as a romantic time of anticipation: "Pregnancy is a honeymoon . . . If things are going to get rough later, at least you'll have this time now when things are peaceful, and quiet." She likened pregnancy to the portrait of maternity found in a diaper ad: "the mother is in this white nursery with white lace, and the baby clothes are all white, and she's wearing a beautiful white nightgown . . . she's just nursing beautifully and this baby's perfect," and acknowledged the difference between that image and reality: "I know it's not going to be like that, but can't I pretend? You know, take a little of the magic through."

Like Marie Bickerson, who was aware of the reality that followed the pregnant "honeymoon" but somewhat wistfully held onto the fantasy of perfection, Dorothy Lee portrayed pregnancy as a romantic prelude to motherhood: "when you're pregnant . . . you have a more romanticized notion of what the future will hold . . . like being a virgin . . . it's a very special time."

Another reason women felt positive about pregnancy was that it made them feel special. Jane Foster described her first visit to the gynecologist during her pregnancy:

They made me feel like Queen for a Day because I was pregnant, I mean, it was wonderful. You went in there and it was, aren't you great, you're pregnant, you look great. They were so positive, so I came out of there saying, hey, I'm pregnant, I'm great! It was just a whole new thing.

Louise Frey, like Jane Foster, found that her pregnancy gave other people a reason to treat her in a new and special way. She described her colleagues' reaction to the news of her pregnancy:

And I said, you know, I think I might be pregnant. And as soon as I said that, they put me on this pedestal, and just pampered me, and told me all their wonderful pregnancy stories, and they just felt honored to be in a room with a pregnant woman. And it was so much fun.

Many of the women talked about enjoying their pregnancies; fourteen women made explicit comments to that effect.[3] Enjoyment took the form of fantasy in some cases, as in Marie Bickerson's idealized image of perfect maternity, or Lauren Fagan's comment that she had "conversations" with the baby[4] growing inside her, for example. In addition to having pleasurable fantasies about the baby, women enjoyed the processes of pregnancy: the bodily changes and their emotional, psychic, intellectual, and social corollaries.

Though pregnancy can be a positive experience, an exhilirating "honeymoon," it can also be a time when women experience frightening or uncomfortable physical problems. Sarah Worthington was concerned about physical problems she was experiencing during this pregnancy:

I see this pregnancy as much more of an obstacle course than the last one . . . I've had a number of problems . . . I am kind of breathless . . . more tired than I expected . . . I have a fibroid now and I've never had a fibroid . . . I know that I shouldn't worry, but I do worry . . . my obstetrician told me that I should bank some of my own blood . . . So I'm sitting there thinking, gee, this could really turn into a disaster.

For Sarah Worthington, pregnancy was not a wholly positive experience, to say the least. She wanted to be pregnant, she had chosen pregnancy, but the experience itself was frightening and uncomfortable. And, as described in chapter 1, Sarah Worthington's concerns during pregnancy were followed by tragedy when her baby died at sixteen days old.

Nancy Hughes also experienced physical difficulties during her pregnancy; she had a "really rough" time during the first sixteen weeks: "I found out I was pregnant, a week later I was sick, in the hospital." She "could not stop vomiting . . . and I'd dehydrate, and I'd go into the hospital." She eventually chose to take medication to control her nausea, though she was reluctant to do so: "I almost didn't have a choice, it was either stay in the hospital, with an IV in me, and throw up all the time," or take the medication.

Four other women also mentioned specific and worrisome physical problems: a placental tear, a positive pap test result, gestational diabetes, a urinary tract infection. In contrast to the feelings of control or agency described by most of the women, another consequence of the choice to become pregnant can be a loss of control. Twenty-one of the thirty-one women described a lack of control over potential pregnancy complications and worried about the unknown long-term effects of their behavior and their choices. Roxanne Thomas was not always successful in her attempts to control her fears. During her second pregnancy, she was "more worried, because you know more." She tried "not to read too much about the complications . . . I find myself flipping through the books . . . I lately have been having this terrible fear that something's wrong." Jane Foster thought about possible problems: "I tend to worry all the time that something's going to go wrong, that there's something wrong with the fetus, or the baby . . . that something will happen." Lauren Fagan felt that she might inadvertently harm her baby:

I was worried about medication . . . I didn't want to take anything . . . things that you don't even think about. They put Nutrasweet in so many things . . . diet soda has Nutrasweet . . . I was eating a bran cereal that I thought was real good . . . and it's made with Nutrasweet. And those things happen and of course you panic, think, oh my God, I've eaten this cereal for two months, what's going to happen to the baby?

Women's stories about pregnancy contained contradictory images, but one constant in the stories was a picture of flux: "For the pregnant subject . . . pregnancy has a temporality of movement, growth and change."[5] This image of pregnancy as an experience of contradictions and transformation was illustrated in the fact that women felt pregnant and not-pregnant at the same time, though popular wisdom and an often-heard joke suggest that it is not possible to be "a little bit pregnant."

The Pregnant Identity: It Is Possible to Be a Little Bit Pregnant

Pregnancy tests detect or "diagnose" the biological reality of pregnancy, but other indicators contribute to women's self-identification as pregnant women. Family members' responses, the labels used by health providers, women's own feelings and perceptions, and the physical changes that make women's pregnancies obvious to others (e.g., "showing") are some of the markers that women use to know that they are pregnant. Women recognize their own pregnancies and identify themselves as pregnant women in part because of these external and internal signs.

Pregnancy is a social category as well as an individual experience and biological phenomenon, and thus women vary in the ways they identify with their pregnancies and with being pregnant women.

Louise Frey took on the pregnant identity soon after she and her husband attempted conception for the first time. Certain that she was pregnant, she responded to her bodily changes through the eyes of a pregnant woman: "I thought, okay, well I'd like to begin the pregnancy in August, and deliver this baby in May. And so, when my period came in September, I didn't even think it was a real period . . . I thought that maybe something was wrong with me. I knew I was pregnant."

She felt sure that she had conceived in August, and during the next four weeks, she remembered saying to herself, "I feel on top of the world, I don't know about this nausea stuff, I'm doing great. I'm invincible!" When she got her period, she was puzzled: "I was like, what is this? I'll have to look this up in a pregnancy book . . . I really stumped myself, 'cause I was so sure that I was in charge. So that was the beginning."

Louise Frey soon relinquished the pregnant identity and acknowledged the fact that she was not pregnant. She regained the pregnant identity, but more slowly, when she did become pregnant. For Louise Frey the decision to become pregnant represented "a new, perhaps momentous, definition of [her] situation": "The decision to become pregnant is a turning point in a woman's identity or social role. The decision changes a woman's relation to her body, to sexuality, to time, to her partner(s), and to her future. From the moment of decision, she becomes an 'about to be pregnant person' or 'mother-to-be.' "[6] Other women, such as Barbara Smith and Laura Aston, were forced to relinquish the pregnant identity following miscarriages. In Laura Aston's case, this experience made her realize that her sense of herself as a pregnant woman was different from her sense that there was a baby.

A Pregnancy Is Not a Baby

During Laura Aston's current pregnancy, she felt that she was *pregnant* until the point when she miscarried during the last pregnancy, but she acknowledged the *baby* only after that point. During her first pregnancy, Laura Aston felt there was a baby inside her as soon as she learned she was pregnant. She had a different response during this, her second pregnancy: "the first time I was pregnant and there was a baby at the same time. This time I was pregnant, but that didn't necessarily mean that there was going to be a baby. It came in two pieces."

Other women also distinguished between the pregnancy, or their pregnant identity, and the baby. Sara Swanson, for example, tried to make the pregnancy more real to herself and her husband: "That's some of what I struggle with, even though it's happening in my body, you know, this whole question of is it really real?" Initially, Sara Swanson felt "that it's not going to be real until the baby's there," even though "the changes started, you know, from the point when I got pregnant." She struggled to give the pregnancy "more definition. I know there's something there, and something's happening, but I'm trying to find ways of capturing it." She wanted to make the pregnancy more real for herself and for her husband, "to find ways of sharing with him." She wanted the pregnancy "to be more available to him, the reality."

The perception that the pregnancy will actually lead to the birth of a baby can occur at one particular moment or it can recur at different times during the pregnancy. Women allowed themselves to think that there really was going to be a baby after the first three months of pregnancy, at the beginning of the second trimester (Laura Aston, Jill Anderson, Marta Betts); after hearing the baby's heartbeat (Sara Swanson, Rachel Howard, Carol McAllister); after getting negative results from the maternal serum alphafetoprotein (AFP) test (Jane Foster, Sarah Worthington); after having an ultrasound (Betty Mell, Jill Anderson, Lauren Fagan, Louise Frey, Anna Simas); after receiving negative amniocentesis results (Barbara Sanders, Anna Simas, Nancy Wilson, Evelyn Michaels); and/or after learning the baby's sex (Jane Doe, Evelyn Michaels, Barbara Sanders.) Only Lauren Fagan told me that she knew that there was a baby there when she first felt the baby move. She said that she first had the sense of the baby as "a separate person" at the time that once was called "quickening":

When intense movement, when it becomes really really strong . . . it's not anything that you can control. In early days of movement, it's like, little, just bits and pieces. Which still take you by surprise . . . he'll just be moving all day long, and turning . . . if I lie down, he'll move, and it's almost like he's communicating . . . you totally have that sense that he's his own person.

She was always fascinated with the baby's movement: "I can literally, sit in front of the TV, we're watching something, and I'll be watching my stomach . . . there's almost a sense of pride, did you see how big that kick was? I mean, this kid is . . . a tough kid . . . there are accomplishments that the baby is making. There's almost a sense that you are a separate person." Lauren Fagan experienced both ultrasound and amniocentesis during her pregnancy, yet she perceived the reality of her baby upon quickening, when she felt the baby move inside her. Other women waited for external evidence—an ultrasound "picture," a negative prenatal diagnosis result, the beginning of the second trimester and the perception that miscarriage was now unlikely—before acknowledging or perceiving that there really was a baby there. The fact that Lauren Fagan alone, of the thirty-one women I interviewed, associated the moment of quickening with her awareness of the baby as distinct from the pregnancy or from herself is consistent with the research of Diane Beeson, Barbara Katz Rothman, and Rosalind Petchesky.

Beeson, Rothman, and Petchesky noted that ultrasound and amniocentesis can influence women's relationships to their pregnancies and their developing fetuses, causing the phenomenon Barbara Katz Rothman has called "the tentative pregnancy."[7] In previous studies, some pregnant women described a period of suspended animation during the time when they were waiting to learn the amniocentesis results. Unwilling to commit themselves fully to a pregnancy that they might terminate in the case of a positive amniocentesis diagnosis, these women waited to wear maternity clothes, postponed telling other people about the pregnancy, and in some cases ignored fetal movement ("quickening") until after receiving negative test results.[8] Rothman, Petchesky, and Beeson, among others, found that pregnant women's consciousness of the baby as a separate person (or person-to-be) often occurs during or after prenatal diagnosis, particularly when women see the image on the ultrasound screen. A question Petchesky, Rothman, Ann Oakley, and others have asked, based on this observation, is whether medical technologies, particularly prenatal diagnostic techniques, have usurped women's own bodily sensations as indicators of the baby's reality. I will return to women's experiences of prenatal diagnosis in chapter 6.

Women may claim the pregnant identity in a tentative way for a variety of reasons. Some women readily accepted the pregnant identity; for example, Jane Lowe went immediately into the "maternal mode": "My body has been in maternal mode a long time now." Lauren Fagan experienced a heightened and positive sense of self- and body-consciousness soon after she learned she was pregnant:

I was real in tune with every little step . . . it was a real big deal to me. I wanted to be pregnant. I was very interested in everything that was going on with me. I was very clued into the physical, feelings . . . I was aware that this was going to happen, then this was going to happen . . . I was real interested in how it felt.

Not all women stepped into the "maternal mode" as easily or thoroughly, however. Some women accepted the pregnant identity only partially or temporarily. Pregnancy can be an ambiguous state in which a woman may feel pregnant but not feel that she is necessarily a "mother-to-be." Some women "grew into" the pregnancy, gradually assuming something of a new identity as their bodies changed and other people acknowledged their new role(s). They did not experience a sudden, complete, or permanent acceptance or an outright rejection of the pregnant identity. Instead they seemed to shift back and forth between feeling pregnant, with all that the pregnant status implies about a woman's changing roles and identity, and not feeling "any different."

Sara Swanson is an example of a woman whose identification with her pregnancy was muted during the beginning weeks of her pregnancy. She was delighted when she learned that she was pregnant, but wanted to assume the pregnant identity in a more pronounced way. She wanted to feel "different," and yearned for the physical changes and public recognition of her new status that would help her to do so. At first, pregnancy "just felt like being sick . . . the symptoms you are having aren't that unique." She had had mononucleosis in the past, and the fatigue she felt during early pregnancy reminded her of that. Her symptoms "didn't feel unique or special in any way." She felt that "until my stomach pops out, I'm not going to really feel pregnant . . . there's something about having that external sign that is confirming and validating." Hearing the baby's heartbeat helped her "know . . . that something was really happening, because I wasn't feeling unique, you know." But she still wanted the pregnancy "to be real in a more public way. I mean, I know I've heard the heartbeat, and we've given the baby an in-utero name . . . those things help me in making it real." She compared herself with a pregnant friend, "who is about two months ahead of me . . . when I saw her for the first time . . . and her stomach was right out there . . . I thought, well there is a pregnant woman." During early pregnancy, Sara Swanson noted, "you could be faking it, you could just be getting a little chubby . . . there's something about the stomach popping out that makes it more definite."

It is possible for a woman to be "a little bit pregnant," to experience her pregnancy and the baby as two different phenomena, and it is possible for women to move in and out of the pregnant identity, sometimes for months. This changing sense of the meaning and the reality of pregnancy may persist until a woman perceives that her pregnancy will actually result in the birth of a baby, and that perception occurs at different moments for different women. By the latter months or weeks of pregnancy, most women's pregnancies are public, and at that point it is harder for women to be somewhat pregnant or to temporarily lose the pregnant identity (until after the birth).

Chosen and Cherished: Precious Pregnancies

The thirty-one women all described their pregnancies as wanted pregnancies, including the women whose pregnancies were a surprise or an "accident," or those for whom conception occurred earlier than planned. Seventeen of the thirty-one women described their pregnancies in ways that led me to think of their pregnancies as more than merely wanted. These pregnancies were chosen and cherished. For these women, the (physical) pregnancy itself "was very much desired for . . . a very long time." These pregnancies were "a long time in coming" for two reasons. One reason was that these women always wanted to have a child or additional children and had been trying to conceive for a long time (defined by the women in terms of months and years.) The other reason was that they had not tried to become pregnant before now due to circumstances—the state of their relationship(s) with lovers or spouses, age, or other considerations—and now, after much consideration and waiting, the "time was right."

Women who thought they could not become pregnant because of their own or a partner's fertility problems and those who had a difficult time getting pregnant described their pregnancies as special. Blossom Hunneycutt and her husband thought they would never be able to have a child:

This pregnancy is kind of unique, in that my husband had cancer when he was young and we didn't think we were going to have any children at all. And when I conceived [first child] we thought it was a real freak thing . . . doctors had told us, your chances look slim . . . I started taking my temperature . . . it was a great surprise.

Blossom Hunneycutt's first pregnancy was more than chosen; it was extraordinary, if not miraculous, and this pregnancy was a second miracle. Nancy Wilson told a similar story. Her first child seemed like a miracle, and this pregnancy also was very special to her:

It took us a long time to have a first child. We went through all . . . the . . . infertility stuff. We weren't quite at the point of in vitro, but we were near there, when I got pregnant with [first child] . . . I've always thought of [first child] as our miracle child . . . I didn't think that . . . would be a possibility . . . we thought maybe we'd only have one . . . Before [first child] we thought we'd have none, and now . . . we'll have two.

Penny Adams and her husband had tried to conceive for nearly a year. When they succeeded and she became pregnant, she could hardly believe it: "I think that the first two weeks of being pregnant I kept walking around saying, can you believe it?" Nancy Wilson, Blossom Hunneycutt, and Penny Adams all described pregnancies that were special because they did not know whether they would ever be able to conceive. Other women, such as Barbara Smith, Laura Aston, and Barbara Sanders, described pregnancies that were "precious" in the context of their previous miscarriages. They did not know if they would ever be able to carry a pregnancy to term.

Lauren Fagan's pregnancy was special because she had wondered if she would ever have "the chance" to become a mother. When she was thirty-five, she and her partner decided to get married, and they decided to attempt pregnancy around the same time. Her pregnancy felt like her "one and only chance." Her feelings about her pregnancy were influenced by its super-chosen quality: "When you're thirty-six and . . . it might be your only child . . . you want it to be, not perfect, but you want everything to be alright, you want it to have all the proper arms and legs . . . and you do, worry that something's going to be wrong, and your one and only chance is not going to be what you wanted it to be."

Like Lauren Fagan, Anna Simas mentioned her feelings about her "only chance" to become a mother. Anna Simas's choice to carry her current pregnancy to term was connected with choices she made during two earlier, unplanned pregnancies, as noted in chapter 3. One of her earlier pregnancies ended in a miscarriage; she chose to terminate the other. After those two experiences, Anna Simas decided that she would carry any subsequent pregnancy, planned or not, to term. Anna Simas told me that this was because she worried that she had lost the chance to have a baby: "What I went through with, um, getting rid of the other one, was, I may have thrown out my only chance. And even though I don't know if I really wanted it, it still might have been my only chance." In a way, her current pregnancy was precious even before it was conceived. She talked about the choices she made during her pregnancy with the seriousness and deliberation consistent with an "only chance" pregnancy. Anna Simas thought that her age (thirty-seven) gave her a different, more grounded perspective on pregnancy, for example. She compared herself with younger pregnant women, saying that she thought she was taking her pregnancy more seriously: "I'm having a real different experience from these younger women . . . it's like, their heads are in the clouds." Lauren Fagan, like Anna Simas, talked about her pregnancy as her "only chance," and compared herself with younger women. She suggested that there "should be a group for older people who are having babies." Like Anna Simas, Lauren Fagan felt there was a "real big difference between people in their twenties and a forty-year-old." She suggested that her "commitment" to the pregnancy was different from that of the younger women: "They don't seem to be as worried, they don't seem to be as concerned." For them, she said, "it's more, okay, I'm having a baby, but I'm going to have one or two other babies, so this is one of many babies, not one baby that I'm going to have and maybe never have another one." She felt that the younger women "don't take the pregnancy as seriously as I have." Their "commitment isn't that strong to the pregnancy," it is not their "one and only chance, you don't think of it that way, it's not as much of a conscious decision as it was for me, you didn't have to struggle for it."

Precious pregnancies have a paradoxical quality. Women whose pregnancies are "super-chosen" may experience a heightened sense of joy, but that joy may be tempered by a heightened sense of the seriousness and difficulty of their pregnancy-related choices. Being pregnant is not a wholly unambiguous state for a pregnant woman, even when her pregnancy is precious.

Ambivalent Anticipations of Motherhood

Pregnancy may be precious for many women, but they may anticipate motherhood with ambivalence nevertheless. In other words, women can cherish the pregnant identity and the experience of pregnancy, and can have positive and nurturing feelings toward their fetuses or their babies at the same time as they have mixed feelings about motherhood and its responsibilities or about the experience of pregnancy itself.

Paradoxically, pregnancy today can be both a positive and a negative experience for pregnant women. When women talked about choosing pregnancy and selecting a health provider, they simultaneously acknowledged the limits of choice and the obstacles that impeded their attempts to enhance their choice or control. Similarly, women talked about their pregnancies in ways that incorporated paradoxes. Pregnancy, like the choices women make while pregnant, can be an experience of contradictions.

Pregnancy is both an exciting, hopeful time and a fearful time for pregnant women. At the beginning of this century pregnancy was a dangerous time because of the very real hazards associated with childbirth (e.g., puerperal, or "childbed" fever caused by lack of sanitation, such as the absence of regular handwashing by doctors).[9] As we end this century, pregnant women and their fetuses or babies face different dangers. Women described their fears about the risks associated with unnecessary cesarean sections, the use of fetal monitors, and fertility drugs; that the women expressed fears and worries associated with these and related dangers is not surprising. Jill Anderson, for example, recalled the DES debacle and wondered about the possible long-range, unanticipated risks of ultrasound.

The same women who talked about their pregnancies in ways that prompted me to call their pregnancies "precious" also expressed ambivalence about pregnancy. Their stories contained ambivalence and contradictions about the physical changes, social roles, and choices associated with pregnancy, childbearing, and motherhood.

Changing Bodies, Changing Selves

Women's ambivalent feelings were revealed as they talked about their pregnant bodies. Fifteen women referred explicitly during our interviews to the physical changes that occur during pregnancy.[10] They shared their feelings about their bodies, such as feeling "big" or "gross." They talked about the social implications of their changing bodies, such as the response(s) of family members or co-workers to the physical "advertisement" of pregnancy.

Body weight was one theme that emerged in the interviews. Jane Lowe, Carol McAllister, and Lauren Fagan enjoyed the physical changes of pregnancy, such as "getting big." For them, taking delight in their growing bodies was part of a positive acceptance of the pregnant identity. Sara Swanson welcomed those changes, but also expressed contradictory feelings about her pregnant body. She wanted people to recognize her pregnancy, and looked forward to the time when she would "show," yet, when a woman in a restaurant told her she didn't look pregnant, Sara Swanson thanked her, interpreting the comment as a compliment. Though she was pleased that she "didn't look pregnant," she also looked forward to growing "big," because she welcomed that public sign of her pregnancy. Roxanne Thomas, in contrast, expressed negative feelings about being "big": "I feel . . . really obtrusive and gross." She compared this pregnancy with her first one: "I don't glow this time . . . I looked pretty great the last time, I just had a little bump in the front, I was kind of thin." Now, though, she said, "I just feel kind of gross . . . I don't talk about it anywhere near as much. Except the physical, grossness that I feel." She described her reaction to compliments about her appearance from colleagues, " 'Oh isn't that a cute outfit,' and I'm like, oh yeah, oh yeah, there's pleats in front of all the outfits, it's another burlap sack, with a different design."

Pregnant women's feelings about gaining weight during pregnancy were connected to the way(s) other people responded to their changing bodies. Penny Adams kept herself slim by exercising regularly. She knew she would gain weight during pregnancy, but had not gained much during her first few months. She noted that her co-workers were monitoring her changing body, as if they were anxious for her to become "big" or "fat": "I'm walking through the halls . . . people who know me, or know I'm pregnant, are sort of checking me out . . . looking to see if I'm gaining any weight." She said the workers "in my department are saying, I can't wait to see you fat, you know, I don't think I'm incredibly thin, but I run, I exercise a lot, you know, so I stay pretty slim." Penny Adams noted that she had "only gained five pounds so far, so that's not a lot." She wondered how her colleagues would respond as her pregnancy progressed: "they keep saying, oh, we just can't wait. I don't know what they'll do when they see me fat."

Penny Adams's experience reflects the fact that the changes in pregnant women's bodies have both personal and social consequences. Women's ambivalence about the pregnant identity may be associated with the pressures on women to conform to socially acceptable standards of attractiveness. The comments of Sara Swanson, Roxanne Thomas, and Penny Adams reflect our societal preoccupation with thinness. Given the contemporary American cultural distaste for large or "fat" bodies, though, it is surprising that more women did not talk about their pregnant bodies in self-deprecating ways. One woman, Lauren Fagan, had anorexia nervosa as a teenager, but she expressed no ambivalence about the weight she gained during her pregnancy.

Sexuality was the second body-related theme that emerged from my analysis of the interviews. A woman's pregnant body is usually recognizable as such at some point during her pregnancy, and pregnant women do not have to wear T-shirts that declare "Baby" (with an arrow), or "Preg State" for people to get the message. A pregnant body also is an overt symbol of sexuality; a pregnant woman can be perceived as a walking advertisement for the fact that she is, or has been, a sexually active person.[11] Sara Swanson, a therapist, discovered that her clients responded to her differently as her pregnancy progressed. As she became visibly pregnant, the people who came to her for counseling discussed their sexuality and raised sexual topics for discussion much more frequently and openly in the counseling sessions than in previous sessions. This indicated to her that they perceived her pregnancy as a sign of sexual experience, and they responded to that sign by talking more openly about their own sexual issues and feelings.

Women's ambivalence about their pregnant bodies may be associated with the fact that the pregnant identity is inconsistent with a professional work identity. Pregnant bodies represent sexuality, femaleness,[12] and maternity, three identities that are often deemed incompatible with workplace requirements and expectations. As recently as 1967, this was so threatening that pregnant women were required to leave their jobs, for example, elementary school teachers.[13] Even in the absence of explicit strictures against combining employment and pregnancy, women may find that their employee role(s) and their mother (or expectant mother) role(s) conflict.

When women employed in the workforce become pregnant, they may experience role strain or conflict, related to their own or other people's workplace expectations. This conflict between workplace and reproductive roles has been described by Emily Martin (1987),

Kristin Luker (1984), and Robbie Pfeufer Kahn (1988), among others. As Martin notes, the "lack of institutional support in the United States makes it very difficult for women to be whole people—productive and reproductive at the same time." [14]

Lauren Fagan described the conflicting feelings she experienced as a pregnant woman and a professional worker: "there's a part of me that wants to present this sort of, this pregnancy's not affecting me in any way whatsoever . . . I'm sure I talk about it ten times more than you should . . . on a professional level . . . there's always been sort of a conflict for me." She described the implicit expectations she perceived, living in a small New England town: "a lot of women . . . they're not working . . . they're having their kids . . . So there was always this, kind of funny little feeling that you're always trotting off to work every day . . . I've always had that conflict." She noted the "pressures on . . . women, to continue to act completely unpregnant when they're working, in the business world," and wondered about her own and other women's expectations of pregnant workers, "I sometimes think we have set up these models for ourselves . . . you don't have to quit your job as soon as you get pregnant, and . . . you shouldn't, and it's wonderful that there are laws now to protect us from getting fired . . . but to a certain extent we went overboard." Now, she said, women cannot legally be fired when they become pregnant, but also, "we can't even act like we're pregnant. We pretend like we're not pregnant, which is impossible, and in doing it you've . . . shortchanged yourself. You've lost, because you need . . . to be pregnant, you need to go through that whole thing."

The conflict that Lauren Fagan experienced, the pressure of wanting both to act pregnant and to act not-pregnant, is related to her ability to fully accept or acknowledge the pregnant identity. At her workplace, Lauren Fagan felt that she should be, or act, not-pregnant, though she wanted to experience her pregnancy fully. As it turned out, her feeling that she should act "not-pregnant" on the job was grounded in reality. She described the punitive response of her work supervisor to her pregnancy: "when I told my boss that I was pregnant, he changed my job to make my commute longer." Her supervisor changed her workplace from its current location, in one town, to another town located an additional forty minutes away from her home. She protested this action, "I said to him . . . my commute is really long, I'm getting tired, and my doctor's really worried," and her boss said, "well, then, if you can't do it, you're out of a job."

Lauren Fagan did not quit, despite the fact that she suspected her supervisor wanted her to leave the job, and she decided to deal with the additional pressure by doing "what I wanted to do" with respect to her work schedule: "I went every day, but I went when I wanted to go, and I came home when I wanted to come home. Which I also felt badly about, but I just, I said, he's going to . . . try to make my day fourteen hours long, I'm not going to let him do that." She felt strong "pressure to continue, to never say I can't do it because I'm pregnant. That was the pressure."

Lauren Fagan chose to keep working, and to do so she developed a strategy to deal with the unrealistic and perhaps punitive expectations of her boss as well as her own role strain. She managed to balance her work responsibilities with her pregnancy, but it was a struggle, and she faced both internal and external pressures as a result. Sarah Worthington also experienced role strain when she began to "show." At her workplace, she noticed that a male co-worker looked surreptitiously at her profile and observed her changing body from time to time. She described his discomfort at the realization that she had other roles than her professional worker role. She was able to cope with the situation by deciding to ignore her co-worker's response to her pregnancy, but—unlike Lauren Fagan—she made no attempt to act not-pregnant.

Penny Adams also shared an observation that illustrates the tension between work and pregnancy-related roles and identities. She liked it when people expressed an interest in her pregnancy, but noted that people's interest sometimes seemed too focused on her body. She described a co-worker's response to her after being away for a few days: "When [she] hasn't been on . . . for a few days, when she's there . . . she looks right at my belly, you know. It's like the rest of me has disappeared, because the eyes go right to my belly." A friend told her that "people are going to start walking up to you and rubbing your belly, and I thought, my God, it seems like such a violation." Many of the other women described the ways strangers sometimes approached them, touching their bellies. To some pregnant women, this kind of behavior seems particularly inappropriate in their workplaces, where they may be struggling to maintain a professional identity.

Just as women can experience role conflict between their pregnant selves and their professional work identities when their pregnancies become public, they anticipate additional conflict(s) that may occur between their mothering and their worker roles following the birth of their babies. Betty Mell anticipated that her mothering role(s) would not be compatible with full-time employment following the birth of her baby. Such conflicts are not inevitable. Robbie Pfeufer Kahn has described what she calls "mixed-zone" workplaces, "which combine the world of the mother with the world of the child." [15] But most women, including Betty Mell, are not lucky enough to work in such contexts. A mother of three when she became pregnant, Betty Mell knew how having children had constrained her work options in the past. Before she became pregnant this time, she had planned to go back to work full-time, and it took her a little while to reconcile the conflict between another pregnancy and a full-time job. This conflict made her ambivalent about the pregnancy at first: "I was looking forward to being able to go back to work." Eventually, though, she made "a big shift . . . it took me a few weeks to come to terms with that." Betty Mell reconciled the conflict between her identities as a worker and a mother by modifying her immediate work plans so she would be able to fulfill the requirements of her role(s) as a mother in a way that made sense to her.

Pregnant women can experience role strain at home as well as at work. The pregnant identity can change a woman's sense of herself in relation to domestic as well as employment arrangements. Lauren Fagan found that her acceptance of the pregnant identity ultimately allowed her to assume a more flexible self-identity at home, but initially her new status made her uncomfortable: "It was hard for me to say I can't do this because I'm pregnant." She found her activities ("going to the doc, taking out the garbage, getting in and out of the car") tiring. Things became "more of a chore," but "it was hard for me to say I need help." By learning to ask for assistance when she needed it, she felt she made "great strides." It was "very helpful to be able to say to my husband, I need you to carry in the groceries . . . my primary job in the next three weeks is to get plenty of rest . . . for the delivery." Asking for help like that had been "an impossible thing for me to say" in the past, she said, noting that she never before had taken into account her "physical limitations, and . . . mental limitations." But during this pregnancy, she realized "you have to do that, and it's not easy . . . it's giving up that sense that you can do everything." Lauren Fagan ultimately viewed this relinquishment of complete independence and control in a positive light, noting "that's just all part of the process . . . to learn . . . when you have a baby

. . . If you take the time to try to figure out what it all means, you can learn a lot from it."

Lauren Fagan's experience is an example of the ways women can transform constraints into control. At first she felt ambivalent about the physical limitations associated with her pregnancy. She was uncomfortable with her changing sense of her own physical abilities and her need for assistance. But she chose to construct an acceptable new sense of herself as a pregnant woman; like Betty Mell, she made "a big shift." Lauren Fagan transformed her lack of control—over her bodily needs and abilities—into an opportunity for change and learning. She chose to interpret the pregnancy as a training period or preparation for her experiences as a mother. In this way losing control became purposeful in her mind: "You have morning sickness, and you lie on the couch all day . . . my house is a mess, the dishes haven't been done, and you say to yourself, this is what it's like, when you have a baby." She reinterpreted the new demands of pregnancy as preparation for her impending life as a mother: "You have to get up in the middle of the night when you have to go to the bathroom, you have to learn to do that and then go back to bed . . . get used to what it takes . . . I think there is a definite reason for the nine months." Lauren Fagan took something she could not control— the discomfort associated with her bodily and role changes during pregnancy—and used it to develop a new balance.

In addition to feeling ambivalent about their physical and social identities as pregnant women, some women are ambivalent about their prospective mothering role(s). For them, the meaning of pregnancy is related to the meaning of impending motherhood. Twelve women expressed ambivalence about becoming mothers or having additional children.[16] When these women mentioned their concerns about taking care of their child(ren), they did so in a tentative way: laughingly, rhetorically, or as an aside. Evelyn Michaels wondered how she would adjust to having a child, a son in particular: "How do you deal with a little boy?" Laura Aston was "somewhere in between being very, very excited and being very, very worried" about becoming a mother. As she anticipated the changes she would face following the birth, Laura Aston wondered about her ambivalent feelings: "Sometimes I think, boy, I'm really not as excited as I should be." She worried about parenting an infant: "newborn babies are nice, for about half an hour, and then, they're just a pain. You have to take care of them all of the time." She looked forward to mothering a toddler: "I would like to have, be delivered of a two-year-old. I can deal with a two-year-old . . . but it's hard for me to deal with kids who don't talk."

Women's and Medical Views of Chosen Pregnancy: Different Worlds of Meaning

The ambivalent and multidimensional qualities that characterized these women's experiences and depictions of pregnancy suggest that the meaning of pregnancy to pregnant women is complicated, variable, and very different from the mainstream medical model of pregnancy. That model, used by obstetricians and other physicians and reflected in medical texts, depicts pregnancy as a physiological and biological phenomenon.[17] Following conception, changes occur in a woman's body that lead ultimately, if all goes well, to the birth of a baby. Pregnancy has certain stages or phases, and is a linear, developmental process; "physicians make decisions about women's bodies based on a set of normal life trajectory expectations."[18] Pregnancy, as one event within that "normal" life trajectory, is perceived in the medical model to have a trajectory of its own.

While it certainly is true that most pregnancies have a beginning, a middle, and an end, what happens during each of these phases may vary considerably from woman to woman. More importantly, each woman's perceptions, feelings, and experiences of these phases are uniquely her own. This does not preclude the identification of some common patterns or similarities among women's pregnancies, such as the phenomenon of "precious pregnancies," for example. But each woman perceives and has the experiences that comprise even these shared patterns in her own way(s).

The medical model of pregnancy is decontextualized. When Dorothy Lee told her present doctor during the intake interview about the problems she had with her first pregnancy, he was not interested: "he had pretty much turned me off." She told him she had been hospitalized during her first pregnancy, and "I mean, they just ignored that." Dorothy Lee saw her current pregnancy in the context of her earlier pregnancy, but her doctor did not. Bernadette Lynn also noted a disjuncture between the medical perspective and the realities of her own life. Her doctor gave her advice when he informed her that she had a placental tear: "they told me to go home and bed rest, and at the time my husband was at work and I have a two-year-old, and I said, how do you bed rest with a two-year-old? They said, do the best you can." Bernadette Lynn's life context was not acknowledged by her doctor in his approach to her pregnancy.

Most obstetrics and gynecology practitioners are taught to focus on the physical or biological aspects of a pregnant woman's situation, with little recognition of other aspects of her life. Medical intake forms and interviews omit important details, such as the nature of the woman's work, whether she may be exposed to occupational or environmental hazards, whether she can afford to pay for the pre-scribed prenatal vitamin supplements, whether she needs assistance with childcare or transportation or other resources that would enable her to obtain the recommended prenatal care. The medical perspec-tive toward pregnancy does not encompass the possible conflicts between a woman's pregnancy and her other roles and responsibili-ties, at work or at home.[19]

The medical view of pregnancy virtually ignores the public dimen-sions of pregnancy, the social corollaries of the physiological manifes-tations of a woman's pregnancy. For example, social values influence people's responses to a pregnant woman and these, in turn, influence her self-image and identity. This was demonstrated in the comments of Penny Adams, Roxanne Thomas, Rachel Howard, and other women who talked about body weight, reflecting our cultural preoc-cupation with physical appearance and the stigma associated with being "big" or fat. Women's descriptions of pregnancy are embedded in a number of contexts: their other pregnancies, other aspects and circumstances of their lives, and the larger social, cultural, and politi-cal environment. Unlike the medical view of pregnancy as a biologi-cal phenomenon, to pregnant women, pregnancy is a physiological, psychological, and social process.

Though the medical model does not address women's social loca-tions or the possible conflicts between disparate aspects of a woman's life (motherhood responsibilities versus other household responsibili-ties or employment responsibilities, for example), the model implic-itly assumes the existence of a conflict between the woman and her developing fetus. In the medical view, once a woman is pregnant she becomes two patients: the (prospective) mother and the fetus. Women's acknowledgment of pregnancy can occur apart from their acknowledgment of the baby or their full awareness of their prospec-tive motherhood, as described by Laura Aston, Lauren Fagan, and

Sara Swanson, but this does not mean that women feel their fetuses are completely separate from themselves. When doctors consider pregnant women and their fetuses as separate patients, with potentially different interests, determining whose interests come first in the case of medical intervention can become a difficult decision.

In the most extreme version of the medical model, the relationship between the fetus and the pregnant woman is that of a parasite and host, as Barbara Katz Rothman has noted.[20] Rather than assuming that the interests of the mother and her fetus are consistent with one another, this extreme variant of the medical model assumes that the needs of the mother and her fetus are opposed. A pregnant woman: "is taught that the baby is her adversary." She is told to "allow the baby's needs to dominate."[21] The implication is that the choices a woman makes during pregnancy may mean sacrificing her needs to those of her fetus or baby. When there is a question, the medical expert is the ultimate arbiter, and medical choices ultimately rest on fetal needs and biological considerations.

The tendency toward biological reductionism on the part of the medical establishment has been amply documented by feminists and others. But while feminists have criticized biological reductionism, they have also recognized the power of female biology and women's physiological, procreative processes, as noted in chapter 2, in the discussion of positive essentialism, one form of radical feminism. Most feminists, though, including those who wish to valorize women's "natural" procreative processes, recognize the social contexts in which those processes occur. The failure to contextualize pregnancy, or any other bodily phenomenon for that matter, is a major criticism of mainstream medicine by feminists and also by "alternative" health practitioners, who acknowledge a person's entire life situation as a part of her health status.

Pregnancy has many dimensions for pregnant women, beginning with the deceptively simple question: "Am I pregnant or not?" For doctors, there is an easy answer to this question. If a pregnancy test indicates that conception has occurred, the woman is pregnant. But for women, it is possible to be, or feel, pregnant and not-pregnant at the same time. In the medical view, pregnancy starts with conception, but for women pregnancy can begin long before conception, as with Nancy Wilson and Barbara Smith, for example, who sought and planned their pregnancies long before becoming pregnant. In the medical model, pregnancy is an objective state. For women, pregnancy is a subjective and changing condition.

Medical texts tend to emphasize the risks and problems experienced by (some) pregnant women. The texts reflect an illness model of pregnancy, not a health or "wellness" model. Pregnancy is often viewed by doctors as an illness, crisis, disease, or disability. Birth is described as a dangerous event and every pregnancy is potentially high-risk. Given these assumptions, it is no surprise that the medical model emphasizes the importance of intervention during pregnancy to assure a better "birth outcome." The medical model incorporates the assumption that more medical intervention will result in a "better" baby. Medical specialists have redefined pregnancy as pathology, "to abolish any idea of its essential normality"[22] and to provide a rationale for the necessity of their expert intervention. This approach to pregnancy has obvious implications for choice. If doctors are the experts on pregnancy, then pregnancy-related choices are within their domain, made when medical expertise determines there are reasons to take action.

Pregnancy is a complex, contradictory, profound, and transformative experience for pregnant women. Women's experiences of pregnancy are influenced by their personal circumstances and social contexts. The experience of pregnancy influences women's sense of their bodies and themselves, their relationships at work and home, and vice versa. For pregnant women, pregnancy has many dimensions and many interconnected layers. The meanings of pregnancy go far beyond its biological or physiological reality. As Sara Swanson said, describing her feeling that she needed to find additional friends once she became pregnant and a prospective mother: "What I've been trying to sort out is, is it a matter of a changing role and having to find a new group?" The feeling started as soon as she became pregnant: "There's really a nine-month period where you're trying to figure out where you fit in."

Pregnancy gave Sara Swanson a new identity, a new sense of herself. Though this new identity did not completely supplant her other identity(ies)— she wanted to continue working outside the home, for example—Sara Swanson felt she was entering a "maternity" (Anna Simas's term) and she hoped to find other women with whom to share the experience. Sara Swanson's experiences were similar in some ways to the experiences of other pregnant women, as

demonstrated in their comments. As a group their experiences were
substantially different from the medical model of pregnancy.

That these women's experiences of pregnancy differed from the
medical model of pregnancy is consistent with previous research by
social scientists and feminists who have discovered dramatic differences between women's and medical assumptions and perceptions.
Emily Martin compared medical depictions of menstruation, childbirth, and menopause with women's own representations of the same
processes, for example.[23] She notes that the images in medical texts
are based on metaphors of production and bureaucracy. Birth is
production and the baby is the product. Women's bodies and organs
(e.g., the uterus) are machines; the obstetrics ward is a factory; physicians "manage" the births of laboring women. Choices during pregnancy are made by doctors (managers) to improve the product or the
production process.

Martin extends the metaphor of industrial production to show
how menstruation and menopause are viewed in the medical model:
menstruation represents failed production and menopause represents
the breakdown of the system of (re)production. A problem with this
part of Martin's analysis, though, is that for women who are attempting to become pregnant, menstruation can indeed mean failure.
Martin does not discuss miscarriage, ectopic (tubal) pregnancy, or
stillbirth. Presumably these pregnancy outcomes would also be categorized by doctors as failed production, and perhaps viewed in the
same way by some pregnant women and women who hope to become pregnant.

Interestingly, Martin's book does not focus explicitly on pregnancy, per se. The two processes, pregnancy and childbirth, are
undeniably and inextricably connected, when a pregnancy is carried
to term and when all goes well, but it is interesting that Martin
seems to focus on the "product" of conception—or the production
moment?—in the same way that she says the medical model does:
childbirth, rather than pregnancy. In Martin's interview guide the
pregnancy questions are linked to labor. The women in Martin's
study were asked only a few questions about pregnancy itself. Most
of the questions about childbearing focused on labor and childbirth.
Women who never had been pregnant were asked: "Looking ahead,
do you have any hopes or fears about pregnancy, about labor? What
have you heard or learned about it from your parents, siblings,

friends, books? If you were to get pregnant, what kind of birth experience would you want?"[24]

Some of the women interviewed by Martin and her research team appeared to accept the medical model. Middle-class women's descriptions of their own body processes reflected an internalization of the mechanistic, medical model. In contrast, working-class or lower-income women described menstruation "phenomenologically" (e.g., describing bleeding or the feelings associated with menstruation, talking about a "life-change").[25] Their descriptions of their body processes did not reflect the dichotomized picture of women's bodies and selves contained in medical texts and in the discourse used by middle-class women.

Martin uses the images of consciousness and resistance found in some women's discourse to suggest an alternative model of women's reproductive processes. She suggests that women are capable of constructing an alternative conception of their experiences, despite the power of the prevailing medical view. In this way Martin's findings are analogous to the stories of the women I interviewed. Their perceptions and depictions of their experiences pose a challenge to medical conceptions of pregnancy.

Other feminists have exposed the assumptions that lurk beneath ostensibly "objective" or "scientific" medical language and practice, and have analyzed differences between the perceptions and discourse of patients and doctors. Alexandra Dundas Todd and Sue Fisher, for example, have analyzed communication between doctors and their women patients. Todd discovered that "women's social, biographical material was repeatedly truncated by doctors who wanted to focus on the medical matter at hand—the body, its control, and its treatment."[26] Fisher's analysis shows how the institutionalized power imbalance between doctors and their female patients influenced treatment decisions in potentially dangerous ways, leading to unnecessary hysterectomies and leaving needed Pap smears not recommended or not done.[27]

Hilary Graham and Ann Oakley have suggested that differences between women's and doctors' perceptions are based on different frames of reference or ideologies.[28] They found that pregnant women and doctors disagreed about the definitions of pregnancy and "successful" reproduction. Doctors used the reference point of "perinatal and maternal mortality rates, and to a lesser degree certain restricted

indices of morbidity." Women (mothers) defined success more holistically, incorporating the quality of their pregnancy and birth experiences, "the subsequent mother-baby relationship" and the way
"motherhood is integrated with the rest of a woman's life." [29]

Barbara Katz Rothman's "midwifery model" is an explicit feminist
alternative to the "man's eye view of women's bodies." In the medical model, "the male body is taken as the norm." [30] In the midwifery
model, women are seen as the norm, their procreative processes are
seen holistically, and pregnancy is viewed as a healthy, normal condition. [31]

The differences between women's and medical perspectives on
pregnancy have parallels in women's, feminist, and medical depictions of choice. Pregnancy is relational, multidimensional, and contextual for women, and women's choices about their pregnancies
have those same qualities. Pregnant women's previous experiences
and their changing feelings and ambivalence about pregnancy and
motherhood influence the choices women make about their pregnancies: choosing a health provider, making choices about "going public" about the pregnancy, and, as we shall see in the next chapter,
having prenatal tests.

Risky Choices: Decisions about Prenatal Diagnosis

When a woman chooses to attempt pregnancy, she risks failing in that attempt, as noted in chapter 3. Once she becomes pregnant, she faces other risks and responsibilities. After learning they were pregnant or confirming a suspected pregnancy by using a home or laboratory pregnancy test, and after choosing a health provider, women faced choices about several other tests as they began their formal medical prenatal care. The maternal serum alphafetoprotein (AFP) test, ultrasound (sonogram), and amniocentesis are three tests commonly used for prenatal screening and diagnosis.[1]

If pregnancy is a clear-cut, developmental, biological phenomenon that proceeds in a linear fashion from conception to birth, the implications for choices are clear: the only relevant "data" for decision-making are those about the pregnancy's physiological trajectory. Doctors use a statistically derived model of the "normal" pregnancy as the standard against which to measure or calculate the "progress" of each woman's pregnancy. Choices, such as whether or not to use a particular prenatal test, are made by the doctor or by the pregnant women and her partner in consultation with her doctor on the basis of the medical model. Decisions occur at different points; certain tests are appropriate at certain times. Medical norms about the stages of pregnancy and childbirth are associated with protocols that require doctors to intervene when women's pregnancies differ from those norms. The role of the physician is to ensure that the pregnancy goes smoothly, resulting in both a healthy mother and a healthy baby. To ensure these outcomes, the physician monitors the pregnant woman for risk factors and initiates interventions if problems arise.

As Michelle Harrison has noted, the medical model of childbirth includes a well-defined time-line. As an obstetrics resident, Harrison felt pressured to follow the medical model. She learned that she was unable to act on her belief—based on her experience with birthing mothers—that it is important to allow each woman's pregnancy and childbirth to "progress" in its own way and time. She was expected to initiate interventions when women's pregnancies and deliveries differed from the "normal" time-line. Her choices were limited to maintaining the normal trajectory of pregnancy and birth; none was made by the pregnant woman. Harrison preferred an approach that involved listening to and observing the pregnant woman. But within the context of an obstetrics and gynecology ward of a major urban medical center, Harrison found she was forced to standardize her approach to pregnant women.[2]

Paradoxically, while the medical approach to pregnancy and child-birth is based on the idea of a normal trajectory, the medical perspective includes an expectation that women will deviate from that trajectory; variation and riskiness are expected. There is no such thing as a no-risk or low-risk pregnancy, as noted by one physician, an advocate of the fetal monitor.[3] Pregnant women also talked about risks, and like doctors, they considered risks as they made choices about their pregnancies.

In describing their feelings and choices about prenatal tests, the women consistently mentioned three concerns: the information provided, reliability, invasiveness and risks of the tests themselves in relationship to their own sense of the "riskiness" of their pregnancies; their previous experience with the test(s); and their feelings about their potential choice(s) following a positive diagnosis, including feelings about disability and abortion. Most of the women mentioned more than one of these concerns; many mentioned all of them. Together, these considerations comprise a complicated picture of choice.

Concerns about the Tests Themselves

Nearly all the women had several blood tests as part of their routine prenatal care. These tests often included the maternal serum alphafetoprotein test (AFP), a blood test used to screen for possible neural tube defects in the fetus, including anencephaly and spina bifida.[4] The alphafetoprotein test is not very invasive, requiring only a sample of the pregnant woman's blood. It involves minimal pain, if any, and has none of the dangers associated with more invasive tests (e.g., amniocentesis or chorionic villi sampling), such as possible injuries to the fetus, infection, or miscarriage. Penny Adams talked about the test with a nurse at her doctor's office. The nurse gave her a brochure, and said "it's up to you." Penny Adams asked her doctor some questions about the test, "and he answered them. He really kind of recommended it because it might give them information." Her husband thought the test "might show something helpful." She was not really interested, though, "because what are we going to do with the information?" Both she and her husband are Catholic and "wouldn't think of terminating." But she agreed to have the test: "they said that they could use some of the information to monitor, and that's why we agreed. They just draw blood, so it's real simple."

Laura Aston also considered the value of the information provided by the AFP test. She carefully read some information her doctor gave her, to see "would it be worth it to have this test, would it be a helpful test . . . it's not a question of risk, but just a question of, is is going to give you any information that would be helpful." After talking with her husband, Laura Aston decided not to have the test, given its inconclusiveness: "It can mean a lot of different things, and you're going to have to get more invasive testing to find out what those things are." It seemed "like a worry rather than something to make you feel better." She felt that prenatal information would be useful if it could help the baby: "like they can do a shunt . . . if there's tests that can tell me something so I can do something helpful . . . then I would get the test. But if it's just a test to say there's something wrong with this baby, and then I have to decide whether to abort . . . I've already decided I'm not going to abort it, so it's not a very helpful test."

The alphafetoprotein test constituted a difficult choice for eight of the women, a somewhat surprising finding. I had expected all of the women to tell me it was a routine, noninvasive test, and therefore not a very significant choice. This was not the case. Six of the eight women knew there was a chance of a false positive result and did not want to subject themselves to the possibility of the additional choices that might follow (i.e., whether to have amniocentesis to confirm the AFP result; what to do if the amniocentesis result was positive). A Swedish study found that women chose not to have the test for two reasons: their anti-abortion feelings, and their feeling that the test was unreliable.[5] Four of the six women who expressed concern about the unreliability of the test chose to have it anyway. The other two women chose not to have the test. Roxanne Thomas and Carol McAllister both had the same health provider, and that may have had something to do with that decision.

Women welcomed information offered by prenatal diagnosis when they felt it would be useful. Their conceptions of useful information took three different forms. Information was useful when it could be used to help a woman and her partner: decide whether to continue or terminate the pregnancy (Barbara Smith, Sarah Worthington, Lauren Fagan, Anna Simas); plan for the birth of a child with a potential problem (Carol McAllister and Laura Aston); or when it could help the health providers monitor the pregnancy, plan for the birth, or "do something" to help the fetus or infant before or immediately after birth (Penny Adams, Roxanne Thomas, Jane Foster, Laura Aston.) Rather than valuing information in and of itself, women welcomed information that would let them or their doctor "do something." Information was useful and desirable to women when it felt empowering to them, but their varied responses to the information available from the alphafetoprotein test demonstrate that not all information feels empowering to all women.

Wanting Visual Information: Prenatal Baby Pictures

Another choice faced by pregnant women in a high-tech age is the choice to "see" the fetus prenatally, by having ultrasound and observing the baby's image on a video screen. Nearly all of the women wanted to see the baby in an ultrasound "photo." The thirty-one women received prenatal care from obstetricians, family practitioners, internists, and midwives. Like most pregnant women in the 1990s who are privileged enough to have prenatal care, thirty of the women had at least one sonogram by the time I talked with them or anticipated having one at some point during the pregnancy. The only woman who had not had an ultrasound and did not anticipate having one was Meg Fryer, whose prenatal care came from a midwife and a holistic doctor. The women's health-care providers suggested and performed ultrasounds for three reasons: to "date" the pregnancy (i.e., determine the date of conception and/or the delivery date); to determine a safe place for the insertion of the needle during amniocentesis; or to check the baby for morphological anomalies toward the end of the pregnancy.[6]

Almost all of the women described their experiences with ultrasound in positive, if not glowing terms. This was true of women who wanted to learn the sex (and hoped that ultrasound would allow them to do so) as well as those who did not wish to learn the baby's sex prenatally. Even women who were not sure they actually would have the procedure talked enthusiastically about the chance to "see" the baby or receive copies of prenatal baby pictures. Roxanne Thomas was not certain that her doctor would suggest ultrasound, for example, but talked almost wistfully about the possibility of having the test, wanting that visual information. Carol McAllister also expressed a desire for a picture of her baby. She chose not to have the alphafetoprotein test with this pregnancy, in part due to her awareness of the risk of a false positive result, and felt she would prefer to have an ultrasound: "if I felt . . . there was a problem I would probably say, let's just do an ultrasound . . . I don't want to mess around waiting for the AFP." She "was curious to get a little picture of the baby." If ultrasound "turned up something funny . . . I'd have to struggle . . . [about choosing amniocentesis] . . . I don't think I'd consider aborting . . . I already talk to my belly, say, hi in there. It feels more like there is a child growing . . . But if she [doctor] says . . . there's something . . . going on that really makes me curious, I'd say wait and do ultrasound."

Sara Swanson anticipated having ultrasound at some point during her pregnancy, and she also welcomed the chance to "see" her baby: "My sister had participated in a study . . . they did one . . . every two months, so she had a lot of pictures . . . that was really neat . . . a way to make it really real, and it was something . . . that you could visibly share with somebody . . . it's [ultrasound] something that I look forward to . . . more information is what it is." She felt that the visual information would make her pregnancy "more comprehensible."

Other women also wanted the visual information available from ultrasound, to confirm "that there was a baby there" (Laura Aston, Marta Betts, Bernadette Lynn); to determine fetal position(s) and development (Greta Erlich); to check on the "dating" of the pregnancy (Rachel Howard, Jane Lowe); and to check the baby for morphological anomalies (Nancy Wilson). All of the women except Meg Fryer had reasons for wanting to have ultrasound. Only three women expressed concerns about the possible risks of the test. Jill Anderson had heard a speaker at a conference who talked about the unknown effects of sonar waves on fetal development, and that made her wonder about the possible long-term risks of the procedure. Jane Foster also worried about the test and wanted the equipment turned off as soon as possible after her baby's image appeared on the screen. And Jane Lowe worried that an early ultrasound might have "done some damage" to her baby. Women's descriptions of their experiences with ultrasound demonstrated that getting prenatal information by seeing the image of their baby for the first time can be a highly emotional experience for pregnant women. Though some doctors may view ultrasound and amniocentesis as "routine" interventions during pregnancy (especially in the case of "high-risk" pregnancies), women's experiences with these tests are far from routine.

Laura Aston chose to have an ultrasound during her second pregnancy for reassurance, because her last pregnancy ended in miscarriage. She found the test exciting, and seeing the baby's image was a relief to her and her husband: "we had brought a videotape, to tape it, and before she put the videotape in she said, 'Let's just check and make sure there's something in there,' in this sort of calm, matter-of-fact voice . . . and she turned it on and right away you could see that there was a baby, and [husband] and I both cried, while she was doing it . . . I don't know what was more, a feeling of relief or excitement . . . when she went out of the room we both just cried . . . such a relief." Laura Aston noted that "during the first trimester we weren't as excited . . . the first time I was pregnant I started feeling like there was a baby there, as soon as I knew I was pregnant. But the second time I didn't feel that way until after the ultrasound."

Rachel Howard also found that her experience with ultrasound was a positive one, despite some physical discomfort.[7] Her doctor suggested ultrasound to verify her conception date. Rachel Howard knew when she had conceived, but after detecting a fetal heartbeat during an early prenatal exam, her doctor thought that the pregnancy might be further along and suggested the ultrasound. He told her, "it's very unusual to get a heartbeat when you're only eight weeks pregnant, so maybe you're really ten weeks . . . and your dates are wrong." She was "pretty sure of the dates," and told him so, but "he says, well, we'd better check, because two weeks is a big difference." The test "was uncomfortable" for her: "you have to have a really full bladder and then they use the hearing instrument, and they rub it across your abdomen and they have to use a lot of pressure to get a good reading." At eight weeks "there's not much to see, but you can see the heart beat . . . you can see this little tiny bit of light, just barely quivering, so that was kind of nice . . . I wasn't nervous about it or anything . . . just . . . anxious to find out how pregnant I really was." As it turned out, "my dates were right." In that sense the experience was an empowering one for Rachel Howard.

Louise Frey described her experience with ultrasound in glowing terms. Because her baby was very active on the morning of her amniocentesis, Louise Frey had two or three ultrasounds and eventually left the doctor's office, returning later for the amniocentesis. She described her response to the four ultrasounds:

I couldn't believe it! To see this little being inside me . . . it was play time, and it was just bouncing off the walls, and scrunching up its knees, and going ping, ping, just all over . . . there was no safe pocket to put in the needle . . . [doctor] was . . . pushing my stomach, to just see if we could get the kid to the other side . . . he would . . . lift his fingers and the baby would [sound of movement] . . . all over the place, just having a blast.

Twenty minutes later the doctor tried again, but the baby still was moving, so Louise Frey went home and returned later to try again:

When I went back, the baby was napping. Upside down, just all curled up . . . it was very easy to draw the amniotic fluid out, no problem . . . But what happened that day, is um, a new layer of bonding, upon seeing, the baby, and seeing this kid scratch its ears, and suck its thumb, rub its eyes, it was like, oh my God, it's a little baby in there. And I knew, I mean it was just so active and full of zest, and I felt like this kid has got to be healthy, and I thought, maybe we shouldn't even have the test.

Seeing the image of her baby was "very reassuring" to Louise Frey. She noted that "the kid looks really happy . . . I really understood why I was so fatigued, why I was so hungry, and it was really obvious that there was something real major going on in my body." Her feelings about ultrasound changed after her experience:

I came out of there feeling like, boy, a month ago I would have had such a cuckoo attitude . . . it felt like, now, I agree, it's probably completely unnecessary, but I feel now, that it's a big cheap thrill. It's a lot of fun, to see what's happening inside you. It was a high day for me, just watching this kid and [doctor] was being really silly with me, and saying, you know, I meant to tell you there's a prenatal child obedience class at [hospital] and I really think you should enroll!

The visual images available through ultrasound confirmed women's sense of the timing (dating) of the pregnancy, made them feel closer to the baby, made the baby more real, and made them feel that the baby was healthy. But getting visual information was not a wholly positive experience for all of the women, and women's responses to the experience included feelings of ambivalence and alienation.

Jill Anderson had a positive experience with ultrasound, but her description contained contradictions. She loved seeing the image of her baby on the screen. She "hated it when they turned the machine off" and she no longer saw the image of her fetus, which looked so much more like a baby than she had expected. She and her husband were quite moved: "it was a powerful image, a really powerful image, I mean, tears came to both of our eyes, you know, it just, I think we hadn't expected, you know, that that was what we would see." She felt sad when the machine was turned off, and felt she had left the baby behind, in the doctor's office. As she and her husband drove back home after the amniocentesis, she could not connect her womb, and what was in her womb, with that image:

I can remember saying to [husband] on the ride back up, that I was having a strange sensation of having left the baby back in the office, you know, that the baby was there in the screen . . . what we saw couldn't possibly be right here with us, in the front seat, in my womb. It just, I mean, I still, didn't feel I could make the connection . . . so I felt I left it there for safekeeping.

Jill Anderson's sensation that the baby was in the ultrasound monitor, no longer in her body, is consistent with Rosalind Pollack Petchesky's observation that procreative technologies, and particularly ultrasound, contribute to making the baby appear to be a separate individual, outside the pregnant woman. One ramification of that sense of separateness is that the woman can become, or feel, extraneous to the whole process. Jill Anderson loved getting the visual information about her baby. At the same time, the experience caused her to feel a sense of alienation from her own body and the reality of the baby within her body.

The experience of seeing the baby's image on the screen was also powerful and somewhat troubling for Betty Mell. She had experienced ultrasound during previous pregnancies, but saw the image on the screen for the first time during this pregnancy: "They wouldn't show me the screen [in the past.] They gave me a picture this time

. . . so I was thrilled, but it was a little spooky . . . it was fascinating . . . seeing the baby, but when she got it at such an angle that the baby turned its face, and I could see the face . . . that was too much for me, I don't know why, I was just overwhelmed, I guess." Though the experience felt a bit spooky, she also enjoyed it: "it was really interesting, and I felt like going every day and watching."

Ultrasound is not invasive in the way that amniocentesis and chorionic villi sampling are invasive; the sound waves that enter a woman's body are invisible. Only two of the women talked about ultrasound in terms of invasiveness: Lauren Fagan and Jane Foster, both of whom worried about "invading" their baby's space and privacy during the test. Jane Foster described her ambivalence:

Although they never have found any problems with ultrasound, it is sound, and they don't know how it is experienced . . . I remember watching this little fetus in there, moving, he was moving his hands around up near his head, and kind of going [moves arms] which is kind of a typical baby gesture, you know, up in the air like that, and I kept thinking he's saying, turn it off, turn it off. And I said to them, okay, that's enough. I just, I felt like I didn't, how long did it need to be there?

The invasion of a woman's womb and her baby's space by ultrasound is less obvious than the invasion by a needle in amniocentesis, for example, but the image produced by the test makes something inside the woman—her fetus—become externally discernible. Something internal, and private, becomes externally knowable and public. Only a few women expressed uneasiness or ambivalence about ultrasound, though, despite concerns about the possible risks of the test. When it came to amniocentesis, however, women expressed clear concerns about the invasive nature of the procedure.

Invasiveness and Risks to the Baby or Woman

One of the paradoxes of choice is that the choice to have something and the choice not to have that same thing—prenatal tests and/or information, in this case—can be equally empowering to different women. Thus, the implications of choice are not clear-cut when the choice itself entails risk. The rational choice model, reflected implicitly in liberal feminism as well as in the medical approach to pregnancy and prenatal diagnosis, suggests that women make (or should make) choices about prenatal tests by considering or balancing these factors: the risk of having a baby with a detectable disability, the risks associated with the tests themselves, such as the miscarriage risk associated with amniocentesis, and the benefits of the test(s), that is, knowing whether the fetus has or is at risk of having a particular genetic anomaly, and being able to choose to terminate the pregnancy or carry it to term on that basis. Women talked about risks when they talked about their pregnancies and about prenatal testing, as noted above, and they did so in a different, more comprehensive way from the medical approach to risk. But the women also reflected the medical notions of risk to some extent, when they talked about the invasiveness of prenatal tests and the related risks to themselves and their fetuses.

Women worried about the invasiveness of amniocentesis, and some, such as Jane Doe, mentioned the "big" needle: "I was nervous . . . I had seen pictures of this horse needle that they were going to stick in my stomach." After having the test, Jane Doe relaxed. She and nearly all of the other women who experienced amniocentesis noted that the procedure itself was not as bad as they expected.

Women expressed other concerns after having amniocentesis: harming the baby, getting inaccurate information, or receiving a positive diagnosis. Lauren Fagan had misgivings after having the test. She had chosen to have amniocentesis because she wanted the genetic information, but did not know if she would choose to terminate her pregnancy in the case of a positive diagnosis. It was reassuring to her to get a negative diagnosis, but her feelings about the test were not completely positive. She felt she had invaded the baby's privacy by having the test, and felt her choice was a selfish one. She felt she had taken a risk, because the baby could have been "poked" by the needle.

Louise Frey, on the other hand, minimized the risks associated with both ultrasound and amniocentesis after having the tests. She originally planned not to have amniocentesis, so minimizing the risks may have been a way for her to reconcile herself to the choice she ultimately made. She clearly enjoyed seeing her baby's image on the screen, as described above, and the pleasure and value of the information were primary in her mind: "I really don't think that the risks, I mean, there's no real documented risks with ultrasound, and I . . . didn't mind going in four times, because I kept seeing what was going on . . . that was really fun. So today I finally got the phone call saying 'you have a chromosomally normal child.' "

Six women talked explicitly about the risks of the tests (especially the risk of miscarriage) in relationship to the risks of having a child with a disability.[8] These women talked about balancing, or weighing, the risk of miscarriage against the risk of having a child with a detectable disability. They seemed to have internalized the medical model of choice with respect to prenatal diagnosis at least to some extent; their thinking was consistent with a rational choice model. Of these six women, three chose to have amniocentesis and three did not have the test. One of the six, Barbara Sanders, chose amniocentesis over chorionic villi sampling on the basis of her concerns about miscarriage. One of them, Laura Aston, was under the age of thirty-five, so the thinking process was somewhat speculative in her case.

Two of the six women, Laura Aston and Nancy Wilson, described their thinking processes in ways that specifically mirrored the rational choice and medical models: risks versus benefits, or risks versus risks. In addition to her interest in obtaining useful information, Laura Aston was concerned "that the risk does not outweigh the benefits." Nancy Wilson also compared the risks of amniocentesis with the risk of having a child with a detectable disability, and "that's partly why we did decide on amnio this time, plus . . . I will be thirty-five, which is when they recommend it." What Nancy Wilson "had to think about was, what's the risk of losing the child, with the amnio, versus the risk of having an abnormality with the child. And they were the same, so the question I asked myself, was, which was the worst outcome. And for us I think having a child with an abnormality that we didn't know about would have been a worse outcome, and that's what finally made me say okay."

Nancy Wilson was willing to risk miscarriage in order to get information about her baby. She arranged to have an "early amnio" at around twelve weeks (usually amniocentesis is performed at sixteen weeks), and made the two-hour drive to the test center on a snowy day. At the center, she learned that the risk of miscarriage was slightly higher with early amnioceteses than later ones. The higher risk may be associated with the fact that most miscarriages occur during the first trimester of pregnancy, and there is no way to determine if the higher miscarriage rate associated with early amniocentesis is attributable to the procedure or not. Nancy Wilson thought again about the risk of losing her pregnancy, and considered traveling back home through the snow and returning in a few weeks for the later test, to minimize the miscarriage risk. She decided to go ahead with the procedure, but the choice was a difficult one; weighing risks against risks is not an easy process.

Jane Foster also considered the risk of miscarriage and the risk of having a child with a detectable condition. She thought about the same two risks considered by Nancy Wilson, but came to the opposite conclusion. She decided not to risk miscarriage, and chose to accept the possibility of having a child with a detectable disability. Risks and benefits are defined and perceived in different ways by different women.

Physicians and genetic counselors label some women's pregnancies as high-risk and then treat them accordingly, providing information about potential problems and recommending prenatal diagnosis, for example. Only some of the women I interviewed fell within the medically defined high-risk category. Eighteen of the thirty-one women were age thirty-five or older at the time of our interview(s). Three of those eighteen women could also be considered "high-risk" on the basis of factors other than age: Sarah Abraham, on the basis of having a chronic disease (lupus); Nancy Wilson, on the basis of her history of cancer and her difficulty in becoming pregnant; and Barbara Smith, on the basis of her history of multiple miscarriages. Not all of these eighteen women identified themselves as high-risk though.

High-Risk and Low-Risk Women, High-Risk and Low-Risk Choices

Women differed in their perceptions of their own "at-risk" status with respect to their pregnancies, just as they differed in their perceptions of high-tech and low-tech medicine (chapter 4). Doctors and genetic counselors generally use three criteria or "risk factors" to determine whether women have "high-risk" pregnancies, any one of which is enough to place a woman in the high-risk category. These factors are: being age thirty-five or over at the time of the expected birth, previously having given birth to a child with a genetic disability, or having a family member with a genetic disability. Doctors and genetic counselors recommend amniocentesis to women with high-risk pregnancies. In some cases, amniocentesis is scheduled by the health provider as a routine part of health-care when at least one of the risk factors is present. Only one of the women I interviewed mentioned having a family member with a genetic condition or disability, Down syndrome. None of the women had ever given birth to a child with a genetic disability. The women who identified their pregnancies as "high-risk" did so on the basis of age alone.

Women between the ages of thirty-five and forty who accept a high-risk pregnancy identity based on age accept two ideas: they are "older mothers;" and older mothers have "high-risk" pregnancies. Betty Mell, age thirty-six, thought she was too old to be pregnant. Anna Simas, age thirty-seven, wanted additional "hand-holding" and monitoring during her pregnancy, due to her age. Three of the women who identified themselves as older mothers with high-risk pregnancies equated this identification with the need for prenatal diagnosis. Barbara Smith and Sarah Worthington, both age forty, felt this way. As Barbara Smith put it, "it certainly seemed to me . . . an absolutely essential test for someone of my age, because the risks of it were less, statistically, than the risks of not having it." Sarah Worthington said she "wouldn't have gone through the pregnancy otherwise. Let's put it this way. I'm forty years old, and without diagnostic tests that are available I wouldn't have risked pregnancy." Her sentiment is not surprising in the United States at the end of the twentieth century, a time when the category of risk has expanded to encompass nearly all pregnant women, and most certainly includes "older" ones.[9]

Lauren Fagan, age thirty-six, expressed similar feelings about prenatal diagnostic tests at first, stating that she needed the tests because she was "at risk" due to her age: "I have talked to women who did not have any of those tests and I thought to myself I don't think I could have gone through the whole pregnancy without those reassurances." Like Sarah Worthington and Barbara Smith, she seemed to accept the notion that the pregnancy of an "older woman" is a high-risk pregnancy, and thus seemed to accept her status as a high-risk woman. Later in the interview, she talked about her concerns: "There's a part of me that thinks I'm being selfish by having this test . . . my selfishness is causing him [baby] to get bothered, and if my selfishness causes him to get poked, and then have this deformity, I'm going to feel even worse." She mused about pregnancy in the past: "for years, for centuries and centuries people had babies without finding out whether they were normal or not beforehand. And now we have all of these tests available to us, and there's something about . . . not just being able to go on faith, that well, everything's going to be alright, and if it's not, I'll have to deal with it." As she continued to talk, Lauren Fagan expressed more ambivalence: "I mean, why do we do all this? We've made a lot of advances in terms of medical procedures . . . and we should take advantage of those, and there's a part of me that says, oh, we should just leave it all to nature."

None of the "younger women," those who were thirty to thirty-four years old, talked about their pregnancies in ways that made me think they accepted the high-risk identity. Meg Fryer and Rachel Howard mentioned their feelings of security about the pregnancy and their good health, for example. Jane Lowe and Roxanne Thomas both worried that something could go wrong with the pregnancy, but neither of them and none of the other younger women talked about particular risk factors or described themselves as being "at-risk." Six of the younger women seemed to feel they were not at risk because they were younger than thirty-five years of age, and some, like Jane Lowe, speculated that they might feel and choose differently in a few years: "I wonder if it will occur . . . if I have another one . . . I bet . . . I won't have one, um, until I'm at least thirty-five, maybe even older . . . Maybe if I heard enough horror stories, I would start thinking about it . . . what I would do next, I probably would have the AFP, and if the level came out weird, then I would proceed to amnio, but I wouldn't go straight to amnio." Laura Aston, Marta Betts, Rachel Howard, and Sara Swanson also made projections, speculating that they might choose to have prenatal diagnosis during future pregnancies.

Louise Frey and Jane Foster, both "older" women, age thirty-five or older, seemed to reject the high-risk identity. They understood their statistical chances of having a fetus with a detectable, genetically linked disability, but did not feel their pregnancies were high-risk pregnancies. It is possible for women to "know" something and simultaneously feel otherwise. As Louise Frey, age thirty-five, said: "I had decided, very early, before we were even talking about the pregnancy to other people, that I'm not a high-risk woman. I'm not having amniocentesis." She and her husband discussed prenatal diagnosis: "it was more [her husband's] thing, he had more concern about genetic disorders than I did, and we do have a Down syndrome child in our family . . . I was just loving being pregnant, I've worked with Down syndrome children, I wasn't interested in talking about abortion, but yeah, we could get the information, and if we got a Downs child, we could at least be prepared for it." So Louise Frey called her doctor's office "and said, I'll do it . . . it was a very quiet decision, I didn't really talk with many people." She knew several women who had chosen to have amniocentesis and "didn't know anyone who had a spontaneous miscarriage as a result, and the odds seemed pretty good." When it came time to decide about having amniocentesis, she chose to have the test: "when I had the opportunity to have the decision by myself, I decided to do it."

For Louise Frey, the rejection of the high-risk identity did not mean rejection of amniocentesis, a prenatal test that doctors routinely recommend to high-risk women. Her choice to have the test can be explained in different ways: she changed her mind after talking with her husband; she changed her mind after talking with her doctor, who told her she had the freedom to choose or reject the test; her feelings about her pregnancy changed as the pregnancy continued; or, most likely, some combination of all those factors. Whatever the actual reason(s) for Louise Frey's eventual choice, if she experienced any feelings of contradiction or cognitive dissonance about the decision, she seemed able to reconcile her actions and beliefs. Later in the interview she mentioned the "minimal risks" involved in amniocentesis and talked about having had a "little high-tech test," for example. By minimizing the test, she was able to live with her decision to have it and maintain her sense of herself as a low-risk woman at the same time.

Jane Foster, age thirty-five, also knew her statistical risk of having a baby with a genetically linked disability: "One of the statistics is, I guess at this age, it's one in three-hundred-ish, for problems, and it's about the same for miscarriage." Accepting the high-risk status to some degree, she considered having amniocentesis. She called a large, regional medical center, one of the places where women in her area go for prenatal diagnosis, and had two telephone conversations with a genetic counselor. She did some reading, and talked with her husband and some friends. She had "a lot of doubts . . . I know people who've done it, without any problems." She considered "that list of possible things to look for . . . things like Tay Sachs if people are Jewish or of Eastern European descent, or all the other things that might warrant it, like sickle cell anemia, and in our case, with no history of any problems, it just seems so unlikely that there would be anything wrong." Ultimately she decided against the procedure: "I know it's a gamble, but I know it's, it's just part of it." Thus Jane Foster seemed to accept the high-risk status without acting on it.

Some women's choices to have or refrain from using amniocentesis and other prenatal diagnostic tests did not seem consistent with their self-identification as high-risk or low-risk women, or their identification of their pregnancies as high-risk or low-risk pregnancies. Some women who were "objectively" at risk, who fell into the medically defined high-risk category, such as Louise Frey, did not feel they were high-risk women. Other women who fell into the medical risk category—due to age—felt they had high-risk pregnancies, but made choices inconsistent with the medical approach to high-risk pregnancies. Three women over the age of thirty-five— Betty Mell, Mary Meyer, and Sara Ashley—decided not to have amniocentesis or other forms of prenatal diagnosis because they associated the tests with a possible decision to terminate the pregnancy. They knew they would not choose abortion following a positive diagnosis, so chose not to have the tests.

It is possible for women to maintain contradictory beliefs about themselves and their pregnancies. Women may feel varying degrees of risk at different moments, days, or years, or in different situations. Just as women may move in and out of the pregnant identity, feeling pregnant to varying degrees at different times (chapter 5), women may shift in and out of a high-risk or low-risk identity. Women's self-attributions of risk, like their definitions of risk, were far more complicated than medical risk definitions and designations.

Women talked about their pregnancies in ways that made me think they partially accepted and partially rejected a high-risk status, or accepted a high-risk status at particular moments but rejected it at other moments. Louise Frey and Lauren Fagan both said they knew they were at risk for having a child with a genetic abnormality due to their age, for example. They also told me they were healthy and had no reason to suspect problems of any kind, and both chose to have amniocentesis. Jane Lowe and Roxanne Thomas worried about the risk of something going wrong, despite the fact that they both were in their early thirties, but neither of them considered requesting or choosing amniocentesis.

Learning the Sex of the Baby

In addition to providing information about possible genetic anomalies, some prenatal tests provide information about the sex of the fetus. The image generated by ultrasound allows a trained observer to learn the sex of the baby (if the baby is in an appropriate position during ultrasound).[10] Amniocentesis provides a full genotype, including the sex chromosomes.[11] All of the women were aware that information about fetal sex is available through prenatal diagnosis, and most women had definite feelings about whether or not they wanted that information. Women described three different responses to the chance to learn the sex of the baby: clear feelings about wanting the information and enthusiasm about knowing the baby's sex; clear feelings about not wanting the information, and enthusiasm about being surprised about the baby's sex at birth; and mixed feelings about getting the information and knowing the baby's sex prenatally.

Lauren Fagan welcomed the chance to learn her baby's sex and said it was hard for her to imagine relating to her child in utero otherwise. She and her husband had named the baby, she felt he was "a real person" and had "conversations" with him. Roxanne Thomas had similar feelings. She did not want to have amniocentesis and was unlikely to have the test, since she was under thirty-five and had no other medical risk factors, but hoped there might be a reason to have ultrasound, as it would provide information that interested her: the sex of her baby.

Not all of the women wanted to learn the baby's sex before birth. Laura Aston did not think she would ask for the information, following ultrasound: "My mother-in-law . . . asked me if we were going to . . . and I said, well, I really don't want to know, but I think [husband] wants to know . . . she had asked him separately, and he said, no, I don't really want to know." I asked her to elaborate and she said, "both of us would kind of like to know, but not really . . . It's exciting news, no matter when you get it . . . I don't want to be sexist about it, so I almost prefer not to know, to delay as long as possible making attributions about this child." Some of her relatives suggested that she might want to know the sex, to know "what to get" for the baby. She dismissed this: "you get baby stuff for it, it doesn't matter if it's pink or blue or whatever."

As Barbara Katz Rothman has noted, knowing the fetal sex can influence women's impressions of their in-utero babies. Rothman found that women's descriptions of their fetuses' movements, in utero, during the last three months of pregnancy were gender-specific when they knew the sex of the fetus: "The word 'lively' was always used to describe a male's movements, never a female's," for instance.[12] One reason Laura Aston did not want to know her baby's sex prenatally was to avoid sex-typing the baby before birth. As it turned out, though, she got that information by mistake, which made her very unhappy. She picked up a piece of paper that had inadvertently been dropped on the floor. On it she read one word: "male."

Jill Anderson also did not want to know her baby's sex, in part because she did not want to make sex-based, stereotypical assumptions about the child. She and her husband also wanted the surprise of learning that information at the moment of birth. To protect herself from inadvertently learning the sex of the baby, Jill Anderson asked the technician at the prenatal diagnosis center not to share that information with her obstetrician, and checked with her doctor's office to make sure her request had been honored. Her doctor thanked her for doing that, saying it made the birth more fun for him and his colleagues, an unusual surprise in this era of high-tech obstetrics. Choosing not to learn the baby's sex allowed Jill Anderson to maintain control over the pregnancy and birth to some extent.

Women sometimes encountered implicit and explicit pressures to learn the sex of the baby. When I asked Sara Swanson whether she wanted to learn the sex of her fetus she said,

No, no I don't. And in fact . . . we're in the process of looking at houses . . . and we told the realtor that we are pregnant, and she was, she puts her hand on my stomach and says, "it's a boy." And I was so outraged, like how dare you presume that we wanted a boy. I didn't say anything at the time, but I said to my husband, I don't want people prejudging . . . I want it to be whatever it is, to just welcome whoever comes out.

In addition to making assumptions about women's preferences for a boy or girl, people sometimes assumed that all pregnant women now learn the baby's sex prenatally. Dorothy Lee was ambivalent about learning her baby's sex during her first pregnancy: "I really wanted a girl and my husband really wanted a boy . . . I felt that once the child was born, I wouldn't care, but if I found out that it was a boy mid-way then my feelings would affect the baby." She asked not to be given the information, "although weekly my husband and I talked about calling them up and finding out." In this pregnancy, "we don't really care if it's a boy or girl . . . it just was so exciting not finding out, we just decided to wait." She was sure she would not ask for the information, "but everyone does ask that. Since we've had amnio everyone assumes that we know. I don't know anyone who's had amnio who hasn't found out."

Meg Fryer was aware that many women learn the sex of the baby before birth, but felt no desire for that information: "It wasn't an issue for our first child, and it won't be an issue with any other children . . . That's part of the delight of childbirth, you find out what sex of child you have." She did not want or need to know: "If we had a nursery and we had to paint it all pink or blue . . . I always puzzle myself about people who have to know . . . to have a nursery . . . perfectly painted . . . or they want clothes . . . for that particular child." Like Jill Anderson, she anticipated with pleasure the surprise of learning the baby's sex at birth. Unlike Jill Anderson, though, Meg Fryer took no action to prevent herself from learning the information, because there was no chance of an information "leak." She had no prenatal diagnosis, the information was unknown, and there was therefore no risk that she would learn it. Because Jill Anderson chose to have ultrasound and amniocentesis, she faced the risk of receiving unwanted information. She took deliberate actions to make sure that the information was not shared. Laura Aston also attempted to make sure the information was kept from her; unfortunately, though, once known, it is sometimes difficult to keep information hidden. In Laura Aston's case, the information became known to her by mistake.

When I first talked with Louise Frey, she was considering whether or not to learn the sex of her baby. When she had ultrasound, she became enthusiastic about the possibility: "I couldn't believe the detail, there's five fingers over there, five fingers over there, wow, I thought, if I can count fingers, maybe I can see genitals." She found herself looking, closely, "I thought, is there a penis there, or is that an umbilical cord?" She asked the doctor "is it possible to see genitals at this stage . . . and they said . . . often times we do see something . . . that kind of got me very interested in focusing in on the little, abdomen . . . the nurse said, oh, I think I know what it is . . . and she said, do you want to know?" Though Louise Frey really had not thought about her answer in advance, she said, "yeah . . . yeah, sure . . . how interesting, what a nifty piece of information, I would really know who it was down there." The nurse said "I won't tell you until after the [amniocentesis] results come back . . . we will say something like this, the baby is chromosomally normal, and it's a male or female." When she got the call with the test results, Louise Frey asked the nurse not to tell her the sex, though she had previously wanted that information: "When they called me up, they said . . . did you want to know the sex? And I said no, not until Friday, I have an appointment on Friday, and I'm not ready to know the sex today." She "said that very spontaneously . . . I thought they would say . . . you have a chromosomally normal male . . . They separated out the two pieces of information for me, and they gave me a second chance, and very spontaneously I just said no . . . I can find out on Friday, if we still want to know." I asked what she thought she would do on Friday, and she said, "I don't know . . . I got real excited about knowing, and then I think over the weekend I got excited about not knowing." She recalled a conversation with her pregnant sister-in-law, who had learned the sex of her baby prenatally and was very excited: "She calls the child by name now, and they're sort of focused on this boy child joining their family." Two cousins, both new parents, had a different view, "talking about how wonderful it was not knowing, and just waiting and seeing . . . I didn't feel real definitive about it, and I thought that as long as I'm not definitive, don't do anything."

Louise Frey was struggling with two unknowns. First, she did not know the sex of her baby, though this information was known to others. Second, she was struggling to clarify her feelings about getting the information. In her case, getting the information was potentially empowering, but not knowing was also potentially empowering. She had a feeling that she knew the baby's sex anyway, based in part on the nurse's remarks during the ultrasound. Her feelings changed after getting the amniocentesis results:

When I knew that I had a healthy baby, I thought, that's all that matters . . . now that we know that, we can just, go on, isn't that all I need to know right now . . . I . . . just started thinking about primitive women . . . not knowing until it happens, and how that's part of the birth experience, the pregnancy experience, that, did I want to take that away from myself, because I did a little high-tech test to make sure I had a healthy baby?

The women who chose to learn the sex prenatally felt empowered by the choice. Barbara Smith, for example, welcomed the chance to get information about her baby's sex, comparing it to other, less clear pieces of information, such as the ambiguous information she received about an "autoimmune phenomenon" that doctors thought had caused her miscarriages. But when it came to the actual information about the sex of the baby, women responded in two different ways, with happiness or disappointment at the news. Barbara Sanders was one of the twelve women who wanted to know the sex,[13] and one of the ten women[14] who asked for and got the information:

We did this little guessing game, what does Mom think, what does Dad think . . . I thought it was a boy, because deep in my heart I wanted a girl . . . I figured it definitely would be a boy, and my husband was convinced it would be a girl . . . I was glad I found out . . . when we first found out I had this slight disappointment, but by the next day I didn't care.

Like Barbara Sanders, Sarah Worthington and Evelyn Michaels were disappointed when they first learned the baby was male. These three women had chosen to get the information, but the information itself was disappointing, at least initially. Nancy Hughes also chose to learn the sex of her baby: "it just made sense" to get that information: "you have the amnio done, you know the sex, it's easier to pick a name, you know what's coming . . . it doesn't spoil anything." When she got the telephone call informing her that her baby was a girl, "it was a surprise . . . I guess because I have a boy . . . I'm just real comfortable with boys . . . you could have knocked me over with a feather, when they told me." In her husband's family, "there are just boys, boys, boys." She "kind of assumed . . . I would again be the mother of a boy . . . I was happy . . . it was a nice surprise . . . the nurse could tell . . . when she told me . . . she seemed real pleased . . . from my reaction. It made her day."

Nancy Hughes's surprised happiness at the news that she was carrying a female baby parallels the surprised delight expressed by Dorothy Lee and Jill Anderson when they learned they had given birth to daughters. Not one of the women was disappointed by the baby's sex when learning this information at birth. The only women who expressed disappointment at the news, albeit fleeting or temporary disappointment, were women who learned the sex prenatally. All of the disappointed women had learned they had male fetuses, and the women who expressed delight at the news of fetal sex were carrying females. This finding is consistent with the research of Barbara Katz Rothman, who found that women who learned prenatally that they were carrying male fetuses expressed disappointment at the news, whether or not they had wanted a son prior to becoming pregnant.[15]

Medical and Women's Conceptions of Risk: Not the Same Thing

From a medical perspective, women's pregnancies are risky when specific risk factors are present. The existence of those risk factors is determined by assessing the woman's age; her previous pregnancies, if any; her health; and her family's genetic history.

For doctors, risks are directly related to choice(s), because when risks exist they determine medical decisions and treatment protocols. Risks obviate choice, to a certain extent, because their presence means that certain options are no longer really options. Options, or choices, become instead the medically appropriate actions taken in response to risk factors for the purpose of controlling or reducing risks.

Women's conceptions of risk were more comprehensive than the medical risk categories, and women experienced risk differently from the medical model. Some women seemed to have internalized the medical conceptions of risk and made choices on that basis; for example, the ten women over age thirty-five who chose amniocentesis and did so on the basis of accepting their own age-related high-risk status. But for these and the other women, risks had both personal and social dimensions, and entailed physiological, or medically defined, as well as nonphysiological factors. Their definitions of risk included risks to themselves as well as their fetuses, and the relationship between risks, responsibility, and choices was complex, embedded in and connected to other choices. A choice to reduce a particular risk sometimes entailed other risks. The second recurring theme in women's descriptions of the ways they considered risks and made choices about prenatal diagnosis was their previous experience with prenatal tests.

Previous Experience with Prenatal Tests

Just as women made choices about attempting pregnancy in the context of the rest of their lives, and experienced pregnancy in the context of their other pregnancies and life circumstances, women's choices about prenatal diagnosis were connected to their previous experience(s) with the tests. Women's previous experiences with the alphafetoprotein test, ultrasound, and amniocentesis prompted them to choose to have particular prenatal tests again after experiencing them in the past; to refrain from, or consider refraining from, particular tests after experiencieng them in the past; and to choose to have particular tests after experiencing different tests in the past.

Carol McAllister convinced herself that the information available from the alphafetoprotein (AFP) test was worth getting during her last pregnancy; to some extent, the potential information did not feel empowering but instead felt burdensome. Her "irrational fear" of getting "bad" information made the test a frightening prospect. But eventually she and her husband chose to take the risk of getting a positive diagnosis, a risk that they might have to make additional, potentially difficult decisions. When it came time to decide about the AFP test during this pregnancy, though, she decided not to have it. She felt the information was not worth getting, in part because of her previous experience. Last time, she struggled over the choice: "I believe in the holistic sense of pregnancy . . . if I took care of myself and the genes were right we would have a healthy baby . . . knowing that there are factors that you can't control." She and her husband decided to have the test during her earlier pregancy: "the decision not to have it was based on a fear that there might be bad information or . . . information hard to deal with, and that really wasn't a good reason . . . because chances are that it wouldn't be positive." They felt that "a fear of the unknown" was not a good reason to refrain from the test. When Carol McAllister received the negative test result, she and her husband experienced "a little bit of a sigh of relief." Nevertheless, when she became pregnant again, she decided not to have the test.

Jane Lowe's feelings about the alphafetoprotein test changed between her last pregnancy and this one. Last time, "I had no questions. I was like, okay, I'll take it, it's just a blood test and it will be . . . one more thing that will make me feel that this pregnancy is healthy. So it didn't even cross my mind not to take it." During the waiting period, though, she remembered feeling "ooh, this is weird, you know, I wanted to know . . . I kind of felt a little anxious about not knowing . . . if I was going to have a normal pregnancy." During this pregnancy, she said, "I really question doing it . . . I've heard some real valid reasons not to do it . . . getting a false result, and hearing the level . . . is too high or too low, and getting all worried about that, and then finding out later that it was just a bad result." This time, she and her husband "talked about it a lot . . . my husband was willing not to do it." She felt "we have a healthy baby, and we don't need to take this test." Researchers in Switzerland interviewed ten women about their experiences with prenatal diagnosis and found that the women who chose not to have prenatal diagnosis, who chose to say "yes to the risk," expressed a feeling that "my baby is healthy."[16] But Jane Lowe considered having the AFP test during this pregnancy despite her feelings about her baby's health: "part of me was like, but if I didn't take it, I um, might be wondering the whole rest of the pregnancy . . . if I did take it, and it came out fine, I'd feel so much better."

Jane Lowe's feelings about ultrasound also changed following her last pregnancy. Ultrasound was recommended to her as a routine part of her prenatal care during her last pregnancy: "she [nurse] just said we do ultrasound here, to date, and to see . . . about the possibility of twins, or to see if there are . . . physical abnormalities." She "didn't question it, and I thought it was actually kind of exciting." She had heard of ultrasound, and was sure she wanted it done. The experience itself was uncomfortable: "you have to fill your bladder, and I remember they made me wait in the waiting room so long . . . I almost died, and I just thought, this is agony . . . this is terrible, they push this thing around on your belly, and they push on your bladder, and I thought oh God, this is hell." But the discomfort associated with the test was the least of her worries. She received a telephone call from the doctor's office following the procedure, and was told that her amniotic fluid level seemed low. She became really worried. Her doctor wanted to do another ultrasound in three weeks, and it was a scary three weeks for her. As it turned out, there was no problem, but the experience influenced Jane Lowe's feelings about prenatal tests. During her current pregnancy, she had two sonograms (ultrasounds) before the sixth month, the first because she had a "soreness" in her breast, and the second for "dating" the pregnancy. When her doctor suggested the dating ultrasound, she was reluctant: "part of me doesn't even like having the ultrasounds done . . . not so much for my body as for the fetus." It was so early in the pregnancy that "all they saw was this tiny little yolk sac." She worried "that they had done it so early, that maybe they had done some damage or something, to this little guy." When she shared her worries with her doctor, he said "oh no, it's just nothing to worry about at all. So that made me feel better."

When her doctor suggested yet another ultrasound, at six months, to check for morphological anomalies, Jane Lowe was "kind of tempted just because of my own paranoia about making sure it's a healthy pregnancy . . . and a little part of me wanted to know the sex, but . . . my husband was so adamantly against doing that, finding out the sex . . . I decided, yeah, I can wait. So we decided not to have the third one, because I just felt that three was too many."

Nancy Wilson also described an experience with ultrasound during her first pregnancy: "At twenty-three weeks we had one . . . because [husband] was nervous about the normalcy of this child . . . it was too late to do amnio, and they really weren't recommending it at thirty-three years old, but [the doctor] said, we can do an ultrasound, and it shows quite a bit, it will show if, physically, the baby's okay." They opted to do that, and the experience was a good one: "He was moving around a lot . . . we could see all of his bones, and that he had a closed spine, and everything was there . . . you could see his face, his skull." Her positive experience helped Nancy Wilson choose whether or not to have ultrasound and amniocentesis during her current pregnancy; she chose to have both tests.

Dorothy Lee's choice to have amniocentesis during her current pregnancy also harkened back to her experience with the test during her last pregnancy. One of her colleagues had experienced a miscarriage following an amniocentesis, which caused her to approach amniocentesis "with a certain amount of apprehension." Dorothy Lee and her husband learned from a genetic counselor about their statistical risk of having a child with a genetic condition: "Looking at the statistics, as you get older, genetic problems increase exponentially. Thirty-five, which was the age I was . . . seemed to be the age at which the increased problems start." During that pregnancy, she felt she would choose to have an abortion if she received a positive test result: "I didn't really dwell on what I was going to do . . . at that point it would have been a lot easier for me to terminate . . . if I knew there was going to be some kind of problem with the baby." This time, though, after having had a baby, she felt "although I'm definitely pro-choice, it would have been a lot more difficult for me to terminate . . . I wasn't sure what I would have done." She chose to have the test anyway, because she "wanted to know." She thought it "would have been harder to go through the entire pregnancy" without having the test. Her choice to have the test was a relatively easy one, in part because it was a choice she had made once before.

Feelings about Post-Test Choices

The third theme in women's descriptions of the ways they made choices about prenatal diagnosis was their consideration of potential options following a possible positive prenatal diagnosis. I expected that women would talk about their feelings about having a child with a disability as they described their thoughts and feelings about prenatal diagnosis. I was surprised at how often the topic did not come up until I asked about it. One woman, Sara Swanson, told me that once she became pregnant, she really had not thought about the risk of having a child with a disability, until our conversation. Near the end of the first interview with each woman, I asked her to talk about her experiences with disability and how she felt those experiences had influenced her feelings and choices about amniocentesis and other prenatal tests.

Feelings about and Experiences with Disability

Most of the younger women had not thought much about the possibility of having a child with a disability, perhaps because doctors and genetic counselors only stress the risk of fetal genetic anomalies when women are over the age of thirty-five unless other risk factors are present. Nearly all the women expressed a concern for the well-being of the fetus, though, or mentioned that they hoped nothing would be "wrong" with the baby. Sara Swanson had thought about raising a child with a disability before she became pregnant, but not since becoming pregnant:

I haven't thought about it . . . you go through your pregnancy with the assumption that you have a healthy baby . . . it's people who have problems during the pregnancy who tend to worry . . . those of us who are fortunate to feel good . . . don't have the same kind of reason to be thinking about the possibility of there not being something fully developed, or some kind of problem.

She expressed ambivalence about the alphafetoprotein test:

Even though I have felt so tired during the first trimester, I have basically felt so good that I felt there really can't be anything wrong. And so to obsess about the possibility that something might be wrong seems kind of crazy . . . to some extent it feels kind of academic to me, but I'm going through it just because it seems something we should do, it's available, it's technology.

When I asked her how she would respond to a positive prenatal diagnosis, she said she "would deal with it." She "would raise the child . . . if it could be done within my care . . . I'm not going to be a martyr, and sacrifice my life, you know, one-hundred twenty percent . . . I don't think that would be helpful for me, or my husband, or my marriage." She continued to reflect, saying "we all have unique qualities, and whether it's a learning disability, or some sort of physical handicap," she would "work with that." She "would learn what I could, to . . . help that child grow to its best potential." Sara Swanson's feelings about disability did not play an explicit part in her choices about prenatal diagnosis, though. For her, another factor was more important, and that was the fact that the test was available, and she felt her doctor would not suggest such a test unless it was useful. She noted that she comes from a medical family, and acknowledged that this may have been an implicit factor for her, influencing her response to the doctor's recommendation. Other women also felt they would choose tests suggested by their health providers, whom they trusted.

Sara Swanson's feelings about having a child with a disability were somewhat abstract, and she only talked about them when I asked her to do so. The possibility of having a child with a disability was not a central concern for the other younger women either, who talked about the topic only when I raised it. Jane Lowe also talked about her feelings in something of an abstract way: "I actually do worry about a lot of things . . . that could go wrong, and how terrible that would be. Like last week . . . I saw this young boy, he had something really wrong with him, I don't know what it was . . . I just felt so sad, looking at him . . . and so scared, that what if I have one, like him." She felt "an incredible sadness, and fear. I just felt so sorry for the mother, the parents and I just know how wonderful it is to have an incredibly healthy baby, and what an incredible miracle that is . . . it's hard enough to raise a healthy baby, I can't imagine raising one who's not . . . I'm sure that the imagining of it is probably worse than the reality, but I imagine it would be just awful." Jane Lowe connected her feelings with a childhood experience of knowing a friend's brother who had cerebral palsy: "I grew up, watching this family, and seeing how hard it was, and just, yeah, how just plain hard, and sad, and all that stuff. So I think I have a real fear of that . . . He seemed like such a burden on the family, and it didn't seem like a happy situation at all." When I asked her if that is the image she has when she thinks about problems a child might have, she said, "yeah . . . I flash back to that . . . I also believe they really love him . . . they chose to raise him at home . . . they really loved him, always . . . it's just a lot of work . . . a lot of pain . . . I could love a disabled child, but . . . I just can't imagine doing it." She felt she probably would choose amniocentesis if she became pregnant again after age thirty-five and speculated that she probably would choose to terminate the pregnancy in the case of a positive diagnosis, though the decision would be a very difficult one.

Laura Aston, another one of the younger women, felt she would not choose to have prenatal diagnosis and would not choose abortion in the case of a positive diagnosis, based in part on her experience with a friend with spina bifida: "her mother didn't know that she was going to have this problem before she was born." Laura Aston noted that her friend "might not be around" if her friend's mother had had an alphafetoprotein test during pregnancy.

These women had strong feelings about disability, based in part on early childhood experiences. Not "at risk" for having a fetus or baby with a genetic disability on the basis of age, the younger women did not actually face choices about amniocentesis, and did not have to consider their feelings about their choices following a positive pre-natal diagnosis. The older women, on the other hand, were aware of their statistical risk of having a child with a genetic condition, Down syndrome in particular. Their experiences with disability, and their own and their husband's feelings about parenting a child with a disability, influenced their choices about prenatal diagnosis.

Three of the older women clearly stated that they would terminate their pregnancy in the case of a positive diagnosis: Barbara Sanders, Barbara Smith, and Sarah Worthington. Each woman felt she would choose not to carry her pregnancy to term if she learned her fetus had a detectable genetic anomaly.

Barbara Sanders knew that amniocentesis did not rule out all disabilities, and she expressed her feelings about having a child with possible problems: "At this point, if he's born with some kind of imperfection I feel that it will be minor enough that we all can live with it . . . I hope he doesn't have any, but anything's possible." She recalled a recent visit with her best friend, who had just had a new baby:

We were sitting around watching TV and she [host of television talk show] had on this set of twins who were still connected, at the head . . . I said to myself, God, anything else is so fine . . . it really made me change all of my standards. And it made me think that if anything is wrong with this kid I'm just going to think of those Siamese twins and just be grateful. So it doesn't really worry me.

Because she mentioned neural tube defects earlier in the interview, I asked her to talk more about that. She told me how she felt about having a child with a neural tube defect: "I've just been saying that Siamese twins are the worst, but . . . it just seemed to me that if the kid had that, all I could picture was just this vegetable, sitting around, and that would have broken my heart. I don't want a vegetable. I want a bright, healthy kid."

Barbara Sanders felt she would choose to terminate her pregnancy if she learned her fetus had Down syndrome: "I certainly couldn't live with it any better." But the risk that felt most real to her was the risk of having a baby with a neural tube defect: "because my sister had a fetus with neural tube defects, I was told that my chances of having one were fifty percent greater . . . that it had happened to my sister made me realize, gee, this could happen to me, too." She compared her feelings about this risk with her knowledge of her statistical chances of having a fetus with a neural tube defect: "when it happens to someone close . . . you realize that you can be a statistic, no matter how miniscule that statistic is . . . because it happened to her . . . I was more concerned." Barbara Sanders considered the feelings of her mother and sister, who were anxious for her to have prenatal diagnosis. She chose to have amniocentesis, and her family's feelings about the test played a role in her choice. Her feelings about her pregnancy were connected with her sister's experience; the risk of having a child with a disability, a neural tube defect in particular, felt very real to her. Her choice to have amniocentesis was also influenced by her husband's feelings: "he just knew that he couldn't live with a kid who was, who had Down syndrome."

Barbara Sanders's feelings about disability were clear: she wanted a healthy child, but had little information about or exposure to people with disabilities. This was not unusual. Women talked about their statistical risks of having a child with a disability, and chose to have prenatal diagnosis, in part, to deal with that risk. Lauren Fagan knew her statistical chance of having a child with Down syndrome, for example. She "always knew" she would have amniocentesis, even before becoming pregnant: "I had already made the decision, and then they raised the issue." Dorothy Lee also knew her statistical chance of having a child with Down syndrome, and felt burdened by that knowledge. She chose to have amniocentesis, and the negative test result was reassuring: "For the first time I could relax . . . .all of a sudden, I just felt better . . . an enormous burden was off, and I could really feel good about it. And I've really felt good since . . . that's what you hope for."

Their knowledge of their statistical chance of having a fetus with a detectable genetic condition, the risk itself, was the explicit or concrete reason why Dorothy Lee and other women chose to have prenatal diagnosis. Experiences with disability or general feelings about having a child with a disability were implicit factors in the decision. Not many women talked about what it might be like actually to have a child with a disability. Three women—Carol McAllister, Sarah Worthington, and Barbara Smith—did talk about this. Carol McAllister referred to a neighbor who had a child with a disability, and imagined how she would parent such a child; Sarah Worthington and Barbara Smith both talked about how difficult it would be for them to have a nonverbal child, or a child with a limited intellectual capacity, such as a child with Down syndrome.

Only two women referred to their own physical disabilities when I asked them to talk about disability: Sarah Abraham, who has lupus; and Jane Foster, who talked about an experience she had with a broken leg. Women's lack of information or clarity about disability (e.g., which disabilities are detectable by prenatal diagnosis, and the range of prognoses for particular anomalies, such as neural tube defects) may contribute to the ambiguity and ambivalence women feel about the tests and their choices in the case of a positive diagnosis. Marsha Saxton has suggested that women and men need to have access to accurate information about disabilities and the resources available to people with disabilities and their families, to have full prenatal choice. The informed choice to have a child with a disability must be one of the options, in order for true choice to exist.[17]

Six women referred to their work experiences with children with disabilities.[18] These experiences influenced their feelings about the possibility of having a child with a disability in two ways: making them feel that they could "deal with" a child with a disability, or making them feel they "could not handle" such a child. Their experiences with children with disabilities also influenced their feelings about prenatal diagnosis and the choice to terminate the pregnancy or carry it term following a potential positive test result. Once again, women with similar experiences responded to those experiences in a variety of ways.

All of the women I interviewed knew quite a lot about prenatal diagnosis. They knew about the medical risk factors used by physicians and genetic counselors to determine when to recommend the tests to pregnant women, and they were aware of the risks associated with the tests themselves. But, though some of them chose to have prenatal diagnosis to get information about potential fetal conditions or genetic anomalies, they did not always know which conditions are detectable with a particular test. Nancy Wilson's primary concern, for example, was cystic fibrosis. When she worried about having a child with a disability, she thought about her experience: "I . . . took care of kids with cystic fibrosis. Kids that died. I also knew a woman who died . . . who had cystic fibrosis. She lived to be twenty-five . . . how terrible that was." She was not sure she would terminate her pregnancy if her fetus had cystic fibrosis, but "it would have been something that I would have wanted to know. That is one thing that they don't routinely screen for, which I didn't realize." Though Nancy Wilson learned that the amniocentesis would not be used to screen her fetus for her most specific worry, she chose to have the test, in part because her husband was concerned about the possibility of having a child with Down syndrome. Fifteen women also considered explicitly their husband's or partner's feelings about parenting a child with a disability as they made choices about prenatal diagnosis.[19]

Nancy Wilson knew that Down syndrome varied in severity, and this information contributed to her uncertainty about the choice she would make in the case of a positive diagnosis, despite her husband's feelings: "I didn't feel one hundred percent sure that doing this would lead to this if the outcome were such and such . . . there are all levels of Down syndrome. I've seen those that aren't going to live more than a couple of years, and I've seen those that live to be thirty." Nancy Wilson realized the information available from amniocentesis was limited, though before having the test, she had thought "they could screen for more than they do, with the amnio. I was surprised at that."

There is no way to determine the severity of a detected condition prenatally by amniocentesis, though ultrasound can provide a picture

of fetal morphological malformations. But some amniocentesis diagnoses are ambiguous by definition, and Dorothy Lee was aware of
this.[20] She referred to two acquaintances of hers who faced ambiguous diagnoses: "both had, um, genetic abnormalities come up, not
Down syndrome, but other, that they, medically don't know what
the outcome is . . . they were told that it's probably not as serious as
Downs, but they don't know what the effect is going to be . . . these
women decided to terminate." Dorothy Lee did not know what she
"would have done" in the case of an ambiguous diagnosis: "you
could have a baby that's . . . perfectly normal."

Even when women knew their (statistical) chance of receiving a
positive prenatal diagnosis, and felt they most likely would choose to
terminate the pregnancy in such a case, they still were not absolutely
certain what they would do if they actually received a positive test
result. All of the twelve women who chose to have amniocentesis or
chorionic villi sampling thought they probably would choose to have
an abortion if they received a positive diagnosis.[21] Three of the twelve
felt certain that they would terminate the pregnancy, but the other
nine women expressed at least some ambivalence. None of the twelve
women received positive diagnoses, so none had to make that choice.
In thinking about and making choices about prenatal diagnosis,
women considered their experiences with disability and their feelings
about having a child with a disability in combination with other
factors, including their feelings about abortion.

Feelings about Abortion

Amniocentesis is sometimes a code word for abortion. This was
true for women I interviewed as well as for other people they knew.
Some of the women and their family members, friends, or colleagues
assumed that a decision to have amniocentesis implied a decision to
have an abortion following a positive diagnosis. But not all women
who had vague or specific concerns about having a child with a
disability felt they would choose to terminate their pregnancy in the
case of a positive prenatal diagnosis.

Women expressed a multiplicity of feelings about abortion. They
were "personally" pro-choice or anti-choice, they opposed or sup-
ported women's right to abortion on a policy level, and they had
mixed feelings about their own potential choice to terminate a pregnancy. Even women who were pro-choice expressed reservations

about choosing to terminate their own pregnancy following a positive diagnosis. Women's feelings about abortion influenced their feelings and choices about prenatal diagnosis.

Women who were pro-choice and those who felt they might choose to abort a fetus with a detectable disability chose prenatal diagnosis with those feelings in mind. Lauren Fagan, Evelyn Michaels, Sarah Worthington, Barbara Smith, and Anna Simas told me that their decision to have prenatal diagnosis was connected to their feeling that they probably would choose to terminate the pregnancy in the case of a positive diagnosis. For all of the women, those who decided against prenatal testing because they opposed abortion, and those who chose prenatal diagnosis because they wanted the choice to terminate the pregnancy in the case of a positive test result, the choice to have or refrain from having the test was virtually the same choice as the decision about terminating the pregnancy.

Six women told me about previous abortions. Four of the six felt they would choose to terminate a pregnancy again, this time in the event of a positive prenatal test result; one felt that she would not choose to have another abortion, and refrained from prenatal diagnosis as a result; and one woman was not sure. Three of the six were already mothers, and they felt that choosing to terminate a pregnancy would be more difficult for them now, after having experienced childbirth and motherhood, than it had been in the past. Jane Lowe felt "an abortion would be hard at this point in my life . . . I've had two abortions . . . I just knew it was the right thing to do . . . but since I've had a baby I've grieved that, those abortions . . . Now that I've had a baby and I see what a miracle it is, and how wonderful it is." She felt it would be very difficult to terminate her pregnancy in the case of a positive prenatal diagnosis: "it would be very tough, but . . . I would probably have an abortion." Dorothy Lee expressed similar feelings: "Having had a baby once, although I'm definitely pro-choice, it would have been a lot more difficult for me to terminate, you know, going through the labor and birth." Jane Lowe and Dorothy Lee both stressed that they still feel strongly that abortion is a woman's right, however.

Betty Mell's previous abortion influenced her choice to carry this pregnancy to term, and also influenced her choice to refrain from prenatal diagnosis. At one point during our first interview, she asked me to turn off the tape recorder. She told me about the guilt and sadness she felt following her abortion, some years ago. It was for this reason, in part, that she decided to continue her current pregnancy, an unplanned one. During our second interview we discussed her feelings again and she said I could refer to our previous untaped conversation. Betty Mell's choice not to have amniocentesis was directly connected to her feelings about abortion. She did not want to have an abortion and did not want to be faced with the possibility of having to make that choice.

Having had an abortion in the past influenced women in different ways, just as having experiences with children with disabilities influenced them in different ways regarding their feelings about prenatal diagnosis. These women knew that embedded within the choice to become pregnant was the possibility of a choice to terminate the pregnancy. They included the consideration of their previous experiences with abortion as part of the decision-making process.

Women who had not had previous abortions (or who did not tell me about previous abortions, anyway) also talked about their feelings about abortion, and how those feelings influenced their choices about prenatal diagnosis. Penny Adams opposes abortion and would not choose to terminate a pregnancy. She did not want to have prenatal diagnosis, unless it could be used to help the doctor "manage" her pregnancy in some way. Roxanne Thomas also said she would not choose to have an abortion, but wanted to have ultrasound to learn the sex of her baby. Laura Aston is pro-choice and believes women have a right to choose abortion, but did not think she could have one: "I just don't think I could have an abortion anyway." She traced her feelings about abortion to her teenage years, when she made a speech on abortion in her tenth-grade English class. She decided to look at all sides of the issue, and concluded that she had to make her mind up for herself but not for anyone else: "for years and years I have thought I wouldn't get an abortion." Yet Laura Aston also saved money at one point, in case she changed her mind: "I always thought you can never know until you get in the situation." Since then, though, she decided she probably could not terminate a pregnancy, "so, you know, that decision having been made, that made some of the other testing decisions, because it's useless to have the test, what good would it do?" Given her feelings about abortion, the choice to refrain from prenatal diagnosis felt like an easy one for her. Since she was younger than thirty-five and had no other medical risk factors that would lead a doctor to recommend amniocentesis, she did not actually face that choice.

Secret Amnios

One reason women were reluctant to tell other people about their choice to have amniocentesis or other prenatal tests was that they did not want the censure they might receive from people who opposed abortion. Six women connected their feelings about going public about their pregnancies with their decision to have prenatal diagnosis. These women expressed a desire to keep to themselves a potential decision to terminate the pregnancy following a positive prenatal diagnosis. To them, going public was a relinquishment of privacy that made choosing amniocentesis more complicated. Sarah Worthington expressed her feelings: "I didn't tell anybody I didn't have to tell . . . only this past week did I talk to people I work with . . . I told [friend] next door . . . I told a couple of people . . . if I'd been told I had a Down syndrome baby I would have had termination of the pregnancy, and I wouldn't want to have to tell that to a whole lot of people." She viewed any choices about her pregnancy as "my own personal decision" and did not want to "have to go back and tell people things, undo the information."

Anna Simas's decision to have amniocentesis was also related to her intention to terminate her pregnancy in the case of a positive diagnosis, and like Sarah Worthington, she felt that both decisions were private ones. To avoid the risk of being judged by other people for her decision, she planned to keep her choices to herself: "There would be the people who would say, um, every life is valid, you know, drive me crazy with that . . . if I went through with it, and if something was wrong, I couldn't tell a damn person. I'd disappear for a few days, report I had a miscarriage and that would be it. It would be nobody's business, except for [partner] and my mother . . . that one is real clear in my mind." Some of her friends knew Anna Simas was considering amniocentesis, but she did not wish to share her feelings about abortion with them, to avoid "justifying myself . . . this is much too serious a situation to let anybody else in on."

Jill Anderson and her husband decided not to share the news of her pregnancy until they got the amniocentesis results: "When we made the decision on the amnio we decided . . . we certainly wouldn't give the news out until we . . . had gotten the results back . . . I know it wouldn't be other people's choice, but it just felt um, like we needed to protect that privacy . . . in the decision-making process that we might have to . . . go through." That protection of their privacy "just fit well . . . for us . . . those early months were just ours, you know . . . they weren't filled with excitement, or in envisioning really a baby . . . they weren't public, they were just, just private."

Women's desire to keep their choices private may have to do with feelings of responsibility and blame. Many women feel responsible, and there is evidence that women are implicitly or explicitly blamed by others, when they miscarry.[22] A woman may feel even more responsible when she chooses an abortion, and may face more social censure than when she experiences a spontaneous (involuntary) abortion, or miscarriage. Women expressed strong feelings of responsibility when describing their choices about prenatal diagnosis, and were aware that other people also had strong feelings about their responsibilities as prospective mothers. Those feelings were illustrated in the unsolicited advice they frequently received from other people.

Unsolicited Advice: Words Not Chosen

Most of the women chose to honor the feelings of people they cared about, such as family members or trusted health providers; they made their choices in a relational context. The ways women's moral and other choices are influenced by their desire to respect and empathize with the feelings and needs of others have been described in the work of Carol Gilligan and others. Feminist theorists and proponents of a new psychology of women have challenged mainstream (malestream) models of decision-making. Questioning the emphasis in developmental pyschology on separation and autonomy, Gilligan identified an alternative contextual and relational ethic of caring. Her approach has been widely adopted by feminists and others seeking to validate women's ways of thinking, feeling, and making choices, though her work and conclusions also have met with some criticism.[23]

Other people's feelings and needs comprised part of the social environment in which women made prenatal choices. Women were aware of that context, in a general sense of understanding social expectations (e.g., norms of maternal behavior) as well as in the specific instances of friends' and family members' desires and expectations. All of the women mentioned other people's feelings about prenatal tests: husbands or partners, health providers, family members, colleagues, strangers, and friends. These feelings played a role in the choices women ultimately made about prenatal tests. None of the women expressed strong feelings of conflict about the social pressures they faced; nevertheless it was clear that relational considerations, particularly a desire to honor husbands' and doctors' feelings about prenatal tests, superseded women's own feelings or inclinations at times.

Pregnant women receive unsolicited and sometimes unwanted advice. Laura Aston was advised to learn the sex of her fetus, as noted above, but also was advised not to get that information: "You don't want to know if it's a boy or a girl." She also received contradictory advice about her childbirth options. One family member told her to "seriously consider an epidural. [You're] not after earning any merit badges, and you'd be a lot more comfortable." Another family member told her not to ask for an epidural: "You'll be fine, you don't want anything that's going to interfere." People told Nancy Wilson that she had planned her pregnancy unwisely: "I'm due in September and everybody says, oh you picked a bad time of year, because you have to go through the summer . . . you should have gotten pregnant so that you had the baby in May."

Women received advice about breastfeeding, weaning, and childrearing, even before their babies were born. Roxanne Thomas was advised to: "toilet at eighteen months . . . take a bottle away at a year or earlier . . . then they got into discipline." People told Bernadette Lynn, "I shouldn't be breastfeeding. How are you going to wean her, and how are you going to breastfeed two kids at once [after the birth of the second child], and she's going to be seven years old and still breastfeeding."

Women also received advice about choosing prenatal tests. People told Bernadette Lynn about their negative experiences with prenatal screening and diagnosis, and told her "I shouldn't have the alphafetoprotein." Penny Adams was given implicit advice by people who asked her if she planned to have prenatal testing: "It feels like advice, because they're recommending it by asking." Other women also were advised by friends, family members, doctors, or strangers to have, or refrain from having, particular prenatal tests. For instance, Barbara Sanders received explicit advice and pressure from her sister and mother, who urged her to have amniocentesis.

These pregnant women responded both positively and negatively to the unsolicited advice they received. Other people's words of wisdom sometimes were welcomed, perceived as an invitation to enter the "maternity," or interpreted as a sign of connectedness with other women. But the advice sometimes felt like an invasion of privacy or like censure. Meg Fryer did not welcome other people's comments, advice, and criticism in the guise of advice offered at shopping malls and other public places: "I usually tell them what I think . . . and they usually don't give me much more advice . . . I was still nursing [son] when I was pregnant with [daughter.] Many people were just, 'that's so dangerous,' 'you're endangering the pregnancy,' that sort of thing."

Penny Adams responded to advice from friends and strangers in a philosophical manner: "I think about what people say, wondering if it fits with me . . . try it on and go, well, maybe this, and maybe this, and then I say no, I don't think so, or maybe discard it, or save it until later." She was not offended by the advice and chose whether or not to let specific pieces of advice (or particular advice-givers) influence her choices.

Pregnant women can choose whether or not to respond to the unsolicited advice they receive from strangers, family members, and others. They also can choose when, and whether, to go public about their pregnancies and choices, up to a point. Once women's pregnancies become public because of the visible changes in their bodies, though, the only choice that remains is whether to accept or reject the advice they are offered.

Invasions of Privacy: The Risks of Visible Pregnancy

Women's choices about telling people about their pregnancies were connected to their ideas about privacy. Women who decided to keep the pregnancy private were able to do so for a while. At a certain point, though, their pregnancies became public knowledge because they became physically apparent to other people. At some point, if only at the time of birth, most pregnant women must relinquish their procreative privacy.

Women experienced invasions of privacy that occurred only because they were pregnant. When they became visibly pregnant, other people were often eager to acknowledge their pregnancies. As Virginia Barber and Merrill M. Skaggs observed: "One of the first things we learn when we become visibly pregnant is that we are suddenly interesting to almost everybody . . . strangers feel free to congratulate us—and caution us . . . There are lots of subtle rebukes about our 'selfishness' in not 'putting the baby first.' "[24] When a woman's pregnancy becomes public, the pregnant woman often becomes a public persona. These pregnant women found that this phenomenon prompted both desirable and unwanted interventions from other people.

Sara Swanson noticed that people treated her like public property when her pregnancy became visible: "People ask you very personal questions . . . and have a very different approach to you . . . they automatically put their hands on your belly, and at no other time would somebody invade your privacy like that." People asked her, "are you having morning sickness, or um, are your breasts feeling tender . . . things that they normally wouldn't ask you. And some of them you know as just casual acquaintances." She was amazed at the ease with which people seemed to approach her: "It's almost like your boundaries get lost when you're pregnant."

Sarah Worthington also noted that people treated her differently when her pregnancy became obvious. She compared her feelings of privacy with the way she was treated: "I'm not one of those people who thinks pregnancy is anyone else's business. People are terribly tacky . . . they make all sorts of jokes . . . make fun of pregnant women and want to touch their stomachs . . . they're just weird. It's a highly personal matter and it's nobody else's business, basically."

In addition to being a time when strangers responded to women in ways that sometimes threatened their privacy, autonomy, or "boundaries" (Sara Swanson's term), pregnancy was a time when these women found they had new connections with other people, especially other women. Sara Swanson described her discovery of those connections: "I was talking with this woman . . . at a restaurant the other night . . . she was huge, and I . . . couldn't believe I was asking a total stranger . . . when is your due date . . . we just started talking, and it's a connection. And I wouldn't have spoken to this woman except for the fact that we were both pregnant . . . it was one of those points where I feel some kind of connection." The common bond between women who are pregnant and those who have experienced pregnancy had both positive and negative dimensions for these women.

Multiple Choices, Multiple Considerations

In making choices about whether to have prenatal tests, women considered many factors: the tests themselves, the information they provide, their invasiveness, reliability, and risks. They considered contextual and experiential factors: previous experiences with the tests, disability and abortion, and their procreative histories (herstories). Women considered their feelings and beliefs and the feelings of other people: spouses, family members, friends, health providers.

Women chose tests when it made sense to them to do so, to get information or in response to their feelings of risk. They chose not to have tests when they felt the information would not be useful and when they felt the tests were too risky. When they talked about their choices, they talked about personal and social influences. The effort to consider multiple influences sometimes made the choices difficult. The consideration of particular factors sometimes made the choices easy. Jane Lowe clearly articulated her ambivalence about prenatal tests and having to make choices about them:

My sisters haven't had any of these tests . . . they have had totally healthy babies and they haven't had to worry . . . it's what all our mothers did. My mother had . . . eight totally healthy babies. It makes me think that I'm just . . . succumbing to modern medicine, and their paranoia about malpractice . . . I could save myself some anxiety, by just not having any . . . I think that the fact that the tests exist . . . makes the issue . . . that they exist and I would choose not to do it, makes me feel . . . if I had taken it, then I would know . . . something. So it's . . . sort of too bad that they came up with these tests, I think. But on the other hand, if . . . the tests came out positive on one of these things, I would be glad to know . . . rather than going nine months and then giving birth to a Down syndrome baby . . . in the end, I guess it's good that there are these tests, just because I guess I would like to have the option . . . it's anxiety provoking, but when they come out fine, that's great.

After I turned off the tape recorder, we continued to talk, and she said that prenatal tests were "a double-edged sword."

The ambivalence reflected in women's descriptions of their feelings and choices about prenatal tests supports the previous research about prenatal diagnosis, which shows that thinking about and choosing to use these tests can make pregnant women feel troubled or worried. Waiting for test results can be stressful and anxiety-producing.

But in addition to their role in making pregnancy a scary or

stressful time, prenatal tests also make women feel "safe," are reassuring, and sometimes contribute to women's feelings of connection to
their fetuses or babies. Prenatal diagnostic tests, including ultrasound
and amniocentesis, both cause and relieve pregnant women's fears.
The women in this study demonstrated those contradictory impacts
in the ways they talked about the tests and their choices about them.

These women's ways of choosing challenge and reflect aspects of
medical depictions of risks as well as medical, rational, and feminist
models of choice. Medical choice models emphasize risks and benefits. Feminist models of choice emphasize choices as well as social
forces that construct and constrain choice(s). Liberal feminism
stresses choice in and of itself and underemphasizes the social context
and differences among women. Radical feminism underemphasizes
women's coping abilities and women's strategies for taking control,
dealing with risks and uncertainties, and transforming constraints
into choices. Women talked in contradictory or paradoxical ways
about the risks and choices they faced during pregnancy, both sup-
porting and refuting medical and feminist approaches to choice.

In some ways, women's choices about pregnancy and prenatal
tests, and the ways they made those choices, were very different from
the medical model of pregnancy and choice. In addition to involving
a multiplicity of sometimes contradictory contextual, experiential,
and relational factors, women's choices were connected with their
past, present, and anticipated choices. There were no completely
discrete or isolated choices; instead, choices were often nested within
one another. The relationship among these women's choices was
complex; their choices coexisted in a kind of maze or network of
other choices, intertwined in time and space. Women's choices
evolved over time from other choices, as Laura Aston noted: "A lot
of things, by now, they're not big decisions, they're like just checking
to make sure that the things that I have thought about for years and
years and years I still think." Her choices during pregnancy entailed
acting on long-established beliefs. Rather than emerging from a process of weighing factors involved in a particular situation, at a specific
time, women's choices emerged in a lifetime process of developing
beliefs and attitudes, and acting on them when particular choices
arose. Laura Aston's description of her way of making choices is a
reminder that pregnancy is part of a lifelong process, and choices
during pregnancy are moments within that process.

Women's experiences of pregnancy and their choices about prenatal diagnosis involved their definitions of risk, and while women's perceptions of risk were far more encompassing than the medical definitions of risk, some women also internalized aspects of the medical model.

Perhaps because women are exposed to the rational choice model of decision-making, through contact with health providers, popular literature, and liberal American culture in general, they were sometimes surprised at their choices or the way(s) they made them. Louise Frey thought she did not want to have amniocentesis, for example, but when she was faced with the decision, she decided she wanted to have the test. She made the decision quickly, changing her mind from her previous position. The choices she made and ways she made them were "not the decisions that, if I wrote a book about my pregnancy before, I would have thought of," she noted.

Barbara Sanders also was surprised at the way she made choices during pregnancy. She described her usual decision process: "I try to think about the best and the worst that could possibly happen . . . and weigh those out." Before getting married, she made her decisions independently. Now, she always talks to her husband: "I always run things by him . . . somehow it seems more complicated, because I always consult him." In making choices, she said, "the main thing is trying to find out as much as I can, about whatever decision is being made." During her pregnancy, though, she made choices differently:

The decisions that I've made while I've been pregnant, have been much more emotional than any other decisions . . . I don't so much weigh all the pros and cons as see what my gut feeling is, and base my decision on my feelings . . . I tend to be much more concerned about my emotional well-being . . . like, with the ultrasound, when the doctor mentioned having it at twenty-eight or thirty weeks, my reason for not having it done was I didn't want to have to worry, and that's a very selfish, emotional basis for doing it, and not an objective, weighing pros and cons . . . emotion is playing a much bigger role.

Some women may feel, as Barbara Sanders did, that their choices during pregnancy were not "rational." The ways they made choices may in fact be very different from the way choices are depicted in the rational choice and medical models of decision-making. But these women's choices were rational, in a way, in that they made sense to them, were appropriate to their circumstances, and consistent with their perceptions. When their choices were different from what they originally thought they would choose, the women often reinterpreted those choices to make them "fit," or reinterpreted the factors that might have led to different choices, as when Louise Frey chose amniocentesis, despite feeling she was not a "high-risk woman." From the standpoints of these women, even choices that seemed inconsistent from other perspectives were consistent with their needs and situations. One of the paradoxes of choice, though, is that at the same time that women's choices felt "right" to them and reflected their situations, women also felt ambivalent about those choices.

The women I interviewed were acutely aware of their own maternal responsibility. Their stories reflected feelings of responsibility and concern for their babies, husbands or partners, other children and family members, and, to a lesser extent, themselves. This was not surprising, since pregnant women have always been interested in the well-being of their fetuses and babies. Woven into the theme of responsibility was another subtle thread, that of social expectations, censure, and blame. These women's choices during pregnancy involved feelings of guilt about their own behaviors and actions.

The women felt guilty both before and after they made choices. Anna Simas struggled to decide about amniocentesis, for example:

I kind of feel . . . I'll go through with it but I don't want to. But I'm doing it out of fear that the technology's there, and if something's wrong with the child . . . I'll feel like, you know, I could have circumvented that circumstance . . . we're talking Spina Bifida and Down syndrome, we can still have no legs, no eyes, be deaf . . . a myriad of other things . . . if I was faced with either of those problems I'd probably never forgive myself . . . A lot of it is just this fear . . . there's this stuff out there that will tell you all about it.

In a few minutes, after talking about where she might have the test, and saying she really did not want to face the decision, she said, "I was talking to the office and they were saying, you know, it isn't required, it isn't required, and I started thinking, it isn't required, and I don't have to do this." She seemed to be searching for a reason not to "choose" the test.

When women talk about choosing amniocentesis or other tests out of fear, or because it is the "right" thing to do, what does this tell us? Anna Simas was afraid she would be blamed if anything went wrong with her pregnancy or baby. She judged her own choices in advance, in a society where pregnant women may indeed be accused of being dangerous to their own fetuses.

The context in which Anna Simas and other women tried to make responsible choices is a context where mother-blaming is the order of the day. The rhetoric of choice obscures the constraints that impede real choices for women, and, in doing so, it also supports women-blaming and mother-blaming. When women do not act in accordance with popular wisdom about appropriate behavior(s) during pregnancy, blame and censure by others and/or feelings of self-blame or guilt may result. These pressures contribute to making women's choices difficult, and their existence provides evidence for the idea that women's choices are largely, if not completely, illusory. Are women's choices real or illusory? That question is the topic of the next chapter.

Pregnancy and Choice in a High-Tech Age

What has been gained by listening to the voices of these women, attempting to see and understand their perceptions and choices from their standpoints? How do women experience pregnancy and make choices about procreative technologies in a high-tech age? Are those choices real or illusory? The women's stories illustrate that there are no simple answers to these questions. The meaning of pregnancy, like the experience of choice, was fluid and variable for different women and for the same woman during different pregnancies or different moments within pregnancy. These women did not experience pregnancy as the clear-cut biological phenomenon of the medical model. For them, pregnancy was an ambiguous, contradictory physiological and social state in which it was possible to feel and act "a little bit pregnant" or simultaneously pregnant and not-pregnant.

This observation extends the work of Barbara Katz Rothman and other researchers who found that amniocentesis can cause pregnant women to experience a limbo-like state, a "tentative pregnancy." Other experiences and concerns also led women to feel tentative about their pregnancies: previous miscarriages or abortions, difficulties in becoming pregnant, their own and other people's responses to their changing bodies and roles.

Women's experiences of choice during pregnancy, beginning with the choice to attempt to become pregnant, also involved ambiguity and contradictions. Women's attempts to become pregnant, to assert some control over their procreative destinies, entailed constraints: a choice to become pregnant did not always result in pregnancy; and once pregnant, women faced additional choices and limitations.

These women chose to become pregnant, chose health providers, chose whether to have prenatal tests, and whether and with whom to share prenatal information. In doing so, they considered multiple factors: their personal and social locations, previous experiences, philosophies of health, wishes of family and friends, feelings about and experiences with disability and abortion, and perceptions of the risks associated with their choices. Women's ways of choosing were complex, entailing diverse, interconnected considerations.

Choices Are Contextual, Relational, and Intertwined

Women's choices about pregnancy and prenatal diagnosis were embedded in a nexus of other choices. Their choices were contextual and relational, influenced by their life situations. When women talked about the choice to become pregnant, they described their personal circumstances—their jobs, schooling, marriages, children. They also described societal constraints that influenced their choices. When women talked about choosing to have an abortion in the case of a positive prenatal diagnosis, for example, they talked about limited societal resources available for childcare and health care, inflexible workplaces, inadequate social and financial supports for people with disabilities and families of children with disabilities.

Women made choices in a "relational" way, by considering and empathizing with the needs, concerns, and situations of others. Rather than acting as isolated, completely independent individuals, these women made choices in the context of connections—with other people and with their own past and future selves. In making choices about prenatal diagnosis, women considered the feelings of their husbands, children, and other family members. Nancy Wilson's and Louise Frey's husbands wanted them to have amniocentesis, and that influenced their choice to have the test, for example. Sara Swanson also considered her relationship with her husband when she thought about choosing prenatal diagnosis and speculated about her potential choices following a positive diagnosis. She felt that having a "special needs child" who needed "120 percent" of her time would not be good for her, her husband, or their marriage. That women made choices by considering the needs of others is consistent with Carol Gilligan's work on moral choices and the ethic of caring. Gilligan's relational model has been widely adopted by feminists and others interested in an alternative to the prevailing "male" model of ethical choices, its abstract principles and hierarchical depiction of ways of making moral choices.[1] Like Carol Gilligan, I am suggesting that women's choices are relational and contextual, but I also found that women's choices were linked, grounded in other choices.

Women's choices about pregnancy and prenatal diagnosis were intertwined. Some choices were embedded in other choices. In a conversation about my research, one woman (not one of the thirty-one women who participated in the study) told me she chose not to become pregnant after age thirty-five because she did not want to face the choices associated with "high-risk" pregnancy. Other choices—choices about prenatal tests—were embedded in her choice not to attempt pregnancy. The women I interviewed also explicitly made choices to avoid others: Betty Mell chose not to have amniocentesis to avoid choosing whether to carry her pregnancy to term in the event of a positive diagnosis.

For some women, the choice to refrain from having prenatal diagnosis was embedded in previous choices about abortion. Though prenatal diagnosis does not inevitably result in a choice of pregnancy termination following a positive diagnosis, few women considered having amniocentesis or chorionic villi sampling unless they planned to have an abortion in the case of a positive test result.[2] Women who chose abortion in the past responded to their current choices with that previous experience in mind; the two choices, past and present, were linked. Women's previous choices influenced their current ones, and they made their current choices by considering potential future choices.

Some choices lead directly to other choices, some choices incorporate others. Choosing to attempt to become pregnant led women to choose a doctor or other health provider. In making choices about health providers, women made choices about high-tech and low-tech medicine, philosophies of health care, prenatal technologies, and birthplace or birthing options. Choosing prenatal diagnosis entailed other choices, such as the choice to accept the risk of miscarriage associated with amniocentesis or the risk of an ambiguous or false test result. Choosing prenatal diagnosis often prompted women to make or consider other choices, such as the choice about learning fetal sex, choices about additional prenatal tests, or choices following a possible positive diagnosis. Women talked about these linked choices when describing their decision-making. Carol McAllister and Roxanne Thomas felt a positive alphafetoprotein test result would lead to the choice of ultrasound or amniocentesis, and both women refrained from the alphafetoprotein test, preferring to "just have an ultrasound" if prenatal testing seemed appropriate. They realized that choosing one prenatal test can place a woman on a path that leads to other choices about other tests. One choice can "force" additional choices and eliminate others; some choices are nested within one another.

Women's choices about pregnancy and prenatal tests are not simple or discrete. Women's lives rarely progress in a completely clear and linear fashion, and women's choices are no less complicated than their lives. Women simultaneously make multiple choices, and their ways of choosing move backward and forward in time, rather than approximating the linear, developmental decision-tree model of rational choice. Women's choices resemble a series of interconnected and overlapping mazes, or the transparent cellophane pages in biology, anatomy, or medical texts, containing different pages (each devoted to a different system: the circulatory system, the skeletal system, for example) that can be viewed beneath and above each other, and which, when placed together, form a complete picture of the human body. Each layer depends on and is related to the others, but each can be seen and described separately.

Just as women's lives take place within intersecting contexts—their pasts, presents, and futures, family and personal connections, work arenas, friendship networks, the larger structures of their communities, nations, and the world—women's choices also intersect. Some choices are nested like Chinese boxes or Russian dolls: one leads to another which leads to another, and so on.

These women experienced pregnancy and made prenatal choices in ways that differed from the medical model of pregnancy, the rational choice model of decision-making, and feminist perspectives on procreative choice. The picture of choice that emerged from the women's stories requires a recognition of ambiguity, multiplicity, and contradictions or paradoxes, as well as connections. Women's choices were linked with one another, intertwined. Women's choices were contextual and relational, connected with their pasts, their present circumstances, and their vision(s) of their futures. Pregnancy was not a monolithic experience, risks were perceived in diverse and paradoxical ways, and women's choices were complicated and fraught with ambiguity.

Pregnant women's stories illustrate that their experiences and choices are far more complicated than the medical model of pregnancy, the liberal feminist model of rational freedom of choice, and the radical and socialist feminist images of patriarchal and/or capitalist social construction and social control. The women's stories provide contradictory evidence for the liberal feminist notion that procreative choices are real and the radical and socialist feminist claims that procreative choices are illusory.

Procreative Choice: Illusory or Real?

The exploration in this book of the ways thirty-one women experienced pregnancy and prenatal choices illustrates the complex relationship between personal autonomy and the social construction of choice. Women live with ambiguity, pursue self-determination, and make choices within the contradictions, constraints, and contexts of their lives. In addition to illuminating the multiple and interwoven factors involved in women's ways of choosing, their stories illustrate the ambiguous, paradoxical character of choice itself: choice is socially constructed and constrained, and, simultaneously, personally and individually experienced.

To some extent and to some women, choosing prenatal diagnosis did not seem like choice at all. Instead, it was merely the responsible, expected thing to do. Some women identified with the risk categories of the medical model of pregnancy (especially maternal age) and quite readily "chose" prenatal diagnosis when they fell into the medical risk category(ies). Some of these women, such as Sarah Worthington and Lauren Fagan, felt there was little or no choice involved. As "older mothers," their "choice" to have prenatal diagnosis was automatic, an anticipated corollary to the choice to become pregnant. Other women felt compelled to "choose" prenatal tests after experiencing pressure to do so from family and friends. Most of the women had internalized strong societal messages about their personal responsibility for the outcome(s) of those choices.

Responsible Choices

Nearly all women are potential mothers or viewed as such at some time during the life course. Women learn "mothering" skills and values as part of female socialization, regardless of whether they ever become biological or social mothers or both. Girls' socialization as mothers-to-be begins early and receives much cultural and social support. When girls play with dolls or care for pets, they often receive explicit and implicit messages: "what a good little mother." The messages continue into adulthood. When behaving in nurturing ways with friends, siblings, or co-workers, women often hear similar comments: "You would be a great mother." Most women are conscious of social expectations concerning women and mothering: that women should want to mother, try to become mothers, experience mothering, and exhibit appropriate behaviors and make "sacrifices" as mothers.

Numerous aspects of women's lives contribute to their sense of themselves as potential mothers. Given the inadequacy of contraceptive technologies, when (fertile) women are sexually involved with (fertile) men the question of potential motherhood is an implicit third party to the relationship. When women choose to become pregnant, give birth, provide care for a child, they experience the possibility and reality of being mothers.

Some women are acutely conscious of mothering expectations they have not fulfilled because they have not chosen or been able to become mothers or because they do not demonstrate "motherly" behaviors.[3] Childless women may retain a sense of themselves as potential mothers for many years, feeling they could have become mothers, or might still become mothers. If recent trends continue, women may continue to feel a sense of their potential motherhood for most of their lives. The chance for women to become biological mothers now extends beyond menopause, through the use of donor eggs and embryo implantation. One article suggests that "[w]omen 40 and older who have tried every other means of beating the biological clock are creating a growing demand for this method of prolonging fertility."[4] Whether women's "demand" promoted the development and use of methods to prolong fertility (e.g., in vitro fertilization) or the development of the methods created the demand, once techniques exist for medically assisted, extended reproduction, doctors will promote them, and women will "choose" to explore them as options.

Women's feelings of maternal responsibility and guilt derive from societal expectations. Women are deemed appropriately maternal when they are nurturing and accepting, when they listen to, understand, and respond to others, and make sacrifices to meet other people's needs.[5] Societal expectations of women as women and as mothers have become conflated: "good" women are "good" mothers. Women who "act like men" face criticism and censure, even in an era that celebrates "sensitive men" who (ostensibly) behave like women. People criticize and question women who choose not to mother, do not act motherly, or defer their mothering responsibilities through abortion, adoption, and other forms of relinquishing custody of children.[6] In an age of high-technology medicine, women's decisions and choices about pregnancy and mothering take place in a context of heightened public scrutiny. When prenatal diagnosis and "technological fixes" for infertility are available, women face additional social pressure to pursue motherhood. Pregnant women face heightened societal expectations regarding their prenatal choices and greater imputations of responsibility for the outcome(s) of their choices than in the past.

The women I interviewed, and indeed, most mothers, acknowledge and accept responsibility for their present and future children, and worry about the ways their behavior and choices will affect their children. Jane Lowe described an experience that illustrates this. She was exposed to chicken pox while pregnant with her first child. She assumed she had (or had been exposed to) chicken pox as a child: "But to be safe, I went and had this titer done." When the test indicated that she had low immunity to the illness, she was worried: "It was like, oh my God, what if I get chickenpox? And this woman at the [health center] *she gave me total fear in my heart about it.*" Jane Lowe was told "it's really unknown, as to the effects of chicken pox on a fetus." The health clinic staff member suggested she might have to think about her "options . . . she was insinuating you might want to have an abortion." Jane Lowe became worried. She had to wait for a three-week gestation period following her exposure, to see if she would get the disease: "that period . . . was like hell, waiting." Then, "to make matters worse, I was exposed again . . . to my niece . . . I touched her chicken pock, not knowing, and I thought, oh my God,

I'm going to get it . . . I waited three weeks again . . . *three weeks of hell.*" She did not get chicken pox, and "I was just so glad, and then, I figured . . . I had been lucky, and maybe when I'm not pregnant I'll try to get exposed and get it, so I don't have to deal with this again." She did not get chicken pox before becoming pregnant again, though, and during her present pregnancy "was exposed again . . . on New Year's Eve . . . *three weeks of hell, again,* although, this time around I figured, if I didn't get it those first two times, there's not much likelihood I'll get it this time. I must have some kind of immunity, you know." Jane Lowe did not know how chicken pox might affect her fetus(es), but she knew enough to be anxious, especially after talking with a health center staff member. Her experience illustrates the potentially powerful impact on a pregnant woman of a few words from a health professional: her already intense feelings of responsibility escalated into terror.

Women often receive unsolicited advice during pregnancy, as noted in chapter 6. They often feel guilty about their behavior during pregnancy, even in the absence of explicit advice or criticism from others. Roxanne Thomas censured herself: "I had no coffee the first time. I had terrible guilt if I had to take a Tylenol. I never took a drink . . . I had one glass of beer this pregnancy . . . I did have guilt about that. You have guilt . . . you carry it around. You're creating a person, inside you." Betty Mell expressed similar feelings: "Well, the first three I was such a good pregnant person. I really took care of my diet, and on this pregnancy, I'm really bad, I just eat anything and everything, and I used to keep away from preservatives . . . make everything from scratch, and now I eat packaged food . . . I feel kind of guilty about that." One way women demonstrated their concern about acting responsibly was by comparing themselves to other women. Rachel Howard described her feelings about eating responsibly during pregnancy: "I just know that you're not supposed to eat things that are bad for you." She compared her approach to that of another woman: "I know someone who is very laissez-faire . . . she didn't quit smoking until she [her pregnancy] was confirmed, two weeks later . . . she's cut down on her coffee to six cups a day . . . to me that is very irresponsible."

Women's feelings of responsibility resulted in contradictory responses to amniocentesis and other prenatal tests. For some women it felt too risky to use the tests. They worried that the fetus would be damaged by the test or the results would be inaccurate. For these women the responsible choice was the choice not to use the test. For other women, those who talked about taking every precaution, wanting to be sure, to have all of the available facts about their pregnancy, having amniocentesis was a way to feel more responsible.

Feelings of responsibility have probably always accompanied pregnancy, but the existence of amniocentesis and other prenatal tests may heighten these feelings for some women. Lauren Fagan chose amniocentesis on the basis of her statistically higher risk of having a baby with a genetic condition (e.g., Down syndrome) due to her age. She felt she was making a responsible choice. But when she described her feelings during and following her amniocentesis, as noted in chapter 6, Lauren Fagan revealed a sense of uneasiness about the implications of her choice: "I felt very much as if it was the first time my baby's life was being invaded. He had this nice little place, that he lived, and all of a sudden I'm bringing in this horrible, outside influence. And . . . I felt very guilty about that . . . I should have just left him alone. He was so happy before I did that." Lauren Fagan felt guilty after exposing her baby to the risk(s) associated with amniocentesis. She tried to make responsible choices based on her perceptions of the risks of pregnancy at her age, but by doing so she later felt irresponsible because of the risks associated with her choices.

All of the women sought to act responsibly, take control of pregnancy, make choices in the best interest of their baby, be "good mothers." But none of the women was free of ambivalence. Ambivalence is a central part of pregnancy in the 1990s. The ambiguity and contradictions that characterized these women's descriptions of their feelings and choices are not merely a side effect of procreative technologies and tests themselves, however. The development and use of amniocentesis and other prenatal tests reflect cultural and social expectations and values about women, pregnancy, motherhood, children, and disability.

The areas for which women, especially mothers, are considered responsible are infinitely expandable. The tendency to "blame Mom" is nothing new, but the advent of procreative technologies has meant an extension of maternal responsibility and an attendant expansion of potential maternal guilt and social censure.[7] It is the pressures on women to conform to social values and norms as much as the new technologies themselves that make the experience of pregnancy so complicated and paradoxical.

Paradoxes of Choice

I noted earlier that prenatal tests and other procreative technologies involve a fundamental paradox: they are tools for liberation, but also tools for the further medicalization and social control of women's procreative processes. Another paradoxical thing about these technologies is that their existence has created a situation where choices *must* be made. The women I interviewed *had* to make choices. The fact that the technologies exist means that women no longer have the option to act as if they do not exist. A paradox of choice is that the choices themselves are, in a sense, forced: the existence of prenatal tests forces women to make choices about them. Women's choices about pregnancy and prenatal technologies involved three additional paradoxes: the choices both reduced and increased risks; one woman's choice was another woman's constraint; and the choices were simultaneously private and public.

Women made procreative choices as a way to attempt to take control or maintain autonomy of their bodies and lives. One goal of women's efforts to control their procreative processes was to identify and minimize risks associated with biology (e.g., chromosomal and other genetic anomalies) and their own actions (e.g., attempting pregnancy as "older" women).[8] The choices were "risky" in two senses: they were made by women to deal with risks (e.g., the risks associated with being an "older mother") and they entailed other risks. A woman's choice to have prenatal diagnosis in response to her statistical risk of having a baby with a genetic condition sometimes had risky implications, because the tests themselves entail other risks.

An additional paradox revealed by the women's stories was that one woman's choice was another woman's constraint; one woman's way of taking control of the pregnancy was another woman's relinquishment of control. This was demonstrated in women's differing perceptions and choices of health providers; their varying images of low-tech and high-tech medicine and of the "risks" associated with pregnancy; and their different choices about "going public" and decisions about prenatal testing. Some women viewed the information available through prenatal diagnosis, including the sex of the fetus, as an unnecessary intrusion into the processes of pregnancy and childbirth. For these women, a "choice" to have prenatal diagnosis removed the serendipitous "magic" of the pregnancy. Women who chose to refrain from having prenatal tests also chose not to face the possibility of additional choices following a positive diagnosis. They chose to accept whatever baby they had. For them, choosing to use prenatal tests represented a relinquishment of control of the pregnancy processes to technology(ies) or to health providers, to some extent.

Just as women who chose to refrain from prenatal tests chose a form of control over their pregnancies and their potential future choices, the women who decided to get as much information as possible also exercised choice in the name of increased autonomy. They equated the choice to have prenatal tests with control, perceiving that the test results enabled them to make additional, informed choices. To women who chose prenatal diagnosis, information felt empowering. Choosing not to have prenatal diagnosis represented a choice to ignore available information, which to these women would constitute evading responsibility, relinquishing control.

In addition, women's experiences of pregnancy and their choices during pregnancy were simultaneously private and public. The notion of procreative autonomy or freedom entails the idea that a woman's choice to become pregnant is a private one, a decision that is hers (and, often, her partner's) alone. But once a woman's pregnancy—itself an outcome of an ostensibly private choice and, frequently, a private process of conception (though not always, given the rising number of pregnancies that occur through medically assisted conception)—became visible to others, she risked experiencing invasions of privacy, including unsolicited advice and other people's assumptions and judgments about her choices during pregnancy.

During pregnancy, women's privacy and autonomy can be violated implicitly, through attitudes and comments by strangers or others about women's behavior, and explicitly, through more direct pressures and concrete social sanctions regarding her choices. Women make choices in an effort to enhance their autonomy, to control their own procreative processes, but those choices sometimes place women in situations of increased social or medical control and increased pressures or constraints on their future choices.

Once a woman chose to have prenatal diagnosis, her pregnant body was invaded by the health provider and the technologies—sometimes called "windows on the womb"—themselves, and previously private or secret information became accessible to her and to other people, including technicians and doctors. When this private information became public (e.g., genetic information or the sex of the fetus), women's choices occurred in a context where additional social pressures were possible. When a private pregnancy becomes public, it may be harder for a pregnant woman to make future choices with the same degree of autonomy. This may be one reason some women chose to keep their choices secret (to have or refrain from having amniocentesis, for example), or to limit other people's access to the information provided by prenatal diagnosis (to restrict the "public" to whom this formerly "private" information is made available).

The family and social pressures the women described suggest that they experienced implicit, informal kinds of social control. More explicit forms of social control of pregnant women also may come into play when information about health prevention or risks is widely shared. As Shulamit Reinharz noted about miscarriage, information about the causes of miscarriage may be used by pregnant women to exert procreative control, but the same information may be used by others to limit women's autonomy. The information is potentially empowering to women, because they can use it to attempt to prevent (or cause) their own miscarriages. On the other hand, such information may also be used against women, in efforts to control women's lives by restraining women in the name of preventing miscarriages.[9]

Even before they become pregnant, as potentially pregnant persons women may face threats to their autonomy, such as exclusions from workplaces deemed dangerous to fetuses or threatening to (female) fertility. Once pregnant, a woman's privacy and bodily autonomy may be threatened, as demonstrated by recent court cases about forced cesarean sections and other mandated interventions during pregnancy and childbirth.[10]

Women's Choices in a High-Tech Age: Illusory and Real

Pregnant women face subtle and not-so-subtle pressures from doctors and others who promote certain behaviors and choices in the interest of healthy fetuses and healthy babies. Though the women experienced subtle pressures from others, none of them described experiences entailing explicit, overt, formal instances of social control or blame. They talked about their choices as individuals who were aware of the ways other people viewed them, and, in some cases, they chose to incorporate those views in their decision-making. They also described their choices as if they made them as fully active and creative agents.

The stories women told about their pregnancies are indicative of the pervasiveness of the ideology of choice in contemporary American culture. These women made choices, again and again, in an attempt to take control of their procreative possibilities, and they perceived themselves as choosers, not passive victims constrained by the limits of biology or the social environment. They tried to exert procreative control by consciously deciding to attempt to become pregnant, and, after becoming pregnant, choosing to carry a pregnancy to term. They made choices about their prenatal care by selecting a health provider, and by deciding whether to have prenatal tests.

Despite these conscious choices, though, the women in the study found, ultimately, that true procreative *control* was elusive. Choice was possible to some degree, but not fully. Though they made deliberate choices, biological processes and societal pressures limited their ability to take full control of their procreative destinies. Yet women continued to make choices, to act as agents, to attempt to exercise autonomy.

Biology—or bodily processes—are not always amenable to technological control or technical fixes. Infertility and miscarriages occur and pregnancies are conceived despite the use of contraception. And, as Sarah Worthington sadly learned, procreative technologies such as prenatal diagnosis cannot prevent, predict, or solve all problems associated with pregnancy and childbearing.

Feminists and women's health activists have struggled for generations to gain and maintain some control by women over their procreative processes, so it may sound heretical to claim that this control is illusory. But some feminists and others now are suggesting that we need to understand that our bodies are ourselves in a slightly different way, to take more account of bodily processes that may require or inspire social changes, instead of the reverse. We may be able to learn from bodily rhythms and processes, intead of always struggling to make our bodies and bodily processes conform to rigid social (and architectural) structures.[11] As noted in chapter 5, Robbie Pfeufer Kahn and Emily Martin, among others, have suggested that most workplaces and work schedules are inhospitable to women's bodily processes (e.g., lactation, menstruation, menopause). This is not inevitable; workplaces can be transformed into more flexible, creative,

humane places. Feminists and disability rights activists are working
to promote and ensure modifications to workplaces, other buildings
(e.g., restaurants, museums, libraries) and transportation systems, to
make them fully accessible and therefore more humane; such efforts
are part of what I mean when I suggest recognizing and adapting our
social environments to our bodily needs. I am not saying here that
biology is destiny. It is possible to recognize and appreciate bodily
processes without reducing one's analysis to a form of biological de-
terminism.

Despite their awareness and description of the constraints on their
choices, such as the limits of their own biology—including the genetic risks associated with age, and problems with infertility—and
the external and internalized pressures to make particular choices,
these women perceived themselves as choosers. During our conversations they demonstrated a sense of agency or intentionality. They felt
they had choices and perceived that they made them. In this sense,
these women do have choice(s): to them, choice is real. Individual
choice and personal autonomy cannot be dismissed entirely by describing the social construction of choice(s). In representing themselves to me as choosers, the women I interviewed portrayed themselves as having an "authentic self . . . profoundly shaped by social
experience yet endowed with capacities for independent, sometimes
creative, thought." For them, personal autonomy was "a dynamic
process and . . . a phenomenon that admits of degrees."[12] Our awareness of the socialization processes that lead women (and men) to
identify with the individualized, liberal notion of choice central to
the American political culture can coexist with our recognition and
validation of women's sense of themselves as choosers.

It is important to recognize the myriad ways in which women's
procreative choices are shaped and constrained: by the limits of biology, medical professionals who communicate the prevailing medical
view of pregnancy, family pressures, economic and situational constraints, religious beliefs, larger cultural values and attitudes about
disability, and political and social inequality, among other influences.
Yet it is not appropriate or accurate to reject entirely the women's
sense of themselves as (partially) autonomous or self-directed, by
dismissing their feelings as mere manifestations of false consciousness, even in the absence of full procreative autonomy.

Within the constraints and the ambiguities of their situations and
their lives, women took charge of their procreative processes in vary-

ing ways and to varying degrees. Women's choices were made in part as coping or survival strategies, consciously or not. Women's choices can help them make sense of the world, to maintain a sense of themselves as agents, people who have some autonomy, some control. The impetus to identify oneself as autonomous and self-determined is particularly acute in a context where choice is such a central concept, as it is in the American political culture and the ideology that sustains it. Choice is perceived as the quality that makes us human (as opposed to other animals, those which ostensibly respond only to stimuli, or passive organisms that behave only in involuntary ways). People need to feel that they have choices and are choosers, to feel fully human and have a sense of self-worth or self-esteem. Passivity is not rewarded in this culture; rather, activity, industriousness, action, and making choices are behaviors that are admired and rewarded.

These women were capable of constructing domains of choice within limited or circumscribed arenas, transforming constraints into new choices, creating windows of choice within confined social roles or situations. Examples of this ability include: Lauren Fagan's decision to be both pregnant and not-pregnant, to act not-pregnant at work while interpreting and responding to her supervisor's demands in the light of her needs as a pregnant woman; Louise Frey's reconstruction of her own choice to have amniocentesis, in which she moved from an attitude that the procedure was inappropriate (because she was not a "high-risk woman") to a feeling that amniocentesis was merely a "little, high-tech test" when she chose to have the procedure after all; Marie Bickerson's construction of her infertility experience, in which she chose to "let go"; and the ways women chose or refrained from choosing prenatal testing in order to exert control over potentially uncontrollable situations.

Women's ways of choosing sometimes resembled quilting, piecing fragments together to construct a new whole, as when women's choices evolved out of the constraints or unanticipated outcomes of earlier choices. Women transformed constraints into new choices, psychically as well as behaviorally, reconstructing their lives and choices like good cooks are able to transform leftovers into a new dish or a cooking mistake into a delectable new meal.[13] Taking what is on hand or "left-over" and working with it, transforming lemons into lemonade, "blooming where one is planted," and other creative maneuvers may be viewed as mere adaptations or adjustments to a

bad situation without challenging or attempting to change that situation. Such choices may be disparaged as "settling," "rationalizing,"
or merely "making do." Another way to see such efforts, though,
is to acknowledge the choice, intentionality, resourcefulness, and
creativity involved. This ability can be celebrated as a self-empow-
ering mode of behavior. Women who attempt to make these kinds of
choices can be recognized for pushing against the boundaries of their
lives and making spaces and places in which choice exists, or scorned
(or blamed or pitied) for being duped by the system, but I believe
that the appropriate analysis is somewhere in between. We need to
credit women (and others) for their survival skills in the face of real
social constraints, whether those constraints are concrete, ideological,
or both. At the same time, we need to move beyond those constrained choices, to try to create situations where women's perceptions of themselves as choosers are mirrored more accurately by the
opportunities for real choice within their larger social and political
contexts.

Implications for Theory and Practice

Feminists and others have analyzed the impacts of procreative technologies on women and society. As noted in chapter 2, liberal feminists
tend to suggest that the technologies provide women with additional
choices regarding their procreative possibilities. Radical and socialist
feminists, on the other hand, describe the ways the technologies are
used for the social control of women rather than providing women
with real choices. I argue here that we need to develop a more
nuanced view of choice, one that recognizes how historical and present patterns of oppression construct and constrain women's choices
but also acknowledges women's agency and capacity for self-determination.

Women were aware of the personal situations and social factors
that influenced and limited their choices. They did not make prenatal
choices blithely, uncritically trusting doctors and medical technologies. They made choices they felt were in the best interest of themselves and their families, in a context of uncertainty and ambiguity.
These women were aware that their choices were not always "real"
choices. But outright coercion was not a facet of their experiences
as they perceived them. Yes, social forces—pro-natalism; sexism;

discrimination against people with disabilities; the primacy of the medical model; the power of medicine, technology, and science; the commercialization of genetic technologies; the hegemonic ideology of choice—influence and limit women's (and men's) choices, and these influences must be scrutinized critically. But women themselves have pushed for access to procreative technologies and advocated medicalization—childbirth options such as twilight sleep or medical interventions for infertility, for example—as Dorothy C. Wertz, Catherine Kohler Riessman, Deborah Gerson, and Arthur L. Greil, among others, have pointed out.[14] Social influences take place in an interactional context—people take actions and are acted upon—and women must not be dismissed—individually or as a group—as passive victims of social forces.

The women's stories suggest another look at feminist perspectives on procreative technologies and women's choices during and before pregnancy. Their ways of choosing provided striking evidence of the importance of understanding women's choices contextually. The women's stories suggest that current feminist perspectives on pregnancy and procreative choice in a high-tech age do not capture fully the paradoxical aspects of choice and may inadequately address differences among women. Women do not comprise a homogeneous group, despite sharing common experiences (or potential experiences) of gender and sex inequality. Inequality is experienced by women in different ways, depending on their personal experiences and social locations. Women perceive and experience procreative choices differently, too, due to differences in social class, family background, procreative histories (herstories), geography, race, sexual orientation, and nationality. We need to construct theories that recognize women's differences, the uniqueness of each individual and her circumstances, but also serve to illuminate the commonalities among women. It should be possible to incorporate an awareness of contradictions and paradoxes into some kind of whole. The notion of the fully autonomous, individual actor is a myth; but I wonder if we really wish to transform such a notion into reality. One promising direction for feminist theory lies in efforts to reconceive the idea of autonomy, moving away from a focus on isolated individualism to an understanding of autonomy in the context of relationships. Some feminist theorists have begun to develop alternative depictions of ethics, building on a relational perspective, for example.[15]

In terms of medical practice and the provision of genetics services, it is important to learn from women's voices because medical proto-cols are based in part on implicit assumptions about women's experi-ences and decision-making. In the absence of adequate information about women's actual choices and feelings about pregnancy and pro-creative technologies, medical practitioners may fail to serve women's needs. Health providers may perceive and portray procre-ative technologies as options that enhance women's ability to make choices. Doctors may advise women to have prenatal tests on the basis of medical risk factors, or they may "offer" tests to women in the name of autonomy, believing that the information available from the tests expands women's procreative control. Genetic counselors may provide information to pregnant women and prospective parents nondirectively, in an effort to promote women's autonomy and self-determination. But even well-intentioned health providers may in-stead contribute inadvertently to a narrowing of women's choices if they do not understand women's actual experiences of pregnancy and prenatal choices. If doctors, genetic counselors, and other health providers do not understand the degree to which the "options" they recommend are perceived by women as prescriptions (or proscrip-tions), they may influence women's decisions—intentionally or not—without providing enough information or allowing room for real choice.[16]

Studying women's experiences of pregnancy and procreative choices also can yield important insights for policy development. Pregnant women have long been the focus of medical and legal interventions, yet their voices are often missing from the policy debates that spawn these interventions. It is pregnant women who are the experts on pregnancy and prenatal choices. An investigation of women's experiences of pregnancy and prenatal choice can provide information that may be used for developing answers to numerous policy questions. Should procreative technologies ever be required for women with high-risk pregnancies? Who will pay for the tests? Should insurance coverage of these tests be mandated? Should public funding (e.g., Medicaid) be used to pay for the tests for poor women? Should prenatal diagnosis be offered to all women, whether or not they intend to terminate the pregnancy in the event of a positive test result? Should all women have access to abortion following a positive prenatal diagnosis? Who will provide and pay for abortions? Who will provide and pay for services necessary for the care of children with disabilities?

Related policy questions concern the degree to which private procreative choices should be matters of public policy in the first place. Mothers have often been blamed for the problems experienced by their children. Children's life-long physical and emotional health may now be attributed to what mothers did or did not do during pregnancy. As this relationship between women's prenatal choices and the well-being of their children receives additional attention from scientists, health-care providers, and policy-makers, those choices will receive increased scrutiny from people in power as well as the general public. If prenatal diagnosis becomes a routine or mandatory component of prenatal care, how can women be protected from being sanctioned or punished for choosing not to have such tests or for carrying a pregnancy to term following a positive diagnosis? To develop policies that will meet people's needs, it is essential to listen to the voices of those most directly affected. In the case of prenatal diagnosis and other procreative technologies, that means listening to pregnant women to whom these tests are suggested and on whose bodies they are performed. A consideration of women's experiences of pregnancy and choice is likely to lead to different or additional policy options from those developed in the absence of women's voices.

I have shared examples of ways women attempted to take procreative control by making choices, and ways they discovered the elusiveness of that control. By suggesting we recognize the limits of procreative choice, and by acknowledging the biological and societal processes that prevent women from having true procreative control, though, I do not intend to make an argument or provide an excuse for complacency or fatalism. As social scientists and social critics, we must acknowledge the social construction of choice. But even as we do so, we must also recognize the validity of women's perceptions and actions. We must not overlook the extent to which women perceive themselves and behave as agents, as people who do have choices—even as we recognize the psychological, political, and ideological components of those perceptions.

At the same time, though, given the elusiveness of "real" choice, and the multiple biological and social influences that diminish women's control, we need to be honest about what does and does not increase control, what does and does not provide women with real choices. It is a disservice to women to present prenatal and other procreative technologies neutrally or as exclusively choice-enhancing.

The technologies are options, but they do not necessarily provide women with control. The future tasks for feminists and other advocates of choice are: to continue to listen to women's stories and acknowledge the validity of their perceptions of their own experiences; to create alternatives to the rational choice paradigm and its individualistic liberalism; and to work collectively to transform illusory choices into real ones, thus extending the realm in which all women experience real procreative choices.

The Women in the Study

All of the following names are pseudonyms selected by the women, at my request, except for the following: Bernadette Lynn: she selected the first name and I added the second name; Marta Betts, Greta Erlich, and Helen Patrick: I chose those pseudonyms for the first three women I interviewed. The age reported here is the woman's age at the time of our first interview. Ethnic identifications are the women's own self-descriptions, in response to my question, "what is your ethnic background?" I adapted Emily Martin's system of income designation for use with this list, as used in her book, *The Woman in the Body* (Boston: Beacon Press, 1987.) The women's household income range is from between $10,000–19,999/year to between $90,000–99,999/year, with the largest number of women, eleven, in the $40,000–59,999 group, followed by seven women in the $20,000–39,999 group. For purposes of this list, I have used three household income groups: (A) 10,000–39,999; (B) 40,000–59,999; (C) 60,000 or more. In five cases I estimated the household income and those are noted.

SARAH ABRAHAM, age thirty-nine, works as a nutritionist. She is white, has an Irish/Scottish/Welsh background, is Catholic, has been married nineteen years to an engineer/manager, has two children, had two additional pregnancies, both resulting in miscarriages, has a college education and some graduate education, and lives in a New England town. She learned about the study by word-of-mouth through her workplace. She participated in one interview. (C)

P E N N Y   A D A M S , age thirty-three, works as a social worker. She has a graduate degree, has been married two years to a health provider, and this is her first pregnancy. She is white, Scottish, German, and Irish, is Catholic and lives in a town/suburban setting in New England. She learned about the study from a co-worker of hers. She participated in two interviews.(C)

J I L L   A N D E R S O N , age thirty-five, works as a child development professional. Her first child was one-month old at the time of our first interview. She is white, has a graduate degree, has a Protestant background, and is married to a business owner. She lives in a New England town, learned about the study from her health provider, and participated in one interview.(B, estimated)

S A R A   A S H L E Y , age thirty-six, works as a health care provider and lives in a New England town. She has a professional certificate and some college education, is white, has a Protestant, English/German background, has been married four months, and this is her second pregnancy. She has a child from a previous marriage. She learned about the study from an acquaintance and participated in one interview.(A)

L A U R A   A S T O N , age thirty-two, works as a mental health professional. She is a doctoral candidate, is married to a computer specialist/contractor, and has a Protestant, Southern U.S./English/German background. This is her second pregnancy. Her first pregnancy ended in a miscarriage. She lives in a New England town. She learned about the study from me. She participated in three interviews.(A)

M A R T A   B E T T S , age thirty, is a graduate student and a part-time educator/writer/consultant. She is Jewish and white. This is her first pregnancy. She is married to an educator, and they live in a New England city. She learned about the study through me and participated in one interview.(A, estimated)

M A R I E   B I C K E R S O N , age thirty-seven, is a full-time mother and craftsperson. She has a graduate degree, comes from a Protestant, German/English background, has been married eight years to someone in the publishing industry, and has one child. She lives in a New England town. She learned about the study from one of the other women in the study and participated in one interview.(B)

JANE DOE, age thirty-five, works as a flight attendant. She has been married four and a half years to a manager. This is her first pregnancy. She has a Protestant, Scandinavian background, has two years of college education, and lives in a rural location in New England. She learned about the study from her health provider and participated in one interview. (c)

GRETA ERLICH, age thirty-five, works as an educational resources administrator. She has one child and is married to an educator. She is white, has a Protestant, Anglo-Saxon background, and lives in a New England town. She learned about the study from me and participated in one interview. (B, estimated)

LAUREN FAGAN, age thirty-six, works as a public relations specialist. She learned about the study from her health provider and participated in one interview. She is white and has a Catholic background. She is married, has a college education, and lives in a small New England town. This is her first pregnancy. (B, estimated)

JANE FOSTER, age thirty-six, works as an educator/writer. She has one child. She is white, Jewish, and has an Eastern European background. She has a graduate degree, and is married to a teacher/farmer. She lives in a rural location in New England. She learned of the study from her health provider and participated in three interviews. (A)

LOUISE FREY, age thirty-five, lives in a rural location in New England. She is white and has a Protestant, German/Italian background. She learned about the study from a notice I posted in a regional maternity/baby store. She works as an educator and has a graduate degree. She is married to an educator and is expecting her first child. She participated in three interviews. (A)

MEG FRYER, age thirty-one, lives in a New England town. She is white and Jewish. She learned of the study through word-of-mouth and participated in one interview. She has two children and is married to a researcher. She is a full-time mother and has a doctoral-level education. (c)

RACHEL HOWARD, age thirty-two, lives in a rural community in New England. She has one child. She has a college education, works part-time in the medical field, and is married to a computer specialist. She is white and comes from a Catholic, French-Canadian/

German background. She learned about the study from her health provider and participated in two interviews. (B)

N A N C Y   H U G H E S , age thirty-eight, lives in a rural/suburban New England location. She is a full-time mother and has worked in the insurance industry. She is white, a high school graduate, and comes from a Catholic, Italian/Irish background. She has one child and is married to a scientist. She learned about the study from her health provider and participated in one interview. (B)

B L O S S O M   H U N N E Y C U T T , age thirty, lives in a New England town. She has one child. This is her second pregnancy. She is white and comes from a Catholic, Italian background. She has a graduate degree and is an educator. She is married to an electrical engineer. She learned about the study from another woman in the study and participated in one interview. (A)

D O R O T H Y   L E E , age thirty-seven, lives in a rural/suburban New England location. She has one child. She is white, Jewish, and comes from an Eastern European background. She has a graduate degree and is a full-time mother. She is married to a business person. She learned of the study from another woman in the study and participated in two interviews. (B)

J A N E   L O W E , age thirty-two, lives in a rural New England community. She has one child and is married to someone in the publishing industry. She has a college education and is a full-time mother. She is white and has a Protestant, Anglo-Saxon background. She learned about the study from another woman in the study and participated in one interview. (A)

B E R N A D E T T E   L Y N N , age thirty, lives in a New England town. She learned about the study from another woman in the study and participated in two interviews. She has one child and is married to someone in the publishing industry. She has a two-year college degree and works as a health professional. She is white and comes from a Catholic/Italian and Russian/Jewish background. (B)

C A R O L   M C A L L I S T E R , age thirty-four, learned about the study from her health provider and participated in two interviews. She lives in a New England town. She is white and Scotch/Irish. She has a graduate degree and works as an educator. She is married to an educator/consultant and has one child. This is her second pregnancy. (A)

BETTY MELL, age thirty-six, lives in a suburban/rural New England location. She has three children. She is white and has a Catholic, Italian background. She has a college degree and works part-time as a health professional. She is married to an electronic engineer. She learned about the study from her health provider and participated in two interviews. (B)

MARY MEYER, age thirty-nine, works as an administrator. She has a two-year college degree and is married to a business person/ analyst. She is white and comes from a Catholic, Irish/French background. She lives in a rural/suburban location in New England. This is her first pregnancy. She learned of the study through her health provider and participated in one interview. (B)

EVELYN MICHAELS, age thirty-seven, lives in a rural New England community. She has a college degree and works in the computer industry, as does her husband. She is expecting her first child. She learned about the study from her health provider and participated in two interviews. She is white and has a Catholic, Anglo-Saxon, and Italian/Irish background. (C)

HELEN PATRICK, age thirty-six, is married and has two children. She is a graduate student and educator. She learned about the study from me and participated in one interview. She is white and comes from a Catholic background. She lives in suburban/rural New England. (B, estimated)

BARBARA SANDERS, age thirty-five, lives in a New England town. She has a college education and works as a self-employed licensed professional. She is white and has a Jewish background. She is married and is expecting her first baby. She learned about the study from her health provider and participated in one interview. (B)

ANNA SIMAS, age thirty-seven, lives in a New England town. She lives with a male partner. She is white and has a Protestant, Anglo-Saxon/Portuguese background. She has a college degree and works in the publishing industry. She is expecting her first baby. She had two previous pregnancies. She learned about the study from her health provider and participated in three interviews. (A)

BARBARA SMITH, age forty, lives in a rural New England community. She has one other child. She has had additional pregnancies which resulted in miscarriages. She is white and has a Protestant background. She has a Ph.D. and is a self-employed scholar, educator, and writer. She is married to a scholar/educator. She learned about the study from her health provider and participated in two interviews.(B)

S A R A   S W A N S O N , age thirty, lives in a New England town. This is her first baby. She is white and comes from a Protestant, Anglo-Saxon background. She is married to a manager. She has a graduate degree and works as a therapist. She learned about the study from an acquaintance and participated in two interviews.(C)

R O X A N N E   T H O M A S , age thirty-two, works part-time in a medical setting. She completed two years of college. She lives in a New England town. She has a Catholic, Polish/Italian background. She has one child. She is married to a retail manager. She learned about the study from her health provider and participated in two interviews. *(b)*

N A N C Y   W I L S O N , age thirty-four, lives in a rural New England community. She is white and comes from a Catholic, French-Canadian/Scottish background. She works as a health professional and has a graduate degree. She is married to a researcher/human services provider. She has one child. She learned about the study from a mutual acquaintance and participated in two interviews.(C)

S A R A H   W O R T H I N G T O N , age forty, lives in a small town in New England. She has one child. She is a college graduate and works as a business consultant. She is married to a business person. She is white and has a Protestant, Scotch/Irish background. She learned about the study from her health provider and participated in two interviews.(B)

A Methodological Note

In designing the study on which this book is based, I was influenced by feminist approaches to social research. Feminist critiques of positivism and objectivity have led to efforts to make methods and topics of research consistent with feminist epistemology and values. Feminist critics of "malestream" scientific thinking have promoted the use of qualitative research methods as well as the articulation of a new view of social research.

There are numerous "feminist" approaches to social research, just as there are many forms of feminism. The following features, though, capture the most important aspects of a feminist approach. First is the attention to "bringing the woman(en) back in," by giving credence to women's voices, injecting into scholarly and activist discussions the voices, views, insights, and experiences of women. Second, a feminist approach to research involves addressing the impacts of patriarchy and sexism on individual and social behavior. As Dorothy E. Smith suggests in her 1987 book *The Everyday World as Problematic,* a "feminist mode of inquiry might then begin with women's experiences from women's standpoint and explore how it is shaped in the extended relations of larger social and political realities"(p. 11).

A third element of a feminist approach to research involves the development of an alternative methodological paradigm, posing a challenge to the assumptions of positivism and objectivity. Important elements of such a research paradigm are the acknowledgment of interaction between the researcher(s) and her subjects, the inclusion of researcher reflexivity and self-awareness as an integral part of scholarly analysis, and the empowerment of women as a research goal.

This book is based on a qualitative study conducted from a feminist perspective. I wanted to provide women with a chance to tell their stories, and hoped I could help bring women's voices into discussions about procreative policy and practice. I tried to show how the women's experiences illuminate some of the social pressures and social structures that constrain and enable women's choices and women's lives. The study also exemplifies some of the features of feminist approaches to research in my attempts to acknowledge my role as researcher, my recognition of the essential human-ness of the research process, and my commitment to the empowerment of women.

As with most research, the specific study focus—initially, in this case, on pregnant women's decision-making about prenatal tests—emerged from a combination of personal, intellectual, political, and practical interests and considerations. In my mid-thirties when I wrote the research proposal, I was aware of the "magic age" of thirty-five with respect to prenatal diagnosis. As a woman whose friends have been struggling with these decisions, and as someone with a background in citizen empowerment and "client" advocacy, I found these questions personally and politically relevant.

When I reviewed the literature, I discovered that most previous social science research about prenatal tests was of two major types. One group of studies examined variables associated with a woman's choice to have prenatal diagnosis, such as age, religion, socioeconomic status, or her feelings about abortion. Other studies concerned the psychosocial impacts of amniocentesis or other prenatal diagnostic tests on women and their families, such as stress or anxiety. Only a few studies explicitly focused on the ways women perceive and choose prenatal tests. Even fewer were conducted from a feminist perspective or focused on the standpoint(s) of women. Most of the previous research attempted to identify predictive models or explain the variation in women's responses to prenatal tests and concentrated on specific issues (e.g., stress or anxiety). I wanted to look more openly at women's experiences, to generate the textured, nuanced data available through intensive, open-ended interviewing. I chose to use in-person, multiple interviews to allow the women to express themselves more fully than if they were choosing from pre-selected answers, as in survey research.

As it turned out, my approach to the research generated unexpected insights. For example, by listening to the women's stories, I discovered that pregnancy in a high-tech age implies multiple choices. This realization led me to broaden the study's initial focus—on pregnant women's choices about prenatal diagnosis—to include an examination of a range of choices faced by pregnant women or women who hope to become pregnant. The findings—such as the two main points of the book—that women considered a multiplicity of relational, contextual, and intertwined factors when making pregnancy-related choices; and that their experiences of pregnancy and choice were characterized by ambiguity and contradictions (and that choice, for them, therefore, was both real and illusory)—emerged from an inductive process that started with the women's own stories. My goal was to develop theory and come to conclusions grounded in the actual experiences of women.

This book is a synthesis of my interpretation of the women's experiences and perceptions, based on my understanding of their words. Though I have included many of the women's own words here—as a way to share their experiences and thoughts in their own voices—the book reflects my choices as researcher. I chose what questions to ask the women, which themes to highlight, which quotes to include. The women's stories yielded a wealth of rich, detailed data. In transcribing and analyzing the tape-recorded interviews, I looked for similarities and differences, patterns, themes and surprises.

Mary Catherine Bateson (1989, repr. 1990) has written eloquently of the nonlinearity of women's lives. Her description of the ways women construct their lives, improvising along the way, weaving old and new threads, unraveling, and reweaving fits well with the form and the content of the women's stories as they shared them with me. I have presented the women's stories in a more conventional temporal chronology here, starting with the choice to attempt to become pregnant.

This book attempts to bridge worlds of meaning by exploring the meaning(s) of pregnancy and choice described by a small group of pregnant women during intensive, in-person interviews. The thirty-one women I interviewed are a relatively privileged group: North

American, white, and middle class. All are high school graduates, and all but one have taken some courses beyond high school. Eleven have graduate degrees. All of the women have male partners or husbands.

The women live in small towns and rural communities in New England. They ranged from thirty to forty years old when interviewed. Eighteen of the women were thirty-five years old or older, the age when amniocentesis is generally recommended by doctors. Eleven women had amniocentesis with this pregnancy; one had chorionic villi sampling. Twenty-eight women told me they had at least one ultrasound during this pregnancy.

Twelve of the thirty-one women were expecting their first baby and sixteen already had one child. Two women were expecting their third child, and one her fourth child. Six women told me they chose to terminate earlier pregnancies, and five told me about earlier miscarriages. There were two sad events during the study: Sara Ashley's baby died during the seventh month of her pregnancy; and, as noted in the book, Sarah Worthington's baby died sixteen days after he was born.

The stories these women told me comprise a picture of pregnancy, technology, and choice from the standpoint(s) of a particular group of women. The women were not randomly selected; they were self-selected participants who took the initiative to contact me after hearing about the study. They all chose to talk with me about their pregnancies and their choices, and, in that sense, they may differ from women for whom these matters are more private, or women who cannot or choose not to talk about these issues for a variety of possible reasons: they find the topic painful, they think their experiences are unimportant, or they have no time to indulge in unpaid conversations with a stranger.

The women in the study share characteristics that make them a relatively homogeneous and privileged group, despite ethnic, experiential, and attitudinal differences. Their commonalities may distinguish them from women with different characteristics; they are clearly not representative of all women, and, possibly, not representative even of all white, middle-class women in New England or the United States. But their experiences show us some of the diverse ways women are experiencing pregnancy and choice in the late twentieth century.

The impact of medical technologies on an individual is mediated by a host of factors: sex, race, age, relative health or illness or disability, socioeconomic status, religion, sexual orientation. Other influences include the structure of the health-care system, and the economic, political, and cultural configurations of a person's locality, region, and country and their global counterparts. In her extensive research on the impacts of class, culture, race, and ethnicity on genetic counseling, Rayna Rapp (1988a, 1988b, 1989) has demonstrated that women deal with choices about prenatal testing in ways that make sense to them, given their own culturally influenced perceptions of disability, health, illness, and parenthood. Though I have contextualized the women's stories to some extent, I do not deal extensively with the impacts of the larger social, political, and cultural forces that constrain and enhance their lives. A full consideration of those impacts is beyond the scope of this book.

The women whose stories comprise this book, by virtue of their social locations, may have choices not available to other women. But the sense of agency demonstrated by this group of women, their ability to shape their lives, is not unique to white, middle-class, (presumably) heterosexual women in New England. In studying middle-class and working-class women in Baltimore, Maryland, for example, Emily Martin (1987) found that black and white working-class women used a language of resistance—to dominant medical and scientific images of women's bodies—to describe their experiences of pregnancy, menstruation, and menopause. Their descriptions challenged the depictions of women's procreative processes contained in medical discourse, and demonstrated a sense of personal agency and the power to construct their own meanings of their experiences.

On the other hand, that the relatively privileged women whose stories appear in this book discovered that their choices were constrained and their ability to attain procreative control was limited suggests that for less privileged women, choice may be even more illusory.

Notes

Notes to Chapter 1

1. This name is a pseudonym. "Sarah Worthington" and the other women I interviewed selected "code names" at my request, and those names are used throughout this book. See appendix A for a description of each woman.

2. Ultrasound, also known as sonography, uses high-frequency sound waves to generate an image of the fetus. The ultrasound "photograph" is taken by running a transducer over the pregnant woman's abdomen, which "translates" the sound waves into a picture on a video screen. Ultrasound is used by doctors and technicians during the first trimester to date the pregnancy, later in the pregnancy to examine the fetus for morphological abnormalities, to assist in the placement of the needle in amniocentesis, and to detect twins and other "multiples." In chorionic villi sampling, which takes place as early as the ninth week of pregnancy, a catheter is inserted into the uterus through the vagina or abdomen to remove a piece of the chorion, the tissue that surrounds the embryo in a pregnant woman's uterus. This piece of tissue is analyzed to detect possible fetal anomalies. The maternal serum alphafetoprotein (MSAFP) screening consists of a blood test usually aroune the fifteenth or sixteenth week of pregnancy. Measurement of the level of alphafetoprotein in the woman's blood is used to detect possible neural tube defects and also (in the case of the "triple test") to indicate the possibility of Down syndrome. Amniocentesis, another test used to detect fetal abnormalities, involves the insertion of a long needle through the woman's abdomen into her uterus usually around the sixteenth week of pregnancy, though "early amnio" may be performed as early as twelve or thirteen weeks. A small amount of amniotic fluid is removed, cultured in a laboratory, and

analyzed. The information is used to produce a karyotype (a picture of the chromosomes,) which in turn provides information about possible fetal anomalies, including Trisomy 21, in which an extra chromosome indicates the presence of Down syndrome in the fetus. The amniotic fluid may be analyzed to provide information about other fetal conditions as well.

3. As Dorothy Wertz has noted, with respect to childbirth, "North Americans lost the sense of nature sometime in the nineteenth century." The medicalization of childbirth has a long history. Increasingly, pregnancy, and conception too, have become medicalized and taken out of the realm of the natural: "Having foreclosed choices that once existed post-natally, medicine now offers new choices prenatally." Dorothy C. Wertz, *Prenatal Diagnosis and Society* (Ottawa, Ontario, Canada: Royal Commission on New Reproductive Technologies, 1993), 24–25. Whether these new choices also foreclose other choices is a topic for much debate by feminists and others. For more on the medicalization of childbirth, see Richard W. Wertz and Dorothy C. Wertz, *Lying-In: A History of Childbirth in America* (New York: Schocken Books, 1977, reprinted [expanded edition], New Haven: Yale University Press, 1989.)

4. Research has indicated that women use and accept prenatal diagnosis technologies, but it is difficult to assess the extent to which women's "demand" for these and other procreative technologies has influenced their rapid inclusion in standard prenatal care and the extent to which the existence and promotion of the technologies by doctors has influenced women's demand, or choice of the tests.

5. This term comes from Kristin Luker, *Taking Chances* (Berkeley and Los Angeles: University of California Press, 1975).

6. Recent reports have suggested a possible connection between chorionic villi sampling (CVS) and limb malformations in children born to women who had the procedure. At the time of this writing, there is much debate in the scientific and medical community about this topic. Whether the problems of Sarah Worthington's baby were in any way connected with CVS is an unanswerable question at the moment.

Notes to Chapter 2

1. Lawrence M. Friedman, *The Republic of Choice* (Cambridge, Mass.: Harvard University Press, 1990), 74.

2. Deborah A. Stone, *Policy Paradox and Political Reason* (Glenview, Ill.: Scott, Foresman, 1988), 87.

3. See John Stuart Mill, *On Liberty,* first published 1859, edited and with an Introduction by Gertrude Himmelfarb (Middlesex, England: Penguin, 1987). For interesting discussions of Mill and the influence of Harriet Taylor on his thinking and writing, see Alice Rossi, ed., *The Feminist Papers* (New

York: Bantam Books. 1974), 183–196; and Rosemarie Tong, *Feminist Thought: A Comprehensive Introduction* (Boulder: Westview, 1989), 17–22. For a good discussion of Mill and negative and positive concepts of liberty and choice see Deborah A. Stone, *Policy Paradox and Political Reason* (Glenview, Ill.: Scott, Foresman, 1988), 87–103. For a good discussion of the difference between "freedom from" and "freedom to," see David Schuman, *A Preface to Politics* (Lexington, Mass.: D. C. Heath, 1981), 150–172.

4. See for example Beth Rushing and Suzanne Onorato, "Controlling the Means of Reproduction: Feminist Theories and Reproductive Technologies," *Humanity and Society* 13, no. 3 (1989): 268–291; and Rosemarie Tong, *Feminist Thought: A Comprehensive Introduction* (Boulder: Westview Press, 1989).

5. For background on Wollstonecraft, Mill, and Taylor, and the distinctions between different forms of liberal feminism, see Rosemarie Tong, *Feminist Thought: A Comprehensive Introduction* (Boulder: Westview Press, 1989). For additional background on Wollstonecraft, Mill, and Taylor, see Sheila Rowbotham, *Women in Movement* (New York: Routledge, 1992). For more on liberalism, feminism, and liberal feminism, see Juliet Mitchell and Ann Oakley, eds., *What Is Feminism?* (New York: Pantheon, 1986); Hester Eisenstein, *Contemporary Feminist Thought* (London: Unwin Paperbacks, 1984); Carole Pateman and Elizabeth Gross, *Feminist Challenges* (Boston: Northeastern University Press, 1986); Susan Moller Okin, *Women in Western Political Thought* (Princeton: Princeton University Press, 1979).

6. Beth Rushing and Suzanne Onorato, "Controlling the Means of Reproduction: Feminist Theories and Reproductive Technologies," *Humanity and Society* 13, no. 3, 1989: 268–291.

7. For an example of a liberal feminist perspective on procreative technologies, see Lori B. Andrews, "My Body, My Property," *Hastings Center Report,* October 1986: 28–38; and idem, *Medical Genetics: A Legal Frontier* (Chicago: American Bar Foundation, 1987).

8. See, for example, the point of view of the collected articles in Michelle Stanworth, ed., *Reproductive Technologies* (Minnesota: University of Minnesota Press, 1987) and see especially the Editor's Introduction, pp. 1–9; and Lynda Birke, Susan Himmelweit, and Gail Vines, *Tomorrow's Child* (London: Virago Press, 1990).

9. For good descriptions and critiques of the rational choice model, see Mary Douglas, *Risk Acceptability according to the Social Sciences* (New York: Russell Sage Foundation, 1985); and Deborah A. Stone, *Policy Paradox and Political Reason* (Glenview, Ill.: Scott, Foresman, 1988) chapter 10.

10. For more on rational choice models, see Hal R. Arkes and Kenneth R. Hammond, *Judgement and Decision Making* (Cambridge: Cambridge University Press, 1986).

11. See, for example, Amos Tversky and Daniel Kahneman, "The Framing of Decisions and the Psychology of Choice," *Science* 21 (1981): 453–458;

Daniel Kahneman and Amos Tversky, "The Psychology of Preferences," *Scientific American* 286 (January 1982): 160–173.

12. For a good description of this approach, see Irwin Rosenstock, "The Historical Origins of the Health Belief Model," *Health Education Monographs* 2 (1974b): 328–335.

13. See, for example, M. H. Becker et al. "The Health Belief Model and Prediction of Dietary Compliance—a Field Experiment," *Journal of Health and Social Behavior* 18, no. 4 (December 1977): 348–366; Marshall H. Becker, "The Health Belief Model and Personal Health Behavior," *Health Education Monographs* 2, no. 4 (Winter 1974), San Francisco: Society for Public Health Education; I. M. Rosenstock, "Patient Compliance with Diabetic Regimens," *Diabetes Care* 8, no. 6 (November-December 1985): 610–616.

14. For a recent adaptation of the rational choice model as an explanation of human behavior, see James S. Coleman, *Foundations of Social Theory* (Cambridge, Mass.: Belknap Press of Harvard University, 1990). That this book was recently awarded the Distinguished Publication Award by the American Sociological Association (1992) is one indication that the rational choice approach is increasingly gaining in importance in American social science.

15. Deborah A. Stone, *Policy Paradox and Political Reason* (Glenview, Ill.: Scott, Foresman, 1988), 193.

16. Mary Douglas, *Risk Acceptability according to the Social Sciences* (New York: Russell Sage Foundation, 1985), 37.

17. Ibid., 67.

18. For a good description of the strategic functions of rational choice models, see Deborah A. Stone, *Policy Paradox and Political Reason* (Glenview, Ill.: Scott Foresman, 1988), chapter 10.

19. This term ("relations of ruling") is Dorothy E. Smith's. See her *The Conceptual Practices of Power* (Boston: Northeastern University Press, 1990); and idem, *The Everyday World as Problematic* (Boston: Northeastern University Press, 1987).

20. Jalna Hanmer, "A Womb of One's Own," in *Test-Tube Women,* ed. Rita Arditti, Renate Duelli Klein, and Shelley Minden (London: Pandora Press, 1984), 438–448.

21. Zygmunt Bauman, *Thinking Sociologically* (Oxford: Blackwell, 1990), 199–200.

22. For good descriptions of the social construction of choice, see, for example, Elizabeth Bartholet, "In Vitro Fertilization: The Construction of Infertility and of Parenting," in Helen B. Holmes, ed., *Issues in Reproductive Technology* (New York: Garland, 1992), 253–260; Christine Crowe, " 'Women Want It': In-Vitro Fertilization and Women's Motivations for Participation," *Women's Studies International Forum* 8, no. 6: 547–552; Deborah Gerson, "Infertility and the Construction of Desperation," *Socialist Re-*

view 19 (1989): 45–64; and Linda Williams, "Biology or Society? Parenthood Motivation in a Sample of Canadian Women Seeking In Vitro Fertilization," in Helen B. Holmes, ed., *Issues in Reproductive Technology* (New York: Garland, 1992), 261–274.

23. Zygmunt Bauman, *Thinking Sociologically* (Oxford: Blackwell, 1990), 202. Though Bauman's discussion of technology is a general one that only comprises a small part of his book, his analysis fits well with both radical and socialist feminist perspectives on procreative technologies and his book makes for enjoyable and interesting reading.

24. Robyn Rowland, "Technology and Motherhood: Reproductive Choice Reconsidered," *Signs* 12, no. 3 (1987): 518.

25. Corlann Gee Bush, "Women and the Assessment of Technology," in Joan Rothschild, ed., *Machina Ex Dea,* (Elmsford, N.Y.: Pergamon Press, 1983), 151–170, quote at 155.

26. See, for example, the analyses contained in Joan Rothschild, ed., *Machina Ex Dea* (Elmsford, N.Y.: Pergamon Press, 1983), 151–170. For a pioneering feminist analysis of science, see Evelyn Fox Keller, *Reflections on Gender and Science* (New Haven: Yale University Press, 1985).

27. This is my term for feminists who wish to abolish the development and use of procreative technologies until and unless they are controlled by women.

28. For more information on FINRRAGE see "Resolution from Finrrage Conference, July 3–8, 1985," in Patricia Spallone and Deborah Lynn Steinberg, eds., *Made to Order* (Oxford: Pergamon Press, 1987), 211–212. A subgroup within the abolitionist camp embraces an anti-abortion position, despite the fact that this stance generally has been associated with anti-feminists. See for example, Alison Davis, "Women with Disabilities: Abortion and Liberation," *Disability, Handicap and Society* 2, no. 3 (1987): 275–284. Davis extends the disability movement critique of the use of prenatal diagnosis for "quality control," arguing that abortion of fetuses with genetic conditions is unethical.

29. Maria Mies, "Why Do We Need All This?" *Women's Studies International Forum* 8, no. 6 (1985): 553–560.

30. For more on the medicalization and social control of women's procreative processes, see, for example, Gena Corea, *The Hidden Malpractice* (New York: Jove/Harcourt Brace Jovanovich, 1977); idem, *The Mother Machine* (New York: Harper and Row, 1985); Gena Corea et al., *Man-Made Women: How New Reproductive Technologies Affect Women* (Bloomington: Indiana University Press, 1987); Barbara Ehrenreich and Deirdre English, *Witches, Midwives and Nurses* (Old Westbury, N.Y: The Feminist Press, 1973b); idem, *Complaints and Disorders* (Old Westbury, N.Y.: The Feminist Press, 1973a); idem, *For Her Own Good* (Garden City, N.Y.: Anchor Press/Doubleday, 1978); Ann Oakley, *Becoming a Mother* (Oxford: Martin Robertson, 1979);

idem, *The Captured Womb* (Oxford: Basil Blackwell, 1984); Barbara Katz Rothman, *In Labor: Women and Power in the Birthplace* (New York: W. W. Norton, 1982); idem, *The Tentative Pregnancy* (New York: Viking Penguin, 1986); idem, *Recreating Motherhood* (New York: W. W. Norton, 1989); idem, "Commentary: Women Feel Social and Economic Pressures to Abort Abnormal Fetuses," *Birth* 17, no. 2 (June 1990): 81; and Richard W. Wertz and Dorothy C. Wertz, *Lying-In: A History of Childbirth in America* (New York: Schocken Books, 1977).

31. See, for example, Suzanne Arms, *Immaculate Deception* (Boston: Houghton Mifflin, 1975); and Doris Haire, *Cultural Warping of Childbirth* (Minneapolis: International Childbirth Education Association, 1972).

32. For additional examples of medical practices potentially harmful to women, see Gena Corea, *The Hidden Malpractice* (New York: Jove/Harcourt Brace Jovanovich, 1977); and Ann Oakley, *The Captured Womb* (Oxford: Basil Blackwell, 1984). Ruth Hubbard has suggested that ultrasound, so commonly used in prenatal diagnosis, "could cause changes either in the placenta or in the embryo." She worries "about what the women are told to caution them about possible ill effects." Ruth Hubbard, in "Prenatal Diagnosis Discussion," in *The Custom-Made Child,* ed. Helen B. Holmes, Betty B. Hoskins, and Michael Gross (Clifton, N.J.: Humana Press, 1981), 106–107.

33. Shulamith Firestone, *The Dialectic of Sex* (New York: William Morrow, 1970). For commentaries on Firestone, see, for example, Beth Rushing and Suzanne Onorato, "Controlling the Means of Reproduction: Feminist Theories and Reproductive Technologies," *Humanity and Society* 13, no. 3 (1989): 268–291; and Rosemarie Tong, *Feminist Thought* (Boulder: Westview Press, 1989), chapter 3.

34. Shulamith Firestone, *The Dialectic of Sex* (New York: William Morrow, 1970), 209–221; also see Beth Rushing and Suzanne Onorato, "Controlling the Means of Reproduction: Feminist Theories and Reproductive Technologies," *Humanity and Society* 13, no. 3 (1989), 275.

35. See, for example, Gena Corea, *The Mother Machine* (New York: Harper and Row, 1985); Mary Daly, *Gyn-Ecology* (Boston: Beacon Press, 1978); Andrea Dworkin, *Right-Wing Women* (New York: Perigee Books, G. P. Putnam's Sons, 1983); Eva Feder Kitay, "Womb Envy: An Explanatory Concept," in *Mothering,* ed. Joyce Trebilcot (Totowa, N.J.: Rowman and Allanheld, 1983), 94–128; Françoise Laborie, "Looking for Mothers You Only Find Fetuses," in *Made To Order,* ed. Patricia Spallone and Deborah Lynn Steinberg (Oxford: Pergamon Press, 1987), 48–57.

36. For examples of the positive essentialist position, see, for example, Gena Corea, *The Mother Machine* (New York: Harper and Row, 1985); Gena Corea et al., *Man-Made Women: How New Reproductive Technologies Affect Women* (Bloomington: Indiana University Press, 1987); Andrea Dworkin, *Right-Wing Women* (New York: Perigee Books, G. P. Putnam's Sons, 1983);

Adrienne Rich, *Of Woman Born* (New York: W. W. Norton/Bantam Press, 1976); Robyn Rowland, "A Child at Any Price?" *Women's Studies International Forum* 8, no. 6 (1985): 539–546; Patricia Spallone and Deborah Lynn Steinberg, *Made to Order: The Myth of Reproductive and Genetic Progress* (Oxford: Pergamon Press, 1987.

37. Beth Rushing and Suzanne Onorato, "Controlling the Means of Reproduction: Feminist Theories and Reproductive Technologies," *Humanity and Society* 13, no. 3 (1989), 278.

38. Rosemarie Tong, *Feminist Thought* (Boulder: Westview Press, 1989), 39; see particularly her chapters 2 and 6.

39. Rosemarie Tong makes this distinction, suggesting Juliet Mitchell's work as an example of dual systems socialist feminism, and the work of Heidi Hartmann, Iris M. Young, and Alison Jaggar as examples of the unified model. See Tong, *Feminist Thought* (Boulder: Westview Press, 1989), chapter 6.

40. Beth Rushing and Suzanne Onorato, "Controlling the Means of Reproduction: Feminist Theories and Reproductive Technologies," *Humanity and Society* 13, no. 3 (1989), 279.

41. Ibid., 281.

42. Wendy Farrant describes the profits associated with ultrasound and maternal serum alphafetoprotein screening in "Who's for Amniocentesis?" in *The Sexual Politics of Reproduction,* ed. Hilary Homans (Aldershot, England: Gower, 1985), 102–103. See also Gena Corea, *The Mother Machine* (New York: Harper and Row, 1985); Timothy McNulty, "Science Turns Birth into a New Industry," *Chicago Tribune,* August 9, 1987; and Robyn Rowland, "Technology and Motherhood: Reproductive Choice Reconsidered," *Signs* 12, no. 3 (1987): 512–528. For a discussion of the way new medical technologies become institutionalized, see Irving Kenneth Zola, *Socio-Medical Inquiries* (Philadelphia: Temple University Press, 1983).

43. Stephen Lyons, "Ultrasound's Quiet Revolution," *Boston Globe,* 26 November 1990, 27.

44. Dorothy C. Wertz, *Prenatal Diagnosis and Society* (Ottawa, Ontario, Canada: Royal Commission on New Reproductive Technologies, 1993), 167; also see Dorothy C. Wertz and John C. Fletcher, "A Critique of Some Feminist Challenges to Prenatal Diagnosis," *Journal of Women's Health* 2, no. 2 (Summer 1993), 173–188.

45. Barry Meier, "Effective? Maybe. Profitable? Clearly," *New York Times,* Sunday, February 14, 1993 (Section Three,) 1, 6.

46. Dorothy C. Wertz, *Prenatal Diagnosis and Society* (Ottawa, Ontario, Canada: Royal Commission on New Reproductive Technologies, 1993), 11–12. These figures come from an international survey conducted by Dorothy C. Wertz and John C. Fletcher of the attitudes of genetics services providers. The majority of geneticists surveyed in the United States (78%), Canada

(68%), the United Kingdom (71%), and France (81%) indicated that "improving the general health and vigor of the population" is important. Substantial percentages of geneticists in the United States (47%), Canada (51%), the United Kingdom (48%), and France (50%) indicated that reduction in the number of genetic carriers in the population is an important goal of genetic counseling. "The prevention of disease or abnormality" was deemed an important genetic counseling goal by the vast majority of geneticists in Canada (98%) and eighteen other nations (97%); and small percentages of geneticists in the United States (7%), Canada (11%), the United Kingdom (19%), and a majority of geneticists in France (69%) felt that this is "absolutely essential." See Dorothy C. Wertz and John C. Fletcher, eds., *Ethics and Human Genetics: A Cross-Cultural Perspective* (Heidelberg: Springer-Verlag, 1989); Dorothy C. Wertz and John C. Fletcher, "Ethics and Medical Genetics in the United States: A National Survey," *American Journal of Medical Genetics,* 29 (1988a): 815–827; and Dorothy C. Wertz and John C. Fletcher, "Attitudes of Genetic Counselors: A Multi-National Survey," *American Journal of Human Genetics* 42, no. 4 (1988b): 592–600. An updated version of this survey is being conducted in thirty-six nations, as of this writing.

47. Ruth Hubbard, "Prenatal Diagnosis and Eugenic Ideology," *Women's Studies International Forum* 8, no. 6 (1985): 567–576, 573.

48. Adrienne Asch, "Reproductive Technology and Disability," in *Reproductive Laws for the 1990s: A Briefing Handbook,* ed. Nadine Taub and Sherrill Cohen (Newark: Women's Rights Litigation Clinic, Rutgers University, 1988), 88.

49. For discussions of the history of eugenics and analyses of the dangers of new developments in genetics, see, for example, Lori Andrews, *Medical Genetics: A Legal Frontier* (Chicago: American Bar Foundation, 1987); Troy Duster, *Backdoor to Eugenics* (London: Routledge, 1990); Neil A. Holtzman, *Proceed with Caution: Predicting Genetic Risks in the Recombinant DNA Era* (Baltimore: Johns Hopkins University Press, 1989); Ruth Hubbard, "Prenatal Diagnosis and Eugenic Ideology," *Women's Studies International Forum* 8, no. 6 (1985): 567–576; Ruth Hubbard and Elijah Wald, *Exploding the Gene Myth* (Boston: Beacon Press, 1993); Daniel J. Kevles, *In the Name of Eugenics: Genetics and the Uses of Human Heredity* (New York: Knopf, 1985); Philip Reilly, *Genetics, Law and Social Policy* (Cambridge, Mass.: Harvard University Press, 1977); and David Suzuki and Peter Knudtson, *Genethics: The Clash between the New Genetics and Human Values* (Cambridge, Mass.: Harvard University Press, 1989).

50. For a discussion of the ideologies of progress and perfection, see Joan Rothschild, "Engineering Birth: Toward the Perfectibility of *Man?*" in *Science, Technology and Social Progress,* ed. Steven L. Goldman (Bethlehem, Pa.: Lehigh University Press, 1989), 93–120.

51. Marsha Saxton, "Born and Unborn: The Implications of Reproduc-

tive Technologies for People with Disabilities," in *Test-Tube Women,* Rita Arditti et al. (London: Pandora Press, 1984) 298–312, 306. See also Marsha Saxton, "Prenatal Screening and Discriminatory Attitudes about Disability," *Genewatch* (January-February 1987), 8–10.

52. Alison Davis, "Women with Disabilities: Abortion and Liberation," *Disability, Handicap and Society* 2, no.3 (1987): 275–284.

53. Beth Rushing and Suzanne Onorato,"Controlling the Means of Reproduction: Feminist Theories and Reproductive Technologies," *Humanity and Society* 13, no. 3 (1989): 268–291, 280.

54. Tabitha Powledge, "Windows on the Womb: Prenatal Testing Is Altering Our Attitudes toward the Unborn," *Psychology Today* 17, no.5 (May 1983): 37–42.

55. A. W. Liley, "The Foetus as a Personality," *Fetal Therapy* 1 (1986):10. Also see C. Granière-Deferre et al., "Feasibility of Prenatal Hearing Test," in *Normal and Abnormal Development of Hearing and its Clinical Implications,* ed. J. J. Eggermont and G. R. Bock (Stockholm: *Acta Otolaryngol* Supplement 421, 1985): 93–101. In the anti-abortion film, *The Silent Scream,* "the science of fetology" is used to justify the position that the fetus is a human being with full human rights. For legal arguments about fetal rights which rely on medical views of the fetus, see Edward W. Keyserlingk, "The Unborn Child: Part 2," *Health Law in Canada* 3, no. 2 (1982): 31–41, and "Clarifying the Right to Prenatal Care," *Health Law in Canada* 4 (1983): 35–38; Margery W. Shaw, "Conditional Prospective Rights of the Fetus," *Journal of Legal Medicine* 5 (1984): 63–116; and Jeffrey A. Parness, "The Abuse and Neglect of the Human Unborn: Protecting Potential Life," *Family Law Quarterly* 20 (Summer 1986): 197–212. For an opposing view, see Lisa Blumberg, "Why Fetal Rights Must Be Opposed," *Social Policy* 18, no. 2 (1987): 40–41.

56. For a more extensive example of this argument, see Barbara Katz Rothman, *Recreating Motherhood* (New York: W.W. Norton, 1989).

57. Katha Pollitt, " 'Fetal Rights'—A New Assault on Feminism," *Nation* 250, no. 12 (26 March 1990): 409–419, 409.

58. Felicity Barringer, "Sentence for Killing Newborn: Jail Term, Then Birth Control," *New York Times,* Sunday, 18 November 1990, 1. In addition to punishing pregnant women in the name of fetal protection, the courts have sentenced mothers to birth control and sterilization. Barringer's front-page article in the *New York Times* described the case of a young woman who was sentenced to birth control after being convicted of the death of her baby in Florida. The seventeen-year-old woman (called a "girl" in the article) admitted suffocating her newborn daughter and was sentenced to two years in prison. As part of her sentence she was also "required to use birth control for 10 years after her release from jail." Also cited in the article was a 1988 Arizona case in which a judge required the lifetime use of contraception for a seventeen-year-old mother of an eighteen-month-old child and a six-month-

old infant, who pleaded guilty to charges of child neglect; and a two-year-old Indiana case in which "a 30–year old woman with a history of personality disorders agreed to be sterilized as part of a plea arrangement" when she was charged with felony child neglect.

59. For more on these and other examples, see George Annas, "She's Going to Die: The Case of Angela C," *Hastings Center Report,* February-March 1988: 23–25; Sharon Begley et al., "The Troubling Question of 'Fetal Rights,' " *Newsweek,* 8 December 1986, 87; Angela Bonavoglia, "The Ordeal of Pamela Rae Stewart," *Ms* , July-August 1987, 92; Janet Gallagher, "Fetus as Patient," in *Reproductive Laws for the 1990s,* ed. Nadine Taub and Sherrill Cohen (Newark: Women's Rights Litigation Clinic, Rutgers University, 1988), 155–205; Debbie Ratterman, " 'Fetal Abuse': A Miscarriage of Justice," *Off Our Backs,* November 1986, 6; and Jennifer Terry, "The Body Invaded: Medical Surveillance of Women as Reproducers," *Socialist Review* 19, no.3 (July-September 1989): 13–43.

60. Zygmunt Bauman, *Thinking Sociologically* (Oxford: Blackwell, 1990), 201. For a feminist articulation of this idea, see, for example, Abby Lippman, "Prenatal Genetic Testing and Screening: Constructing Needs and Reinforcing Inequities," *American Journal of Law and Medicine* 16, nos. 1–2 (1991): 15–20.

61. Rita Arditti, Renate Duelli Klein, and Shelley Minden, *Test-Tube Women* (London: Pandora Press, 1984), 2.

62. For example, Rosemarie Tong describes forms of feminism I have not mentioned: psychoanalytic feminism, exemplified by the work of Nancy Chodorow and Dorothy Dinnerstein; existentialist feminism, exemplified by the work of Simone de Beauvoir, and postmodern feminism, such as the work of Helene Cixous, Luce Irigaray, and Julia Kristeva. See Rosemarie Tong, *Feminist Thought: A Comprehensive Introduction* (Boulder: Westview Press, 1989).

63. Some of the most notable feminist empirical investigations of the ways women actually perceive and make procreative choices include Diane Beeson, "Technological Rhythms in Pregnancy: The Case of Prenatal Diagnosis by Amniocentesis," in *Cultural Perspectives on Biological Knowledge,* ed. Troy Duster and Karen Garrett (Norwood, N.J.: Ablex Publishing, 1984), 145–181; Monika Leuzinger and Bigna Rambert, "'I Can Feel It—My Baby Is Healthy': Women's Experiences with Prenatal Diagnosis in Switzerland," *Reproductive and Genetic Engineering* 1, no. 3 (1988): 239–249; Kristin Luker, *Taking Chances* (Berkeley and Los Angeles: University of California Press, 1975); idem, *Abortion and the Politics of Motherhood* (Berkeley and Los Angeles: University of California Press, 1984); Emily Martin, *The Woman in the Body: A Cultural Analysis of Reproduction* (Boston: Beacon Press, 1987); and Barbara Katz Rothman, *The Tentative Pregnancy* (New York: Viking Penguin, 1986).

Notes to Chapter 3

1. This term comes from Kristin Luker, *Taking Chances* (Berkeley and Los Angeles: University of California Press, 1975).

2. Previous researchers also have found that in recounting miscarriage experiences women often begin with the decision to have the child. See Shulamit Reinharz, "The Social Psychology of a Miscarriage: An Application of Symbolic Interaction Theory and Method," in *Women and Symbolic Interaction,* ed. Mary Jo Deegan and Michael R. Hill (Boston: Allen & Unwin, 1987), chapter 13.

3. For historical analyses of methods used to control procreation, see Angus McLaren, *Reproductive Rituals* (London: Methuen, 1984); Barbara Ehrenreich and Dierdre English, *For Her Own Good* (Garden City, N.Y.: Anchor Press, Doubleday, 1973).

4. See, for example, Carole Joffe, *The Regulation of Sexuality* (Philadelphia: Temple University Press, 1986); Shulamith Firestone, *The Dialectic of Sex* (New York: William Morrow, 1970).

5. Organizations such as the National Women's Health Network; National Black Women's Health Project; Boston Women's Health Book Collective; Feminist Majority Foundation; National Latina Health Organization; and National Abortion Rights Action League, and numerous other national, regional, and local feminist advocacy and self-help groups continue to work to enhance women's ability to control their own procreative processes and options. See Boston Women's Healthbook Collective, *The New Our Bodies, Ourselves* (New York: Simon & Schuster, 1992), for addresses of these and other feminist and women's health organizations.

6. See Regina H. Kenen, *Reproductive Hazards in the Workplace* (New York: Harrington Park Press, 1993).

7. See Miriam D. Mazor and Harriet F. Simon, eds., *Infertility — Medical, Emotional and Social Considerations* (New York: Human Sciences Press, 1984); Judith N. Lasker and Susan Borg, *In Search of Parenthood: Coping with Infertility and High Tech Conception* (Boston: Beacon Press, 1987); and Arthur L. Greil, *Not Yet Pregnant* (New Brunswick, N.J.: Rutgers University Press, 1991).

8. For analyses of the social construction of infertility, see Jennifer L. Stone, "Contextualizing Biogenetic and Reproductive Technologies," *Critical Studies in Mass Communication* 8, no. 3 (September 1991): 309–332; and Deborah Gerson, "Infertility and the Construction of Desperation," *Socialist Review* 19 (1989): 45–64. For analyses of the relationship between the development of procreative technologies and women's ostensible need or desire for the technologies, see, for example, Christine Crowe, "'Women Want It': In-Vitro Fertilization and Women's Motivations for Participation," *Women's Studies International Forum* 8, no. 6 (1985): 547–552; and Robyn Rowland, "A

Child at Any Price?" *Women's Studies International Forum* 8, no. 6 (1985): 539–546.

9. Shulamit Reinharz, "The Social Psychology of a Miscarriage: An Application of Symbolic Interaction Theory and Method," in *Women and Symbolic Interaction,* ed. Mary Jo Deegan and Michael R. Hill (Boston: Allen & Unwin, 1987), 235.

10. Ibid., 244.

Notes to Chapter 4

1. See Sandy Smith, "Baby Boycott," *Southern Exposure* 18, no. 2 (Summer 1990): 28–31.

2. From New Hampshire Public Radio, WEVO, Concord, New Hampshire, New Hampshire News report, February 25, 1993.

3. Carol McAllister, Betty Mell, Jill Anderson, Dorothy Lee, Sarah Worthington, Evelyn Michaels, Mary Meyer, Sarah Abraham, Roxanne Thomas, Nancy Hughes, Jane Doe, and Sara Swanson.

4. Jill Anderson, Dorothy Lee, Jane Foster, Jane Lowe, Blossom Hunneycutt, Anna Simas, Bernadette Lynn.

5. For a good discussion of the tendency to "blame Mom," see for example, Janna Malamud Smith, "Mothers: Tired of Taking the Rap," *New York Times Magazine,* 10 June 1990, 32; for recent manifestations of mother-blaming that also entail victim-blaming, see Jan Hoffman, "Pregnant, Addicted—and Guilty?" *New York Times Magazine,* 19 August 1990, 33. For more on this theme, see Robin Gregg, " 'Choice' as a Double-Edged Sword: Information, Guilt and Mother-Blaming in a High-Tech Age," *Women and Health* 20, no. 3 (1993): 53–73.

Notes to Chapter 5

1. Iris Marion Young, "Pregnant Embodiment: Subjectivity and Alienation," *Journal of Medicine and Philosophy* 9 (1984), 45–62, quote at 54.

2. Of course, not all women choose pregnancy and not all pregnancies are chosen ones. Many women become pregnant inadvertently, when contraception fails or when they have inadequate or no access to contraception and/or information about sexuality and procreation.

3. Penny Adams, Jill Anderson, Marta Betts, Marie Bickerson, Jane Doe, Lauren Fagan, Jane Foster, Louise Frey, Blossom Hunneycutt, Jane Lowe, Carol McAllister, Mary Meyer, Sara Swanson, Nancy Wilson.

4. I use both terms, "baby," and "fetus," because the women used both. The women usually referred to their fetuses as "babies," and used the term "fetus" when discussing a medical procedure in the abstract (e.g., explaining their understanding of the functions of prenatal diagnosis: to get information about the fetus). When describing their own experiences with prenatal tests,

though, the women almost invariably used the word "baby." (e.g., "I saw the baby on the screen").

5. Iris Marion Young, "Pregnant Embodiment: Subjectivity and Alienation," *Journal of Medicine and Philosophy* 9 (1984): 45–62.

6. Shulamit Reinharz, "The Social Psychology of a Miscarriage: An Application of Symbolic Interaction Theory and Method," in *Women and Symbolic Interaction,* ed. Mary Jo Deegan and Michael R. Hill, (Boston: Allen & Unwin, 1987b), chapter 13, 232.

7. Barbara Katz Rothman, *The Tentative Pregnancy* (New York: Viking Penguin, 1986).

8. See Diane Beeson, "Technological Rhythms in Pregnancy: The Case of Prenatal Diagnosis by Amniocentesis," in *Cultural Perspectives on Biological Knowledge,* ed. Troy Duster and Karen Garrett (Norwood, N.J.: Ablex, 1984), 145–181; Diane Beeson and Mitchell S. Golbus, "Anxiety Engendered by Amniocentesis," *Birth Defects Original Articles Series* 15, no. 5c (New York: Alan R. Liss, 1979): 191–197; idem, "Decision Making: Whether or Not to Have Prenatal Diagnosis and Abortion of X-Linked Conditions," *American Journal of Medical Genetics* 20 (1985): 107–114; Rosalind P. Petchesky, "Foetal Images: The Power of Visual Culture and the Politics of Reproduction," in *Reproductive Technologies,* ed. Michelle Stanworth (Minneapolis: University of Minnesota Press, 1987), chapter 3; and Barbara Katz Rothman, *The Tentative Pregnancy* (New York: Viking Penguin, 1986).

9. For descriptions of past and present hazards associated with childbearing, see, for example, Barbara Ehrenreich and Deirdre English, *For Her Own Good* (Garden City, N.Y.: Anchor Press/Doubleday, 1978); Ann Oakley, *Becoming a Mother* (Oxford: Martin Robertson, 1979); idem, *The Captured Womb* (Oxford: Basil Blackwell, 1984): Barbara Katz Rothman, *Giving Birth* (New York: Penguin Books, 1984); and Richard W. Wertz and Dorothy C. Wertz, *Lying-In: A History of Childbirth in America* (New York: Schocken Books, 1977).

10. Sara Ashley, Roxanne Thomas, Rachel Howard, Penny Adams, Sara Swanson, Jane Doe, Lauren Fagan, Anna Simas, Sarah Worthington, Nancy Wilson, Laura Aston, Jane Lowe, Betty Mell, Carol McAllister, Louise Frey.

11. This assumption contains another, implicit assumption, that of heterosexuality. The assumption that a woman's pregnancy is a sign that she is, or has been (hetero)sexually active does not take other possibilities into account: (1) that the woman is sexually active/involved with another woman, and the pregnancy was accomplished through alternative insemination or (2) that the woman is celibate and/or has no sexual partner, and the pregnancy was conceived through alternative insemination.

12. Pregnancy is a female phenomenon, and receives both the social support and the social censure associated with femaleness. All "pregnant persons" are women. The term "pregnant person" has been used in legal

arguments to excuse discrimination against women. By de-feminizing pregnancy, the term implies that anyone can become pregnant, and that, therefore, discrimination based on a "person's" pregnancy is not sex discrimination. One of the most famous cases of this sort was *Geduldig v. Aiello,* Supreme Court, 1974. 417 U.S. 484, 944 S. Ct. 2485, 41 L. Ed. 2d 256. The decision in that case was that discrimination based on pregnancy is not discrimination based on sex. See J. Ralph Lindgren and Nadine Taub, *The Law of Sex Discrimination* (St. Paul, Minn.: West Publishing, 1988).

13. This practice was outlawed by the Supreme Court in the case of *Cleveland Board of Education v LaFleur,* 414 U.S. 632 (1973). The Court ruled that dismissing teachers from their jobs or forcing them to take leaves of absence in the early stages of pregnancy was a violation of due process. See J. Ralph Lindgren and Nadine Taub, *The Law of Sex Discrimination* (St. Paul, Minn.: West Publishing, 1988).

14. Emily Martin, *The Woman in the Body* (Boston: Beacon Press, 1987), 100. Some employers do attempt to meet the needs of their workers who are parents, but unfortunately they comprise a small minority. For a review of the literature on the extent and impacts of family employee benefits on women in the workforce, see Beth Miller, "Private Welfare: The Distributive Equity of Family Benefits in America," Ph.D. dissertation, Waltham, Mass., Brandeis University, 1992.

15. Robbie Pfeufer Kahn, "The Language of Birth," Ph.D. dissertation, Waltham, Mass., Brandeis University, 1988, 348.

16. Laura Aston, Anna Simas, Evelyn Michael, Betty Mell, Penny Adams, Mary Meyer, Sarah Abraham, Jane Doe, Jane Foster, Dorothy Lee, Jane Lowe, Sarah Worthington.

17. See, for example, Jack A. Pritchard, Paul C. MacDonald, and Norman F. Gant, *Williams Obstetrics,* 17th edition. (Norwalk, Conn.: Appleton-Century-Crofts, 1985). For a critique of what she calls the practice of "obstructrics," see Robbie Pfeufer Kahn, "The Language of Birth," Ph.D. dissertation, Brandeis University, 1988.

18. Arthur W. Frank, "Bringing Bodies Back In: A Decade Review," *Theory, Culture and Society* 7 (1990): 139.

19. Models of pregnancy are analogous to models of childbirth and mothering. The implicit model of the "good mother" is still the mother who stays at home to care for her children. Mothers who do not conform to this model are seen as deviant. But while analyses of motherhood and pregnancy are sometimes analogous, it is important not to conflate the two. Motherhood can occur without pregnancy and vice versa. Though I think that motherhood begins during pregnancy, if not before, the practical work of caretaking of infants and children (work that can be done by mothers and others) is a topic that merits its own treatment. The relationship that develops in pregnancy: woman/mother to fetus/baby or child, is often a precursor to the

relationship of the mother and the child after birth, especially when the birth mother and the social mother are the same person.

20. Barbara Katz Rothman, *In Labor: Women and Power in the Birthplace* (New York: W. W. Norton, 1982), 273.

21. Ibid., 276.

22. Ann Oakley, *The Captured Womb* (Oxford: Basil Blackwell, 1984), 2.

23. Emily Martin, *The Woman in the Body* (Boston: Beacon Press, 1987).

24. Ibid., 207.

25. Ibid., 105–109.

26. Alexandra Dundas Todd, *Intimate Adversaries* (Philadelphia: University of Pennsylvania Press, 1989), 121.

27. Sue Fisher, *In the Patient's Best Interest* (New Brunswick, N.J.: Rutgers University Press, 1987).

28. Hilary Graham and Ann Oakley, "Competing Ideologies of Reproduction: Medical and Maternal Perspectives on Pregnancy," in *Women, Health and Reproduction,* ed. Helen Roberts (London: Routledge, 1981), 50–74.

29. Ibid., 54–55.

30. Barbara Katz Rothman, *In Labor* (New York: W. W. Norton, 1982), 24.

31. Rothman's perspective here is analogous to other feminist scholarship in which women's experiences are assumed to be the norm and/or which challenge male-based theory. See, for example, Carol Hardy-Fanta, *Latina Politics, Latino Politics: Gender, Culture and Political Participation in Boston* (Philadelphia: Temple University Press, 1993); Carol Gilligan, *In a Different Voice* (Cambridge, Mass.: Harvard University Press, 1982); and Mary Field Belenky, Blythe McVicker Clinchy, Nancy Goldberger, and Jill Mattuck Tarule, *Women's Ways of Knowing* (New York: Basic Books, 1986).

Notes to Chapter 6

1. Women also encountered other tests during pregnancy. Two women were given the option of having a blood test to detect HIV; two were tested for gestational diabetes. Other prenatal tests include the non-stress test, used to determine the fetal heart rate, and the contraction-stress test, used to determine how the placenta and fetus respond to contractions. Both stress tests are conducted toward the end of pregnancy, when a doctor feels the baby is overdue or is concerned about fetal growth. For more information, see Boston Women's Healthbook Collective, *The New Our Bodies, Ourselves* (New York: Simon & Schuster, 1992).

2. Michelle Harrison, M.D., *A Woman in Residence* (New York: Penguin Books, 1982).

3. This observation comes from a story Robbie Kahn relates about her experience as a childbirth consultant in a municipal hospital in the 1970s. Talking with the hospital's chief of obstetrics, she learned that a major

advocate of the fetal monitor had said at a colloquium that "there is no such thing as a normal labor and delivery." Robbie Pfeufer Kahn, "The Language of Birth" (Waltham, Massachusetts: Ph.D. Dissertation, Brandeis University, 1988), 160.

4. The maternal serum alphafetoprotein test is a blood test conducted at sixteen to nineteen weeks of pregnancy, to detect indicators of neural tube defects in the fetus. In approximately 5 percent of the tests, the high AFP level in the woman's blood is due to factors other than fetal neural tube defects. The women I interviewed were aware of the risk of a false positive result, and some chose not to have the test for this reason (Sometimes the test is repeated to confirm the positive result; often an ultrasound is done following a positive AFP). A newer form of the test, the "triple test," now has replaced the older version in many places. In this test, two additional markers are measured in the pregnant woman's blood (human chorionic gonadotrophin and unconjugated estriol), to assess the risk of Down syndrome in the fetus. To the best of my and their knowledge, none of the women I interviewed was offered the triple test.

5. Kerstin Berne-Fromell, Gunilla Josefson, and Berndt Kjessler, "Who Declines from Serum Alphafetoprotein Screening, and Why?" *Acta Obstetrica Gynecol Scand* 63 (1984): 687–691. In a related article, the authors reported little difference in anxiety in women who chose and those who declined AFP screening. See Kerstin Berne-Fromell, Berndt Kjesller, and Gunilla Josefson, "Anxiety Concerning Fetal Malformations in Women Who Accept or Refuse Alpha-fetoprotein Screening in Pregnancy," *Journal of Psychosomatic Obstetrics and Gynecology* 2, no. 1 (1983): 94–97. In a Swedish study of midwives' attitudes toward AFP screening, the researchers found that the majority of the midwives surveyed felt it would be better not to use the test routinely, because of the anxiety it produces, but said they would probably have the test if they became pregnant, especially as they approached age forty. See M. L. Johansson, "Midwives' Attitudes to Alphafetoprotein Screening," *Journal of Psychosomatic Obstetrics and Gynecology* 2–4 (1983): 237–242.

6. High-resolution ultrasound may become an alternative, as opposed to a prelude or corollary, to amniocentesis. Researchers at Harvard Medical School have suggested that women at high risk of having a baby with a neural tube defect can be screened just as well with ultrasound, without the miscarriage risk and high expense associated with amniocentesis. Of the quarter of a million women who have amniocentesis each year to detect neural tube defects, about one in fifteen receive a positive diagnosis. Amniocentesis costs around twelve hundred dollars; in about one in five hundred women, normal fetuses are miscarried following the procedure. An article in the *New England Journal of Medicine* about the Harvard study (30 August 1990) reported that "the chance that amniocentesis would cause a miscarriage of a normal fetus was greater than the chance that ultrasound would fail to

identity a fetus with the defect." Gina Kolata, "Alternative Screening of Neural Tube Defects," *New York Times,* 30 August 1990, B 14. Since that study, ultrasound equipment has improved and more practitioners have become adept at reading ultrasound "pictures," making it even more possible that the technique will supplant amniocentesis in some cases.

7. Eleven other women mentioned the discomfort of having to have a full bladder during ultrasound. Barbara Smith, though, compared her earlier ultrasounds with her more comfortable experience during this pregnancy: "What amazed me was the difference in this ultrasound. How much, or how fast technology has changed . . . the earlier ultrasounds . . . you had to have a full bladder and you arrive there bursting to the seams...[now] you can go earlier in the pregnancy . . . you don't have to have a full bladder . . . the first thing that I did was rush to the bathroom when I got to the doctor's office." She noted another change: "It was very much the same . . . except the doctor, the ultrasound doctor must be coining money on ultrasounds. The first time, it was in a small, rather ratty building. Then it moved to a new buiding, and now, in the space of a year, she's now gotten to two floors. She's wonderful . . . very good, but I can see that it's . . . lucrative."

8. Laura Aston, Greta Erlich, Jane Foster, Barbara Sanders, Anna Simas, Nancy Wilson.

9. I am grateful to Susan E. Bell for noting that Sarah Worthington's statement is a historically situated pronouncement. Definitions of risk come and go, but they seem to be infinitely expandable when it comes to women's procreative processes.

10. The ultrasound procedure may be done at any time during pregnancy, and women frequently have more than one ultrasound during pregnancy. For more details on ultrasounds, see chapter 1, note 2.

11. For more information on amniocentesis, see chapter 1, note 2.

12. Barbara Katz Rothman, *The Tentative Pregnancy* (New York: Viking Penguin, 1986), 130.

13. Sara Ashley, Jane Doe, Greta Erlich, Lauren Fagan, Nancy Hughes, Evelyn Michaels, Barbara Sanders, Anna Simas, Barbara Smith, Roxanne Thomas, Nancy Wilson, Sarah Worthington.

14. Jane Doe, Greta Erlich, Lauren Fagan, Nancy Hughes, Evelyn Michaels, Barbara Sanders, Anna Simas, Barbara Smith, Nancy Wilson, Sarah Worthington.

15. Barbara Katz Rothman, *The Tentative Pregnancy* (New York: Viking Penguin, 1986), chapter 5.

16. Monika Leuzinger and Bigna Rambert, " 'I Can Feel It—My Baby Is Healthy'—Women's Experiences with Prenatal Diagnosis in Switzerland," *Reproductive and Genetic Engineering* 1, no. 3 (1988): 239–249.

17. See Marsha Saxton,"Born and Unborn: The Implications of Reproductive Technologies for People with Disabilities," in *Test-Tube Women,* ed.

Rita Arditti, Renate Duelli Klein, and Shelley Minden (London: Pandora Press, 1984), 298–312; and idem, "Prenatal Screening and Discriminatory Attitudes about Disability," *Genewatch* (January-February 1987): 8–10.

18. Jill Anderson, Sara Ashley, Marta Betts, Anna Simas, Roxanne Thomas, Nancy Wilson.

19. Penny Adams, Jill Anderson, Sara Ashley, Laura Aston, Jane Doe, Lauren Fagan, Jane Foster, Louise Frey, Jane Lowe, Carol McAllister, Evelyn Michaels, Barbara Sanders, Anna Simas, Sara Swanson, Roxanne Thomas.

20. For a good discussion of ambiguous diagnoses, see Barbara Katz Rothman, *The Tentative Pregnancy* (New York: Viking Penguin, 1986), chapter 6.

21. Jill Anderson, Jane Doe, Lauren Fagan, Louise Frey, Nancy Hughes, Dorothy Lee, Evelyn Michaels, Barbara Sanders, Anna Simas, Barbara Smith, Nancy Wilson, Sarah Worthington.

22. See Shulamit Reinharz, "Controlling Women's Lives: A Cross-Cultural Interpretation of Miscarriage Accounts," in *Research in the Sociology of Health Care* 7, ed. Dorothy Wertz (Greenwich, Conn.: JAI Press, 1987a), 2–37.

23. See Carol Gilligan, *In a Different Voice* (Cambridge, Mass.: Harvard University Press, 1982); Anne Colby and William Damon, "Listening to a Different Voice," in *The Psychology of Women,* ed. Mary Roth Walsh (New Haven: Yale University Press, 1987), 321–329; and Judy Auerbach, Linda Blum, Vicki Smith, and Christine Williams, "Commentary on Gilligan's *In a Different Voice,*" *Feminist Studies* 2, no. 1 (Spring 1985): 149–161.

24. Virginia Barber and Merrill Skaggs, *The Mother Person* (Indianapolis: Bobbs-Merrill, 1975), 13.

Notes to Chapter 7

1. See Carol Gilligan, *In a Different Voice* (Cambridge, Mass.: Harvard University Press, 1982); and Mary Roth Walsh, *The Psychology of Women* (New Haven: Yale University Press, 1987). For an earlier articulation of a "different voice" in psychology, see Jean Baker Miller, *Toward a New Psychology of Women* (Boston: Beacon Press, 1976); for a "lay" description of some of the theorists of the Stone Center, Wellesley College, and their relational psychology, see Christina Robb, "A Theory of Empathy," *Boston Globe Magazine,* 16 October 1988, 19.

2. Research shows that most women and couples choose to terminate pregnancy following a positive prenatal diagnosis. For a review of the literature on people's abortion decisions related to prenatal diagnosis, see Dorothy C. Wertz, *Prenatal Diagnosis and Society* (Ottawa, Ontario, Canada: Royal Commission on New Reproductive Technologies, 1993).

3. Articles in the popular press have addressed the pressures on mothers

maternity on women's careers in television (particularly as television news-casters), for example, see Caryn James, "What's a Mother to Do?" *New York Times,* Sunday, 17 March 1991, H 33.

4. Richard Saltus, "Demand Grows for Fertility Extension," *Boston Globe,* 28 October 1990, 35.

5. For discussions of the ways the socialization of girls into maternal roles and behaviors affect women's ways of seeing and relating to the world, see, for example, Carol Gilligan, *In a Different Voice* (Cambridge, Mass.: Harvard University Press, 1982); Sara Ruddick, "Maternal Thinking," in *Mothering,* ed. Joyce Trebilcot (Totowa, N.J.: Rowman and Allanheld, 1983), 213–230; Nancy Chodorow, *The Reproduction of Mothering* (Berkeley and Los Angeles: University of California Press, 1978).

6. Of 12.2 million heterosexual married couples aged thirty-five to forty-four in 1988, 1.1 million, or 9 percent, were childless (more than 500,000 of whom were childless by choice), according to the National Center for Health Statistics. But choosing to be childless is still an option that receives scrutiny (if not censure) from friends and family. Three out of five people questioned in a recent poll by the Associated Press said that "couples with children are happier." Leslie Dreyfous, "More Couples Choosing Not to Have Children," *Keene Sentinel* (N.H.), 16 March 1991, 27. For a fascinating discussion of feminist perspectives on mothering and childlessness, see Ann Snitow, "Motherhood—Reclaiming the Demon Texts," *Ms.* 1, no. 6 (May-June 1991): 34–37.

7. My focus in this book is on women's choices and their feelings of responsibility, but I wish to note here that health providers—physicians, genetic counselors, and others—also face additional choices, social scrutiny, and feelings of responsibility concerning pregnancy in a high-tech age. Some of their feelings of responsibility may stem from training (e.g., the commitment to a nondirective approach on the part of genetic counselors), personal and professional experience, ethics, collegial expectations, workplace protocols, or concerns about legal liability. Further consideration of this topic is beyond the confines of the present book, however.

8. Actually, prenatal tests only reduce or eliminate the risk of having a baby with a genetically linked (and detectable) disability when a woman terminates her pregnancy following a positive diagnosis. In and of themselves the tests neither prevent nor reduce risk; rather, the information they provide may be used by women and their partners to prevent the *outcome* of the risk: the birth of a baby with the detected disability. Prenatal testing can prevent or reduce risks in the case of pre-conception or pre-implantation testing, when the pregnancy is not conceived or the embryo implanted following a positive diagnosis, but none of the women experienced this form of prenatal diagnosis.

9. Shulamit Reinharz, "Controlling Women's Lives: A Cross-Cultural

Interpretation of Miscarriage Accounts," in *Research in the Sociology of Health Care* 7, ed. Dorothy C. Wertz (Greenwich, Conn.: JAI Press, 1987), 2–37.

10. For more on this theme, see Robin Gregg, " 'Choice' as a Double-Edged Sword: Information, Guilt and Mother-Blaming in a High-Tech Age," *Women and Health* 20, no. 3 (1993): 53–73. For examples of fetal protection at the expense of pregnant women's rights, see, for example, Katha Pollitt, " 'Fetal Rights'—A New Assault on Feminism," *Nation* 250, no. 12 (26 March 1990): 409–419; Dawn Johnsen, "A New Threat to Pregnant Women's Autonomy," *Hastings Center Report,* August 1987: 33–40; Janet Gallagher, "Fetus as Patient," in *Reproductive Laws for the 1990s,* ed. Nadine Taub and Sherrill Cohen (Newark: Women's Rights Litigation Clinic, Rutgers University, 1988), 155–205; George Annas, "She's Going to Die: The Case of Angela C.," *Hastings Center Report,* February-March 1988: 23–25; Angela Bonavoglia, "The Ordeal of Pamela Rae Stewart," *Ms.* July-August 1987: 92; Sharon Begley et al., "The Troubling Question of 'Fetal Rights,' " *Newsweek,* 8 December 1986, 87; Debbie Ratterman, " 'Fetal Abuse': A Miscarriage of Justice," *Off Our Backs,* November 1986, 6; and Jennifer Terry, "The Body Invaded: Medical Surveillance of Women as Reproducers," *Socialist Review* 19, no. 3 (July-September 1989):13–43.

11. Robbie Pfeufer Kahn, "The Language of Birth," Ph.D. dissertation, Brandeis University, 1988; Emily Martin, *The Woman in the Body: A Cultural Analysis of Reproduction* (Boston: Beacon Press, 1987). For related arguments, see Arthur W. Frank, "Bringing Bodies Back In: A Decade Review," *Theory, Culture and Society* 7 (1990): 131–162; and Irving K. Zola, "To Our Innermost Parts- Reflections on Nancy Mairs' *Remembering the Bone House-An Erotics of Place and Space*," *Kaleidoscope* 22 (Winter-Spring 1991): 48–50.

12. Diana T. Meyers, *Self, Society and Personal Choice* (New York: Columbia University Press, 1989), Preface, xii.

13. In a newspaper article about former Maine Senator Margaret Chase Smith, Jack Thomas mentioned Smith's nationally syndicated newspaper column. In one column, Smith wrote about leftovers, wondering why men resisted them. She saw them as "integral to life, something old to be mixed with something new, a tinge of the past to be blended with the present." Jack Thomas, "Eyewitness to a Century," *Boston Globe,* 9 April 1991, 53.

14. See, for example, Dorothy C. Wertz and John Fletcher, "A Critique of Some Feminist Challenges to Prenatal Diagnosis," *Journal of Women's Health* 2, no. 2 (Summer 1993): 173–188; Catherine Kohler Riessman, "Women and Medicalization: A New Perspective," *Social Policy* 14 (1983): 3–18; Arthur L. Greil, *Not Yet Pregnant* (New Brunswick, N.J.: Rutgers University Press, 1991); and Deborah Gerson, "Infertility and the Construction of Desperation," *Socialist Review* 19 (1989): 45–64.

15. See, for example, Susan Sherwin, *No Longer Patient* (Philadelphia: Temple University Press, 1992); Helen Bequaert Holmes and Laura M.

Purdy, eds., *Feminist Perspectives in Medical Ethics* (Bloomington: Indiana University Press, 1992).

16. Presently there is much discussion in the genetics community about the implications of a nondirective counseling approach. See, for example, Seymour Kessler, "Psychological Aspects of Genetic Counseling VII. Thoughts on Directiveness," *Journal of Genetic Counseling* 1, no. 1 (1992): 9–17; and Janice Edwards, Lynn Godmilow, and Scott Polzin, "Can Non-Directiveness Be Non-Helpful? Three Views," *Perspectives in Genetic Counseling* 12, no. 3 (1990): 1, 6–7. The issue is an important one that cannot be fully addressed or resolved in these pages.

Selected Bibliography

Andrews, Lori B. 1986. "My Body, My Property." *Hastings Center Report*, October: 28–38.

———. 1987. *Medical Genetics: A Legal Frontier*. Chicago: American Bar Foundation.

Annas, George J. 1988. "She's Going to Die: The Case of Angela C." *Hastings Center Report*, February-March: 23–25.

Arditti, Rita, Renate Duelli Klein, and Shelley Minden, eds. 1984. *Test Tube Women*. London: Pandora Press.

Arkes, Hal R., and Kenneth R. Hammond. 1986. *Judgement and Decision Making*. Cambridge: Cambridge University Press.

Arms, Suzanne. 1975. *Immaculate Deception*. Boston: Houghton Mifflin.

Asch, Adrienne. 1988. "Reproductive Technology and Disability." In *Reproductive Laws for the 1990s: A Briefing Handbook*, ed. Nadine Taub and Sherrill Cohen, 59–89. Newark: Women's Rights Litigation Clinic, Rutgers University.

Ashford, Janet Isaacs, ed. 1983. *The Whole Birth Catalog*, Trumansburg, N.Y.: The Crossing Press.

Auerbach, Judy, Linda Blum, Vicki Smith, and Christine Williams. 1985. "Commentary on Gilligan's *In a Different Voice*." *Feminist Studies* 2, no. 1 (Spring): 149–161.

Barber, Virginia, and Merrill M. Skaggs. 1975. *The Mother Person*. Indianapolis: Bobbs-Merrill.

Barringer, Felicity. 1990. "Sentence for Killing Newborn: Jail Term, Then Birth Control." *New York Times* Sunday, 18 November, 1.

Bartholet, Elizabeth. 1992. "In Vitro Fertilization: The Construction of Infertility and of Parenting." In *Issues in Reproductive Technology, An Anthology*, ed. Helen B. Holmes, 253–260. New York: Garland Publishing.

Bateson, Mary Catherine. [1989] 1990. *Composing a Life*. New York: Atlantic Monthly Press.

Bauman, Zygmunt. 1990. *Thinking Sociologically*. Oxford: Blackwell.

Becker, Howard. 1986. *Writing for the Social Sciences*. Chicago: University of Chicago Press.

Becker, M. H., L. A. Maiman, J. P. Kirscht, D. P. Haefner, and R. H. Drachman. 1977. "The Health Belief Model and Prediction of Dietary Compliance: A Field Experiment."*Journal of Health and Social Behavior* 18, no. 4 (December): 348–366.

Becker, Marshall H. 1974. "The Health Belief Model and Personal Health Behavior." *Health Education Monographs* 2, no. 4 (Winter). San Francisco: Society for Public Health Education.

Beck-Gernsheim, Elisabeth. 1990. "The Changing Duties of Parents: From Education to Bio-engineering?" *International Social Science Journal* 42, no. 4: 451–463.

Beeson, Diane. 1984. "Technological Rhythms in Pregnancy: The Case of Prenatal Diagnosis by Amniocentesis." In *Cultural Perspectives on Biological Knowledge,* ed. Troy Duster and Karen Garrett, 145–181. Norwood, N.J.: Ablex Publishing.

Beeson, Diane, and Rita Douglas. 1983. "Prenatal Diagnosis of Fetal Disorders—Part I: Technological Capabilities." *Birth* 10, no.4 (Winter): 227–241.

Beeson, Diane, and Mitchell S. Golbus. 1979. "Anxiety Engendered by Amniocentesis." *Birth Defects Original Articles Series* 15, no. 5c (New York: Alan R. Liss): 191–197.

———. 1985. "Decision Making: Whether or Not to Have Prenatal Diagnosis and Abortion of X-Linked Conditions." *American Journal of Medical Genetics* 20: 107–114.

Begley, Sharon, Pat Wingert, Janet Huck, and Vicki Quade. 1986. "The Troubling Question of 'Fetal Rights.' " *Newsweek,* 8 December, 87.

Belenky, Mary Field, Blythe McVicker Clinchy, Nancy Goldberger, and Jill Mattuck Tarule. 1986. *Women's Ways of Knowing*. New York: Basic Books.

Bell, Colin, and Helen Roberts. 1984. *Social Researching*. London: Routledge and Kegan Paul.

Berne-Fromell, K., B. Kjessler, and G. Josefson. 1983. "Anxiety Concerning Fetal Malformations in Women Who Accept or Refuse Alpha-fetoprotein Screening in Pregnancy." *Journal of Psychosomatic Obstetrics and Gynecology* 2, no. 1: 94–97.

Berne-Fromell, Kerstin, Gunilla Josefson, and Berndt Kjessler. 1984. "Who Declines from Serum Alphafetoprotein Screening—and Why?" *Acta Obstetrica Gynecol Scand* 63: 687–691.

Birke, Lynda, Susan Himmelweit, and Gail Vines. 1990. *Tomorrow's Child.* London: Virago Press.

Black, R. B. and R. Furlong. 1984. "Impact of Prenatal Diagnosis in Families." *Social Work in Health Care* 9, no. 3: 37–50.

Blatt, Robin J. R. 1988. *Prenatal Tests.* New York: Vintage Books.

Blumberg, Lisa. 1987. "Why Fetal Rights Must Be Opposed." *Social Policy* 18, no. 2: 40–41.

Bonavoglia, Angela. 1987. "The Ordeal of Pamela Rae Stewart." *Ms.* July-August, 92.

Boston Women's Healthbook Collective. 1992. *The New Our Bodies Ourselves.* New York: Simon & Schuster.

Boutelle, Ann Edwards. 1984. "The Amniocentesis Experience." In *Infertility—Medical, Emotional and Social Considerations,* ed. Miriam D. Mazor and Harriet F. Simon, 190–197. New York: Human Sciences Press.

Bowles, Gloria, and Renate Duelli Klein, eds. 1983. *Theories of Women's Studies.* London: Routledge and Kegan Paul.

Bush, Corlann Gee. 1983. "Women and the Assessment of Technology: To Think, to Be, to Unthink, to Free." In *Machina Ex Dea,* ed. Joan Rothschild, 151–170. Elmsford, N.Y.: Pergamon Press.

Chodorow, Nancy. 1978. *The Reproduction of Mothering.* Berkeley and Los Angeles: University of California Press.

Colby, Anne, and William Damon. 1987. "Listening to a Different Voice." In *The Psychology of Women,* ed. Mary Roth Walsh, 321–329. New Haven: Yale University Press.

Coleman, James S. 1990. *Foundations of Social Theory.* Cambridge, Mass.: Belknap Press of Harvard University Press.

Corea, Gena. 1977. *The Hidden Malpractice.* New York: Jove/Harcourt Brace Jovanovich.

———. 1985. *The Mother Machine.* New York: Harper and Row.

Corea, Gena, Renate Duelli Klein, Jalna Hanmer, Helen B. Holmes, Betty Hoskins, Madhu Kishwar, Janice Raymond, Robyn Rowland, and Roberta Steinbacher. 1987. *Man-Made Women: How New Reproductive Technologies Affect Women.* Bloomington: Indiana University Press.

Cote, G. B. 1983. "Reproductive Drive and Genetic Counselling." *Clinical Genetics* 23: 359–362.

Crowe, Christine. 1985. " 'Women Want It': In-Vitro Fertilization and Women's Motivations for Participation." *Women's Studies International Forum* 8, no. 6: 547–552.

Daly, Mary. 1978. *Gyn-Ecology.* Boston: Beacon Press.

Daniels, Cynthia. 1991. "Fertile Women Need Not Apply." *Dollars and Sense,* January-February, 9.

Davies, B., and T. Doran. 1982. "Factors in a Woman's Decision to Undergo

Genetic Amniocentesis for Advanced Maternal Age." *Nursing Research* 31: 56–59.

Davis, Alison. 1987. "Women with Disabilities: Abortion and Liberation." *Disability, Handicap and Society* 2, no. 3: 275–284.

Dixson, Barbara, Teri L. Richards, Sylvia Reinsch, Vanessa Edrich, Melinda Matson, and Oliver Jones. 1981. "Midtrimester Amniocentesis-Subjective Maternal Responses." *Journal of Reproductive Medicine* 26, no. 1 (January): 10–16.

Donchin, Anne. 1986. "Future of Mothering: Reproductive Technology and Feminist Theory." *Hypatia* 3 (Fall): 121–137.

Douglas, Mary. 1985. *Risk acceptability according to the Social Sciences.* New York: Russell Sage Foundation.

Dreyfous, Leslie. 1991. "More Couples Choosing Not to Have Children." *Keene Sentinel* (N.H.), 16 March, 27.

Duster, Troy. 1990. *Backdoor to Eugenics,* London: Routledge.

Duster, Troy, and Karen Garrett. 1984. *Cultural Perspectives on Biological Knowledge.* Norwood, N.J.: Ablex Publishing.

Dworkin, Andrea. 1983. *Right-Wing Women.* New York: Perigee Books, G. P. Putnam's Sons.

Edwards, Janice, Lynn Godmilow, and Scott Polzin. 1990. "Can Non-Directiveness Be Non-Helpful? Three Views." *Perspectives in Genetic Counseling* 12, 3: 1.

Ehrenreich, Barbara, and Deirdre English. 1973a. *Complaints and Disorders.* Old Westbury, N.Y: The Feminist Press.

———. 1973b. *Witches, Midwives and Nurses.* Old Westbury, N.Y: The Feminist Press.

———. 1978. *For Her Own Good.* Garden City, N.Y.: Anchor Press/Doubleday.

Eisenstein, Hester. 1984. *Contemporary Feminist Thought.* London: Unwin Paperbacks.

Elias, Sherman, and George J. Annas. 1987. *Reproductive Genetics and the Law.* Chicago: Year Book Medical Publishers.

Farrant, Wendy. 1985. "Who's for Amniocentesis? The Politics of Prenatal Screening." In *The Sexual Politics of Reproduction,* ed. Hilary Homans, 102–103. Aldershot, England: Gower.

Fine, Michelle, and Adrienne Asch. 1988. *Women with Disabilities.* Philadelphia: Temple University Press.

Finger, Anne. 1990. *Past Due: A Story of Disability, Pregnancy and Birth.* Seattle, Wash.: Seal Press.

Firestone, Shulamith. 1970. *The Dialectic of Sex.* New York: William Morrow.

Fisher, Sue. 1987. *In the Patient's Best Interest.* New Brunswick, N.J.: Rutgers University Press.

Frank, Arthur W. 1990. "Bringing Bodies Back In: A Decade Review." *Theory, Culture and Society* 7: 131–162.

Franklin, Sarah, and Maureen McNeil. 1988. "Reproductive Futures: Recent Literature and Current Feminist Debates on Reproductive Technologies." *Feminist Studies* 14, no. 3 (Fall): 545–560.

Friedman, Lawrence M. 1990. *The Republic of Choice: Law, Authority and Culture.* Cambridge, Mass.: Harvard University Press.

Gallagher, Janet. 1988. "Fetus as Patient." In *Reproductive Laws for the 1990s,* ed. Nadine Taub and Sherrill Cohen, 155–205. Newark: Women's Rights Litigation Clinic, Rutgers University.

Gaskin, Ina May. 1978. *Spiritual Midwifery.* Summertown, Tenn.: The Book Publishing Co.

Gerson, Deborah. 1989. "Infertility and the Construction of Desperation." *Socialist Review* 19: 45–64.

Gilligan, Carol. 1982. *In a Different Voice.* Cambridge, Mass.: Harvard University Press.

Glaser, Barney G., and Strauss, Anselm L. 1967. *The Discovery of Grounded Theory: Strategies for Qualitative Research.* Chicago: Aldine Publishing.

Graham, Hilary. 1984. "Surveying Through Stories." In *Social Researching,* ed. Colin Bell and Helen Roberts, 104–124. London: Routledge and Kegan Paul.

Graham, Hilary, and Ann Oakley. 1981. "Competing Ideologies of Reproduction: Medical and Maternal Perspectives on Pregnancy." In *Women, Health and Reproduction,* ed. Helen Roberts, 50–74. London: Routledge and Kegan Paul.

Granière-Deferre, C., J.-P. Lecanuet, H. Cohen, and M. C. Busnel. 1985. "Feasibility of Prenatal Hearing Test." In *Normal and Abnormal Development of Hearing and its Clinical Implications,* ed. J. J. Eggermont and G. R. Bock, 93–101. Stockholm: *Acta Otolaryngol* Supplement 421.

Gregg, Nina. 1987. "Reflections on the Feminist Critique of Objectivity." *Journal of Communication Inquiry* 2, no. 1 (Winter): 8–18.

Gregg, Robin. 1993. " 'Choice' as a Double-Edged Sword: Information, Guilt and Mother-Blaming in a High-Tech Age." *Women and Health* 20, no. 3: 53–73.

———. 1994. "Explorations of Pregnancy and Choice in a High-Tech Age." In *Qualitative Studies in Social Work Research,* ed. Catherine Kohler Riessman, 49–66. Newbury Park, Calif.: Sage Publications.

Greil, Arthur L. 1991. *Not Yet Pregnant.* New Brunswick, N.J.: Rutgers University Press.

Haire, Doris. 1972. *Cultural Warping of Childbirth.* Minneapolis: International Childbirth Education Association.

Hanmer, Jalna. 1984. "A Womb of One's Own." In *Test-Tube Women,* ed. Rita Arditti, et al., 438–448. London: Pandora Press.

Harding, Sandra. 1986. *The Science Question in Feminism*. Ithaca and London: Cornell University Press.

Hardy-Fanta, Carol. 1993. *Latina Politics, Latino Politics: Gender, Culture and Political Participation in Boston*. Philadelphia: Temple University Press.

Harrison, Michelle. 1982. *A Woman in Residence*. New York: Penguin Books.

Hess, Beth. 1990. "Beyond Dichotomy: Drawing Distinctions and Embracing Differences." *Sociological Forum* 5, no. 1 (March): 75–93.

Hoffman, Jan. 1990. "Pregnant, Addicted—and Guilty?" *New York Times Magazine,* Sunday, 19 August, 33.

Holmes, Helen B. 1989a. "Hepatitis—Yet Another Risk of In Vitro Fertilization?" *Reproductive and Genetic Engineering* 2, no. 1: 29–37.

———. 1989b. Review of *In Vitro Fertilization and Other Assisted Reproduction,* by Howard W. Jones, Jr., and Charlotte Schrader, eds. In *Reproductive and Genetic Engineering* 2, no. 3: 289–293.

———, ed. 1992. *Issues in Reproductive Technology, An Anthology*. New York: Garland Publishing.

Holmes, Helen B., Betty B. Hoskins, and Michael Gross, eds. 1981. *The Custom-Made Child*. Clifton, N.J.: Humana Press.

Holmes, Helen Bequaert, and Laura M. Purdy, eds. 1992. *Feminist Perspectives in Medical Ethics*. Bloomington: Indiana University Press.

Holtzman, Neil A. 1989. *Proceed with Caution: Predicting Genetic Risks in the Recombinant DNA Era*. Baltimore: Johns Hopkins University Press.

Homans, Hilary, ed. 1985. *The Sexual Politics of Reproduction*. Aldershot, England: Gower.

Hubbard, Ruth. 1982. "Legal and Policy Implications of Recent Advances in Prenatal Diagnosis and Fetal Therapy." *Women's Rights Law Reporter* 7, no. 3 (Spring): 201–224.

———. 1985. "Prenatal Diagnosis and Eugenic Ideology." *Women's Studies International Forum* 8, no. 6: 567–576.

Hubbard, Ruth, and Mary Sue Henifin. 1984. "Genetic Screening of Prospective Parents of Workers." In *Biomedical Ethics Reviews,* ed. James M. Humber and Robert T. Almeder, 73–120. Clifton, N.J.: Humana Press.

Hubbard, Ruth, and Elijah Wald. 1993. *Exploding the Gene Myth*. Boston: Beacon Press.

Jacobus, Mary, Evelyn Fox Keller, and Sally Shuttleworth. 1990. *Body/ Politics: Women and the Discourses of Science*. New York: Routledge.

James, Caryn. 1991. "What's a Mother to Do?" *New York Times,* 17 March, H 33.

Joffe, Carole. 1986. *The Regulation of Sexuality*. Philadelphia: Temple University Press.

Johansson, M. L. 1983. "Midwives' Attitudes to Alphafetoprotein Screening." *Journal of Psychosomatic Obstetrics and Gynecology* 2–4: 237–242.

Johnsen, Dawn. 1987. "A New Threat to Pregnant Women's Autonomy." *Hastings Center Report,* August: 33–40.

Kahn, Robbie Pfeufer. 1988. *The Language of Birth.* Ph.D. dissertation. Waltham, Mass.: Brandeis University.

Kahneman, Daniel, and Amos Tversky. 1982. "The Psychology of Preferences." *Scientific American* 286 (January): 160–173.

Kamerman, Sheila, and Alfred Kahn. 1978. *Family Policy: Government and Families in Fourteen Countries.* New York: Columbia University Press.

Kantrowitz, Barbara, Pat Wingert, Jeanne Gordon, and Sue Hutchison. 1986. "Three's a Crowd." *Newsweek,* 1 September, 68.

Keller, Evelyn Fox. 1984. *Reflections on Gender and Science.* New Haven, Connecticut: Yale University Press.

Kelly, Liz. 1988. *Surviving Sexual Violence.* Minneapolis: University of Minnesota Press.

Kenen, Regina. 1993. *Reproductive Hazards in the Workplace.* New York: Harrington Park Press.

Kessler, Seymour. 1981. "Psychological Aspects of Genetic Counseling." *American Journal of Medical Genetics* 8: 137–153.

———. 1992. "Psychological Aspects of Genetic Counseling VII. Thoughts on Directiveness." *Journal of Genetic Counseling* 1, no. 1: 9–17.

Kevles, Daniel J. 1985. *In the Name of Eugenics: Genetics and the Uses of Human Heredity.* New York: Knopf.

Keyserlingk, Edward W. 1982. "The Unborn Child: Part 2." *Health Law in Canada* 3, no. 2: 31–41.

———. 1983. "Clarifying the Right to Prenatal Care." *Health Law in Canada* 4: 35–38.

Kitay, Eva Feder. 1983. "Womb Envy: An Explanatory Concept." In *Mothering,* ed. Joyce Trebilcot, 94–128. Totowa, N.J.: Rowman and Allanheld.

Klein, Renate, and Robyn Rowland. 1988. "Women as Test Sites for Fertility Drugs: Clomiphene Citrate and Hormonal Cocktails." *Reproductive and Genetic Engineering* 1, no. 3: 251–273.

Kolata, Gina. 1988. "Confident Obstetricians Discovering New Frontiers in Prenatal Diagnosis." *New York Times,* Thursday, 12 May, B7.

———. 1989a. "Gender Selection or Gendercide?" *The Knoxville News-Sentinel,* Sunday, 22 January, Section F, 1–2.

———. 1989b. "Operating on the Unborn." *New York Times Magazine,* Sunday, 14 May, 34–48.

———. 1990. "Alternative Screening of Neural Tube Defects." *New York Times,* 30 August, B 14.

Kolder, Veronica, Janet Gallagher, and Michael Parsons. 1987. "Court-Ordered Obstetrics Intervention," *New England Journal of Medicine* 316 (May 7): 1192–96.

Kolker, Aliza, and B. Meredith Burke. 1988. "Amniocentesis and the Social Construction of Pregnancy." In *Alternative Health Maintenance and Healing Systems for Families,* ed. Doris Wilkinson and Marvin B. Sussman, 95–116. New York: Haworth Press.

Kunisch, Judith. 1989. "Electronic Fetal Monitors: Marketing Forces and the Resulting Controversy." In *Healing Technology,* ed. Kathryn Strother Ratliff, 41–60. Ann Arbor: University of Michigan Press.

Laborie, Françoise. 1987. "Looking for Mothers, You Only Find Fetuses." In *Made to Order,* ed. Patricia Spallone and Deborah Lynn Steinberg, 48–57. Oxford: Pergamon Press.

―――. 1988. "New Reproductive Technologies: News from France and Elsewhere." *Reproductive and Genetic Engineering* 1, no. 1: 77–85.

Lasker, Judith N., and Susan Borg. 1987. *In Search of Parenthood: Coping with Infertility and High-Tech Conception.* Boston: Beacon Press.

Lather, Patti. 1988. "Feminist Perspectives on Empowering Research Methodologies." *Women's Studies International Forum* 11, no. 6: 569–582.

Lauritzen, Paul. 1990. "What Price Parenthood." *Hastings Center Report,* March-April: 38–46.

Leuzinger, Monika, and Bigna Rambert. 1988. " 'I Can Feel It—My Baby Is Healthy': Women's Experiences with Prenatal Diagnosis in Switzerland." *Reproductive and Genetic Engineering* 1, no. 3: 239–249.

Levesque, Louise. 1977. "There Is More to Childbirth Than Having a Baby." Ph.D. dissertation. Waltham, Mass.: Brandeis University.

Levesque-Lopman, Louise. 1988. *Claiming Reality: Phenomenology and Women's Experience.* Totowa, N.J: Rowman and Littlefield.

Lewin, Tamar. 1987. "Courts Acting to Force Care of the Unborn." *New York Times,* 23 November, 1.

Liley, A. W. 1986. "The Foetus as a Personality." *Fetal Therapy* 1: 8–17.

Lindgren, J. Ralph, and Nadine Taub. 1988. *The Law of Sex Discrimination.* St. Paul, Minn.: West Publishing.

Lippman, Abby. 1991. "Prenatal Genetic Testing and Screening: Constructing Needs and Reinforcing Inequities." *American Journal of Law and Medicine* 16, nos. 1–2: 15–50.

Lippman-Hand, Abby and F. Clarke Fraser. 1979a. "Genetic Counseling: Parents' Responses to Uncertainty." *Birth Defects Original Article Series* 15, no. 52: 325–339.

―――. 1979b. "Genetic Counseling: Provision and Reception of Information." *American Journal of Medical Genetics* 3:113–127.

―――. 1979c. "Genetic Counseling—The Postcounseling Period: I. Parents' Perceptions of Uncertainty." *American Journal of Medical Genetics* 4: 51–71.

―――. 1979d. "Genetic Counseling—The Post Counseling Period: II. Making Reproductive Choices." *American Journal of Medical Genetics* 4: 73–87.

Luker, Kristin. 1975. *Taking Chances.* Berkeley and Los Angeles: University of California Press.

———. 1984. *Abortion and the Politics of Motherhood.* Berkeley and Los Angeles: University of California Press.

Lyons, Stephen. 1990. "Ultrasound's Quiet Revolution." *Boston Globe,* 26 November, 27.

Martin, Emily. 1987. *The Woman in the Body: A Cultural Analysis of Reproduction.* Boston: Beacon Press.

Mazor, Miriam D., and Harriet F. Simon, eds. 1984. *Infertility—Medical, Emotional and Social Considerations.* New York: Human Sciences Press.

McKinlay, John B. 1981. "From Promising Report to Standard Procedure: Seven Stages in the Career of Medical Innovation." *Milbank Memorial Fund Quarterly: Health and Society* 59, no. 3: 374–411.

McLaren, Angus. 1984. *Reproductive Rituals.* London: Methuen.

McNulty, Timothy. 1987. "Science Turns Birth into a New Industry." *Chicago Tribune,* 9 August.

Meier, Barry. 1993. "Effective? Maybe. Profitable? Clearly." *New York Times,* Sunday, February 14, Section Three, 1, 6.

Meyers, Diana T. 1989. *Self, Society and Personal Choice.* New York: Columbia University Press.

Miall, Charlene. 1985. "The Stigma of Involuntary Childlessness." *Social Problems* 33: 268–282.

Mies, Maria. 1983. "Towards a Methodology for Feminist Research." In *Theories of Women's Studies,* ed. Gloria Bowles and Renate Duelli Klein, 117–139. London: Routledge and Kegan Paul.

———. 1985. "Why Do We Need All This?" *Women's Studies International Forum* 8, no. 6: 553–560.

Mill, John Stuart. [1859] 1987. *On Liberty,* first published 1859, edited and with an Introduction by Gertrude Himmelfarb. Middlesex, England: Penguin, 1987.

Miller, Beth. 1992. "Private Welfare: The Distributive Equity of Family Benefits in America." Ph.D. Dissertation. Waltham, Mass.: Brandeis University.

Miller, Jean Baker. 1976. *Toward a New Psychology of Women.* Boston: Beacon Press.

Mishler, Elliot G. 1986. *Research Interviewing.* Cambridge, Mass.: Harvard University Press.

Mitchell, Juliet, and Ann Oakley. 1986. *What Is Feminism? A Re-Examination.* New York: Pantheon Books.

Morgan, Kathryn Pauly. 1989. "Of Woman Born? How Old-Fashioned—New Reproductive Technologies and Women's Oppression." In Christine Overall, ed., *The Future of Human Reproduction,* 60–79. Toronto, Ontario: The Women's Press.

Mydans, Seth. 1990. "Science and the Courts Take a New Look at Mother-hood." *New York Times,* 4 November, 6E.

Nebraska Sociological Feminist Collective, eds. 1984. "Feminist Ethics and Social Science Research." *Humanity and Society* 8, no. 4, November (Special Issue).

Nielson, Carol. 1981. "An Encounter with Modern Technology: Women's Experiences with Amniocentesis." *Women's Health* 6: 109–124.

Oakley, Ann. 1979. *Becoming a Mother.* Oxford: Martin Robertson.

———. 1981. "Interviewing Women: A Contradiction in Terms." In *Doing Feminist Research,* ed. Helen Roberts, 30–61. London: Routledge.

———. 1984. *The Captured Womb.* Oxford: Basil Blackwell.

———. 1987. "From Walking Wombs to Test-Tube Babies." In Michelle Stanworth, *Reproductive Technologies,* 57–80, Minneapolis: University of Minnesota Press.

O'Brien, Mary. 1981. *The Politics of Reproduction.* Boston: Routledge and Kegan Paul.

Okin, Susan Moller. 1979. *Women in Western Political Thought.* Princeton: Princeton University Press.

Overall, Christine. 1987. *Ethics and Human Reproduction.* Winchester, Mass.: Allen & Unwin.

———, ed. 1989. *The Future of Human Reproduction.* Toronto: The Women's Press.

Parness, Jeffrey A. 1986. "The Abuse and Neglect of the Human Unborn: Protecting Potential Life." *Family Law Quarterly* 20 (Summer): 197–212.

Pateman, Carole, and Elizabeth Gross. 1986. *Feminist Challenges.* Boston: Northeastern University Press.

Petchesky, Rosalind Pollack. 1983. "Reproduction and Class Divisions of Women." In *Class, Race, and Sex: The Dynamics of Control,* ed. Amy Swerdlow and Hanna Lessinger. Boston: G. K. Hall.

———. 1987. "Foetal Images: The Power of Visual Culture and the Politics of Reproduction." In *Reproductive Technologies,* ed. Michelle Stanworth, chapter 3. Minneapolis: University of Minnesota Press.

———. 1990a. *Abortion and Woman's Choice: The State, Sexuality and Reproductive Freedom.* Boston, Northeastern University Press.

———. 1990b. "Giving Women a Real Choice." *The Nation,* 28 May, 8–11.

Pollitt, Katha. 1990. " 'Fetal Rights'—A New Assault on Feminism." *Nation* 250, no. 12 (26 March): 409–419.

Powledge, Tabitha. 1983. "Windows on the Womb: Prenatal Testing Is Altering Our Attitudes toward the Unborn." *Psychology Today,* 17, no. 5 (May): 37–42.

President's Commission for the Study of Ethical Problems in Medicine and Biomedical and Behavioral Research. 1983. *Screening and Counseling for*

Genetic Conditions. Washington, D.C: U.S. Government Printing Office, February.

Pritchard, Jack A., Paul C. MacDonald, and Norman F. Gant. 1985. *Williams Obstetrics,* 17th edition. Norwalk, Conn.: Appleton-Century Crofts.

Rapp, Rayna. 1984. "The Ethics of Choice: After My Amniocentesis, Mike and I Faced the Toughest Decision of Our Lives." *Ms.* 12, no. 10 (April): 97–100.

———. 1988a. "Moral Pioneers: Women, Men and Fetuses on a Frontier of Reproductive Technology." In *Embryos, Ethics and Women's Rights,* ed. Elaine Hoffman Baruch, Amadeo F. D'Adamo, Jr., and Joni Seager, 101–116. New York: Harrington Park Press.

———. 1988b. "The Power of 'Positive Diagnosis': Medical and Maternal Discourses on Amniocentesis." In *Childbirth in America,* ed. Karen L. Michaelson, 103–116. South Hadley, Mass.: Bergin and Garvey.

———. 1989. "Chromosomes and Communication: The Discourse of Genetic Counseling." In *New Approaches to Human Reproduction,* ed. Linda M. Whiteford and Marilyn L. Poland, 25–41. Boulder, Colo.: Westview Press.

Ratliff, Kathryn Strother. 1989. *Healing Technology: Feminist Perspectives.* Ann Arbor: University of Michigan Press.

Ratterman, Debbie. 1986. " 'Fetal Abuse': A Miscarriage of Justice." *Off Our Backs,* November, 6.

Reilly, Philip. 1977. *Genetics, Law and Social Policy.* Cambridge, Mass.: Harvard University Press.

Reinharz, Shulamit. 1979. *On Becoming a Social Scientist.* San Francisco: Jossey-Bass.

———. 1983. "Experiential Analysis: A Contribution to Feminist Research." In *Theories of Women's Studies,* ed. Gloria Bowles and Renate Duelli Klein, 162–191. London: Routledge and Kegan Paul.

———. 1987a. "Controlling Women's Lives: A Cross-Cultural Interpretation of Miscarriage Accounts." In *Research in the Sociology of Health Care* 7, ed. Dorothy Wertz, 2–37. Greenwich, Connecticut: JAI Press, 1987.

———. 1987b. "The Social Psychology of a Miscarriage: An Application of Symbolic Interaction Theory and Method." In *Women and Symbolic Interaction,* ed. Mary Jo Deegan and Michael R. Hill, chapter 13. Boston: Allen & Unwin.

———. 1988. "What's Missing in Miscarriage?" *Journal of Community Psychology* 16 (January): 84–103.

———. 1992. *Feminist Methods in Social Research.* New York: Oxford University Press.

Rice, Nancy, and Richard Doherty. 1982. "Reflections on Prenatal Diagnosis—Consumers' Views." *Social Work in Health Care* 8, no. 1 (Fall): 47–57.

Rich, Adrienne. 1976. *Of Woman Born*. New York: W.W. Norton/Bantam Press.

Riessman, Catherine Kohler. 1983. "Women and Medicalization: A New Perspective." *Social Policy* 14: 3–18.

Robb, Christina. 1988. "A Theory of Empathy." *Boston Globe Magazine*, 16 October, 19.

Robbins, Sonia Jaffe. 1990. "Depoliticized Motherhood: How Women's Magazines Construct Mothers." Paper presented at Eastern Sociological Society, Boston, Mass., March.

Roberts, Helen. 1981a. *Doing Feminist Research*. London: Routledge.

———. 1981b. *Women, Health and Reproduction*. London: Routledge and Kegan Paul.

Rose, Hilary. 1987. "Victorian Values in the Test-Tube: The Politics of Reproductive Science and Technology." In *Reproductive Technologies*, ed. Michelle Stanworth, 151–173.

Rosenstock, Irwin M. 1974a. "The Historical Origins of the Health Belief Model." *Health Education Monographs* 2: 328–335.

———. 1974b. "The Health Belief Model and Preventive Health Behavior." *Health Education Monographs* 2: 354–438.

———. 1985. "Patient Compliance with Diabetic Regimens." *Diabetes Care* 8, no. 6 (November-December): 610–616.

Rossi, Alice, ed. 1974. *The Feminist Papers*. New York: Bantam Books.

Rothman, Barbara Katz. 1982. *In Labor: Women and Power in the Birthplace*. New York: W. W. Norton.

———. 1984. *Giving Birth*. New York: Penguin Books.

———. 1986. *The Tentative Pregnancy*. New York: Viking Penguin.

———. 1989. *Recreating Motherhood*. New York: W. W. Norton.

———. 1990. "Commentary: Women Feel Social and Economic Pressures to Abort Abnormal Fetuses." *Birth* 17, no. 2 (June): 81.

Rothschild, Joan. 1983. *Machina Ex Dea: Feminist Perspectives on Technology*. Elmsford, N.Y.: Pergamon Press.

———. 1989. "Engineering Birth: Toward the Perfectabiity of *Man?*" In *Science, Technology and Social Progress*, ed. Steven L. Goldman, 93–120. Bethlehem, Pa.: Lehigh University Press.

Rowbotham, Sheila. 1992. *Women in Movement*. New York: Routledge.

Rowland, Robyn. 1985. "A Child at Any Price?" *Women's Studies International Forum* 8, no. 6: 539–546.

———. 1987. "Technology and Motherhood: Reproductive Choice Reconsidered." *Signs* 12, no. 3 (Spring): 512–528.

Ruddick, Sara. 1983. "Maternal Thinking." In *Mothering*, ed. Joyce Trebilcot, 213–230. Totowa, N.J.: Rowman and Allanheld.

Rushing, Beth, and Suzanne Onorato. 1989. "Controlling the Means of

Reproduction: Feminist Theories and Reproductive Technologies." *Humanity and Society* 13, no. 3: 268–291.

Ruzek, Sheryl Burt. 1979. *The Women's Health Movement*. New York: Praeger.

Saltus, Richard. 1990a. "Demand Grows for Fertility Extension." *Boston Globe*, Sunday, 28 October, 35.

———. 1990b. "Bias Issue Looms over Insurers." *New York Times*, 12 November, 33.

Saxton, Marsha. 1984. "Born and Unborn: The Implications of Reproductive Technologies for People with Disabilities." In *Test-Tube Women*, ed. Rita Arditti et al., 298–312.

———. 1987. "Prenatal Screening and Discriminatory Attitudes about Disability." *Genewatch* (January-February): 8–10.

Schuman, David. 1981. *A Preface to Politics*. Lexington, Mass.: D. C. Heath.

Schur, Edwin M. 1984. *Labeling Women Deviant*. Philadelphia: Temple University Press.

Schwarz, Michiel, and Michael Thompson. 1990. *Divided We Stand: Redefining Politics, Technology and Social Choice*. New York: Harvester Wheatsheaf.

Scutt, Jocelynne. 1990. *Baby Machine: Reproductive Technology and the Commercialisation of Motherhood*. London: Merlin Press.

Seals, Brenda F., Edem Ekwo, Roger A. Williamson, and James W. Hanson. 1985. "Moral and Religious Influences on the Amniocentesis Decision." *Social Biology* 32, nos. 1–2 (Spring-Summer): 13–28.

Shaw, Margery W. 1984. "Conditional Prospective Rights of the Fetus." *Journal of Legal Medicine* 5: 63–116.

Sherwin, Susan. 1992. *No Longer Patient*. Philadelphia: Temple University Press.

Silvestre, Danielle, and Fresco, Nadine. 1980. "Reactions to Prenatal Diagnosis." *American Journal of Orthopsychiatry* 50, no. 4 (October): 610–617.

Simon, Herbert. 1986. "Alternative Visions of Rationality." In *Judgement and Decision Making*, ed. Hal R. Arkes and Kenneth R. Hammond, 97–113. Cambridge: Cambridge University Press.

Sjogren, Berit, and Nils Uddenberg. 1987. "Attitudes toward Disabled Persons and the Possible Effects of Prenatal Diagnosis." *Journal of Psychosomatic Obstetrics and Gynecology* 6: 187–196.

Smith, Dorothy E. 1974. "Women's Perspective as a Radical Critique of Sociology." *Sociological Inquiry* 44: 7–13.

———. 1987. *The Everyday World as Problematic*. Boston: Northeastern University Press.

———. 1990. *The Conceptual Practices of Power*. Boston: Northeastern University Press.

Smith, Janna Malamud. 1990. "Mothers: Tired of Taking the Rap." *New York Times Magazine,* 10 June, 32.

Smith, Richard W., and Ray M. Antley. 1979. "Anger: A Significant Obstacle to Informed Decision Making." *Birth Defects Original Article Series* 15, no. 5c: 257–260.

Smith, Sandy. 1990. "Baby Boycott." *Southern Exposure* 18, no. 2 (Summer): 28–31.

Snitow, Ann. 1991. "Motherhood—Reclaiming the Demon Texts." *Ms.* 1, no. 6 (May-June): 34–37.

Spallone, Patricia, and Deborah Lynn Steinberg. 1987. *Made to Order: The Myth of Reproductive and Genetic Progress.* Oxford: Pergamon Press.

Stanley, Liz, and Sue Wise. 1983. *Breaking Out: Feminist Consciousness and Feminist Research.* London: Routledge and Kegan Paul.

Stanworth, Michelle. 1987. *Reproductive Technologies.* Minneapolis: University of Minnesota Press.

Stone, Deborah A. 1988. *Policy Paradox and Political Reason.* Glenview, Ill.: Scott, Foresman.

———. 1990. "Fetal Risks, Women's Rights." *The American Prospect* (Fall): 43–53.

Stone, Jennifer L. 1991. "Contextualizing Biogenetic and Reproductive Technologies." *Critical Studies in Mass Communication* 8, no. 3 (September): 309–322.

Suzuki, David, and Peter Knudtson. 1989. *Genethics: The Clash Between the New Genetics and Human Values.* Cambridge, Mass.: Harvard University Press.

Taub, Nadine, and Sherrill Cohen, eds. 1988. *Reproductive Laws for the 1990s.* Newark: Rutgers University, Women's Rights Litigation Clinic, Institute for Research on Women.

Terry, Jennifer. 1989. "The Body Invaded: Medical Surveillance of Women as Reproducers." *Socialist Review* 19, no. 3 (July-September): 13–43.

Thom, Mary. 1988. "Dilemmas of the New Birth Technologies." *Ms* 16, no. 1 (May): 70–76.

Thomas, Jack. 1991. "Eyewitness to a Century." *Boston Globe,* 9 April, 49.

Todd, Alexandra Dundas. 1989. *Intimate Adversaries.* Philadelphia: University of Pennsylvania Press.

Tong, Rosemarie. 1989. *Feminist Thought: A Comprehensive Introduction.* Boulder: Westview Press.

Trebilcot, Joyce. 1984. *Mothering, Essays in Feminist Theory.* Totowa, N.J.: Rowman and Allanheld.

Tversky, Amos, and Daniel Kahneman. 1981. "The Framing of Decisions and the Psychology of Choice." *Science* 21: 453–458.

Verjaal, Marianne, Nico J. Leschot, and Pieter E. Treffers. 1982. "Women's

Experiences with Second Trimester Prenatal Diagnosis." *Prenatal Diagnosis* 2: 195–209.

Walsh, Mary Roth. 1987. *The Psychology of Women.* New Haven: Yale University Press.

Wasserfal, Rahel. 1990. "Epistemological Choices and Ethical Conflicts of an Israeli Anthropologist Working with Moroccan Women in Israel." Presented at Practicing Feminist Anthropology, *International Interdisciplinary Congress on Women.* New York: Hunter College, June 5.

Wendell, Susan. 1989. "Toward a Feminist Theory of Disability." *Hypatia* 4, no. 2 (Summer): 104–124.

Wertz, Dorothy C. 1993. *Prenatal Diagnosis and Society.* Ottawa, Ontario, Canada: Royal Commission on New Reproductive Technologies.

Wertz, Dorothy C., and John C. Fletcher. 1988a. "Ethics and Medical Genetics in the United States: a National Survey." *American Journal of Medical Genetics* 29: 815–827.

———. 1988b. "Attitudes of Genetic Counselors: A Multi-National Survey." *American Journal of Human Genetics* 42, no. 4: 592–600.

———. 1993. "A Critique of Some Feminist Challenges to Prenatal Diagnosis." *Journal of Women's Health* 2, no. 2 (Summer): 173–188.

———, eds. 1989. *Ethics and Human Genetics: A Cross-Cultural Perspective.* Heidelberg: Springer-Verlag.

Wertz, Richard W., and Dorothy C. Wertz. 1977. *Lying-In: A History of Childbirth in America.* New York: Schocken Books. Expanded edition, New Haven: Yale University Press, 1989.

Whiteford, Linda M., and Marilyn L. Poland. 1989. *New Approaches to Human Reproduction.* Boulder, Colo.: Westview Press.

Williams, Linda. 1992. "Biology or Society? Parenthood Motivation in a Sample of Canadian Women Seeking In Vitro Fertilization." In *Issues in Reproductive Technology: An Anthology,* ed. Helen B. Holmes, 261–274. New York: Garland.

Young, Iris Marion. 1984. "Pregnant Embodiment: Subjectivity and Alienation." *Journal of Medicine and Philosophy* 9, no. 56: 45–62.

Zola, Irving Kenneth. 1983. *Socio-Medical Inquiries.* Philadelphia: Temple University Press.

———. 1990. "Bringing Our Bodies and Ourselves Back In: Reflections on a Past, Present, and Future 'Medical Sociology.'" Address given upon receipt of the Leo G. Reeder Award for Distinguished Scholarship, August 14, Medical Sociology Section, American Sociological Association, Washington, D.C.

———. 1991. "To Our Innermost Parts—Reflections on Nancy Mairs' *Remembering the Bone House—An Erotics of Place and Space. Kaleidoscope* 22 (Winter-Spring): 48–50.

Index

abortion, 86, 87, 100, 109, 116–20, 129; amniocentesis and, 100, 178 n.2; experiences, feelings, and choices about prenatal diagnosis, 117–20; John Stuart Mill and, 10; negative liberty and, 10; positive liberty and, 10–11

Abraham, Sarah, 31, 96, 114, 149

abstract thinking about disability, 111–12

access (or lack thereof): to prenatal care, 40; to primary health care, 40, 172 n.2; to procreative technologies, 34

ACOG (American College of Obstetricians and Gynecologists), vii, 23

Adams, Penny, 33, 57, 58, 60, 69, 72, 75, 79, 87, 88, 118, 121, 122, 150

Addams, Jane, viii

advanced maternal age (AMA): amniocentesis and, 50, 95; assumptions about, 44–45

advice, unsolicited, 120–22, 139–40

AFP (alphafetoprotein) test, 4, 65, 85, 86, 87–88, 98, 106, 107–8, 110, 112, 121, 132, 161 n.2, 175 n.1, 176 n.4; Swedish midwives' views of, 176 n.5

age: choice and, 133; decision to attempt pregnancy and, 29, 33–34; "only chance" pregnancies and, 70; perceptions of risk status in pregnancy and, 97, 112; recommendations for amniocentesis and, 50

agency, 30, 58. See also women as agents of own lives

alienation: and ultrasound, 92–93; of women from own fetuses, 25

ambiguity: of choice, 5, 129, 132, 133, 157; of feelings about prenatal diagnosis, 114; of pregnant state, 114; of prenatal diagnosis results, 116, 178 n.20

ambivalence, 127, 137; about AFP, 110; and bodily changes in pregnancy, 73, 77; and choice of health provider, 48; and disability, 114; about impending motherhood, 70–71, 77; about learning fetal sex, 102–3; and mother/worker role conflict, 76; about prenatal diagnosis and high-tech pregnancy, 98, 116, 124–25; about ultrasound image, 92–93

amnio. See amniocentesis

amniocentesis, 66, 85, 87, 89, 92, 93, 98–99, 103, 106, 115–16, 125, 127, 131, 132, 137, 143, 158, 161 n.2, 175 n.1; automatic recommendation of, 35, 50, 88–89; code word for abortion, 116; concerns about invasiveness of ("the big needle"), 94; feelings about abortion and, 116–20; secrecy and, 119–20

Anderson, Jill, 31, 46, 50, 51, 55, 60, 65, 71, 90, 92, 102, 103, 105, 119, 150

anencephaly, 86

anti-abortion feelings, 88, 116

anticipation of motherhood, 70–71

anxiety about pregnancy, 7

Ashley, Sara, 32, 100, 150, 158

"assisted reproduction," 3
Aston, Laura, 33, 50, 51, 58–59, 64, 65, 69, 77, 79, 87, 88, 89, 90, 95, 98, 101, 103, 112, 118, 121, 125, 150
autonomy and choice, 133, 138, 139, 141–46; pregnant women's, threats to, 25–26

babies as products, 22–23
baby versus pregnancy, 64–67
Barber, Virginia, 122
barriers impeding procreative choice, 34, 48, 171 n.6
Bateson, Mary Catherine, ix, 157
Beeson, Diane, 66
Bell, Susan E., 177 n.9
Betts, Marta, 65, 89, 98, 149, 150
Bickerson, Marie, 36, 51, 61, 62, 143, 150
biological determinism, 142
biological reductionism, 80
biology and procreative control, 141–42. *See also* myth of procreative choice/control
blame, 120, 127, 128; for miscarriage, 175 n.22
Blatt, Robin J. R., vii
bodies, feelings about changes in, 71–73
body image, changes during pregnancy, 71–73
bonding, and ultrasound, 91
Boston, health providers in, versus more rural areas, 41
Boston Women's Health Book Collective, vii
"bounded rationality," 14–15. *See also* rational choice model
breastfeeding advice, 121
burden of knowledge, 114
bureaucracy metaphors and women's bodies, 82. *See also* Martin, Emily

Carder, Angela, 26
censure or judgment by others, 48, 119, 120, 122, 123, 127, 128, 135, 137
cerebral palsy, 111
cesarean sections, forced, 140, 180 n.10
childbirth, 82, 117, 121
childhood experiences with disability, 111
Chodorow, Nancy, 170 n.62

choice: and American political theory/ideology, 9–11; to attempt pregnancy, 32–34, 55; as central concept in American culture, 9, 143; complicated process of, 5, 124; and control, conflated, 26–27; ethical and political, 4; explicit and implicit, 30–32; and feeling fully human, 143; of health provider, 40–53, 131; to learn sex of baby, 89, 100–105; after positive prenatal diagnosis, 117–20; repeated attempts at, in effort to take control, 5–6; rhetoric of, 9; whether to have prenatal diagnosis, 85–88, 90, 93–100
choosers, women's sense of selves as, 142, 144. *See also* agency; *contrast with* illusory choices; social construction; social control
chorionic villi sampling (CVS), 87, 95, 116, 131, 158, 161 n.2, 162 n.6
"code names" of women, 161 n.1
cognitive dissonance, 48, 99
"commitment" to the pregnancy (Lauren Fagan), 70
commodification: of babies, 22–23; of reproduction, 22; of women's bodies, 19
commonalities among women's experiences, 5–6, 32–33
comparing pregnancies, 32
compulsory sterilization, 24
conception: deliberate attempts, 30; planned, 32–34; time (Jill Anderson), 31
conceptive techniques, 3
confirmation of pregnancy, 54–58
conflation of pregnancy and motherhood, 174 n.19
connections among women during pregnancy, 123
constraints: impeding choice of health provider, 40–48, 52; on other choices, 130
contexts and decision-making, 31, 32–34, 120, 130, 145, 157; intersecting, 132
contextual aspects of pregnancy, 79
continuum, 49
contraception decisions, 30
contraceptive failures, 34–35
contradictions. *See* ambivalence; paradox
contradictory evidence for choice as real, illusory, 133

contradictory impacts of prenatal tests, 125
contradictory responses to choice, 136
control: assumptions about, 6; conflated with choice, 26–27; elusiveness of, 5; illusory aspects of, 6, 8, 148; quest for, 5
cystic fibrosis, 115

"dating" of pregnancy, 88–9, 92, 108
Davis, Alison, 24
de Beauvoir, Simone, 170 n.62
decision analysis, 14
decontextualization of pregnancy, 78–79, 80. *See also* medical model of pregnancy
DES, 19, 71
determinism, technological, 18
dilemma of choice versus control, 47
Dinnerstein, Dorothy, 170 n.62
directiveness, 50
disabilities: inadequate social supports for, 130; lack of exposure to people with, 113; women's own, 114
disability, 86, 95, 96, 110–16, 117, 173 n.8; attitudes about, 142; and choice of prenatal diagnosis, 111–16; discrimination, 145; experiences with, 110–16; feelings about raising a child with, 10–11; perception of burden on family, 111
disability rights movement: and activism regarding access, 142; and prenatal diagnosis, 24
Disabled Women for Life (United Kingdom), 24
diversity of women's experiences, 32, 54
doctors as managers, 82
Doe, Jane, 65, 94, 151
domains of choice within constraints, 143
"double-edged sword," prenatal tests as, 124
Down syndrome, 97, 98, 112–13, 114, 115, 116, 119, 124, 127, 137, 161 n.2

"early amnio," 95
ectopic (tubal) pregnancy, 82
egalitarian or "welfare" feminism, 12
elective abortion, 32
elusiveness of control, 141, 147. *See also* illusory choices

embedded choices, 116, 125, 130–31, 132
embryo implantation, 3
emotional "insurance," 59–60
enjoyment of pregnancy, 61
epidural, advice about, 12
Erlich, Greta, 89, 149, 151
essentialism: negative versus positive, 20; positive, and power of female biology, 80
ethic of caring, 120
eugenics, 23–24
euphoria as response to positive pregnancy test, 55
existentialist feminism, 170 n.62
experiences, as individual and particular, 5
experiential factors in choice, 111–12, 113, 114–16, 117–19
exploitation of physicians and patients by manufacturers, 22–23
expropriation of women's bodies, 19

factors in choosing health provider, 43–44
Fagan, Lauren, 33, 62, 65–66, 69, 70, 72, 73, 74–75, 76, 77, 79, 88, 94, 97–98, 100, 101, 113, 117, 133, 137, 143, 151
failures of procreative technologies, 35
false consciousness, 142–43. *Contrast with* agency
false positive and AFP, 87–88, 89, 107
family influence on choice of prenatal diagnosis, 113, 120, 124, 142
family practitioner: holistic approach of, 47; preference for, 41–42
fears during pregnancy, 62–63, 111
female as norm, as opposed to male as norm, 84, 175 n.31
feminism: and liberalism, 11. *See also* liberal feminism; radical feminism; socialist feminism
feminist: "abolitionist" stance regarding procreative technologies, 19–20; approaches to social research, viii, 155–56; critique of biological reductionism, 80; critique of objectivity, 83, 155; critique of procreative technologies, 8; epistemology, 155; health activism; 141. *See also* liberal feminism; radical feminism; socialist feminism
"fetal containers," women as, 23, 25
fetal protection, 169 n.58

fetal rights: and anti-abortion film *(The Silent Scream)*, 169 n.55; used to thwart women's autonomy, 25–26
fetal sex, 101; feelings about, 105; and prenatal perceptions of baby, 101–2. *See also* choice, to learn sex of baby
fetology, 25
fetus, focus on, 25, 92
"fetus" versus "baby" (language), 172 n.4
FINRRAGE (Feminist International Network of Resistance to Reproductive and Genetic Engineering), 19
Firestone, Shulamith, 20
Fisher, Sue, 83
Fletcher, John C., 167–68 n.46
Foster, Jane, 38, 46, 50, 51, 61, 63, 65, 88, 90, 96, 98, 99, 114, 151
Frey, Louise, 44–45, 56, 57, 61, 64, 65, 91, 94, 98–99, 100, 103–4, 126, 127, 130, 143, 151
Fryer, Meg, 45, 48, 49, 60, 88, 89, 98, 103, 122, 151

gamble, pregnancy as, 99
genetic counseling, 159
genetic counselors, 96, 98, 109, 110, 146, 179 n.7
genetic information available from amniocentesis, 94
geneticists, and goals of genetic counseling, 23, 167–68 n.46
genetics: information, 4; markers, 4; "revolution," 4
Gerson, Deborah, 145
GIFT (gamete intrafallopian transfer), 3
Gilligan, Carol, 120, 131
"going public," 138; about amniocentesis, 119–20; about miscarriage, 58–60; about pregnancy, 58–59
"good mothers," 135, 137
"good pregnant person," 136
Graham, Hilary, 83
Greil, Arthur L., 145
guilt about "wrong" decisions, 48, 127–28, 136. *See also* censure or judgment by others

Harrison, Michelle, 86
hazards during pregnancy, 71
health behavior model, 14
health maintenance organization (HMO),

and limited choice of health providers, 42–43
health provider, selection of, 40–53, 141
heterosexuality, assumption of, 173 n.11
high-pressure approach, of health providers, 51
"high-risk": pregnancy, worries about care during, 41; women, medical and women's definitions of, 96–100
high-tech: age, 54; medicine, 49–51; women, versus low-tech women, 49–51
holistic approach to health care, 51, 88; of family practitioners, 47
home births, 10–11, 44–45
home-pregnancy-test kits. *See* pregnancy tests
homophobia, 48
hopes for baby, 113–14
Howard, Rachel, 32, 33, 41, 45, 65, 79, 89, 90, 91, 98, 136, 151
Hughes, Nancy, 62, 105, 152
human genome research, 4; and controversy, 4–5
Hunneycutt, Blossom, 2, 68–69, 152
husband's feelings: about learning fetal sex, 109; about prenatal diagnosis, 115, 124, 130

ideology: of choice, 141, 143, 145; impacts of, on choices, 48
illness model of pregnancy, 81
illusory choices, 128, 129, 133, 141, 157, 159
images of pregnancy, 61–63
images of resistance in women's discourse, 83, 159. *See also* Martin, Emily
implicit planning of pregnancy, 35
inconclusiveness of AFP test, 87
individual, emphasis on in liberal feminism, 13–14
inducements to doctors to use technologies, 23
inequality between women and men, 12
infertility, 36–37, 52, 68, 135, 141, 143, 171 nn.7, 8; secondary, 36–37. *See also* precious pregnancies
information: available from AFP test, 86–88; empowering, 104, 140
informed choice: and information about disability, 114; in liberal feminism, 16
internalization of medical model, 95

intervention in pregnancy, 2, 3
"intuition" and awareness of pregnancy, 54–55, 57
invasions of privacy: babies, in amnio, 94, 137; pregnant women's, 122–23, 139–40
invasiveness of prenatal tests, 86, 87, 93
IUD, 19
IVF (in vitro fertilization), 3

joy: at learning of pregnancy (Jane Lowe), 55; and precious pregnancies, 70

Kahn, Robbie Pfeufer, 74, 76, 141

Lee, Dorothy, 49, 61, 78, 102, 105, 109, 114, 116, 117, 152
"left-overs," as metaphor for women's ways of choosing, 143, 180 n.13
liberal feminism: and American liberalism, 11; emphasis on individual, 12; limits of, 15; and procreative choice, 11, 133, 144; and procreative technologies, 12; and women's choices of health providers, 52; and women's choices of prenatal tests, 93–94, 125. *See also* egalitarian or "welfare" feminism; libertarian or "classical" liberal feminism; *contrast with* radical feminism; socialist feminism
liberalism in American politics, 9–11, 142
libertarian or "classical" liberal feminism, 12, 163 n.6
liberty: libertarian feminist definition of, 12; John Stuart Mill's view, 10; negative versus positive definitions of, 10
life circumstances and choice to become pregnant, 33–34. *See also* social location(s)
limits of procreative choice. *See* myth of procreative choice/control
"live free or die," as statement of libertarian liberalism, 10
loss of boundaries in pregnancy, 123
Lowe, Jane, 32, 43, 46, 54–55, 57, 66, 72, 89, 90, 98, 100, 107–9, 111, 117, 124, 135, 136, 152
low-intervention versus high-intervention style of medical care, 49–51

"low-tech" medicine, 49–51. *Contrast with* "high-tech" medicine
Luker, Kristin, 74
Lynn, Bernadette, 78–79, 89, 121, 149, 152

McAllister, Carol, 33, 43, 45, 48, 49, 52, 65, 72, 88–89, 107, 114, 132, 152
male: bias in scholarship, viii; feeling at "Mountain Clinic," 46; and medical control of women's procreative processes, 52. *See also* woman doctor
malestream approaches, 131, 155; feminist critiques of, 120
marketing of prenatal diagnosis, 23
Martin, Emily, 73, 82–83, 141, 149, 159
Martineau, Harriet, viii
maternal/fetal conflict, 79, 80
"maternal mode" (Jane Lowe), 66, 67
maternal responsibility, 127; and guilt feelings, 48, 135, 137
maternal serum alphafetoprotein screening. *See* AFP
meaning of pregnancy: for different women, 129; women's versus medical perceptions, 78–81
medical control of women's procreative processes, 7, 18–19, 52, 139–40; and maternal/fetal conflict, 80
medical experts, 80; intervention of, and "better baby," 81
medicalization of pregnancy, 162 n.3
medical model of pregnancy, 78, 79, 80, 129, 132, 133, 142, 145; and amniocentesis decision, 95; compared with women's perceptions, 78–84; and illness orientation, 81; and other "choices," 85–86, 125
Mell, Betty, 31, 41, 45, 51, 65, 76, 77, 92–93, 97, 100, 117, 118, 131, 136, 153
menopause, 82
menstruation, 82
metaphors and women's procreative processes, including menopause and menstruation, 82
methodology of study, 155–59
Meyer, Mary, 100, 153
Michaels, Evelyn, 33, 60, 65, 77, 105, 117, 153
midwife, 41, 43, 44–45, 49
"midwifery model" (Barbara Katz Rothman), 84

Mies, Marie, 19
Mill, Harriet Taylor, 162 n.3
Mill, John Stuart, 10, 12, 162 n.3
miracle pregnancies, 69
miscarriage, 32, 35, 37–39, 52, 82, 87,
    90, 95–96, 99, 104, 109, 120, 129, 131,
    140–41; failure of doctors to mention,
    37–38; influence on feelings during sub-
    sequent pregnancies, 38–39, 69; in rela-
    tion to "going public," 58–60
mixed message presented by women's
    stories, 52
"mixed-zone" workplaces (Robbie
    Pfeufer Kahn), 76, 141–42
monopoly over ob/gyn care in area
    where several of the women live, 52
mother-blaming, 128, 137, 147
motherhood, 117, 134
"mother-to-be," 64
"Mountain Clinic," 46–47. *See also*
    "Town Clinic"
myth of procreative choice/control, 27,
    34–39, 51–52, 141; biology and, 141.
    See also infertility; miscarriage

nested choices. *See* embedded choices
neural tube defects: lack of information
    regarding range of presentation or
    prognosis, 114; perception of, 113
nondirectiveness, 146
"normal" pregnancy, 85
Norplant, 19

Oakley, Ann, 66, 83
objective versus subjective views of preg-
    nancy, 80–81
"obstacle course," pregnancy as, 6, 8, 38
obstetrician, choice of, 41
"obstructrics" (Robbie Pfeufer Kahn),
    174 n.17
"only chance" pregnancy, 69–70

paradox: of choice, 2–5, 51, 93, 127, 133
    138–40; of medical expectations of
    "normal trajectory" in pregnancy, 86;
    of precious pregnancies, 70
paradoxical: aspects of pregnancy experi-
    ence, 71; aspects of risks and choices,
    125, 145; risks involved in "going pub-
    lic," 59–60
pathology, pregnancy as, 81
patriarchy, 19–21, 27, 155

Patrick, Helen, 149, 153
"perfection ideology," 24; and capital-
    ism, 26; and disability rights move-
    ment, 24
Petchesky, Rosalind Pollack, 66, 92
phases of pregnancy, 78
phenomenological descriptions of men-
    struation, 83
philosophy of care, 42, 47–48, 49, 50,
    131
policy development, women's voices
    and, 146
Pollitt, Katha, 25
postmodern feminism, 170 n.62
precious pregnancies, 68–70
pregnancy: attempts to "capture" the ex-
    perience, 65; as gamble, 38–39; high-
    tech, 1–2; as "honeymoon," romantic
    time, 61–62; loss, 37; loss of control
    and, 62–63; medical model of, 78, 79,
    80, 81; monitoring during, 1; as pathol-
    ogy, 81; and physical problems, 62–
    63; as preparation for being a mother,
    77; and redefinition of self, 64; schedul-
    ing/planning of, 29–30, 32–34; stories,
    1–2; as symbol of sexuality, 73; tests
    during, 1–2, 175 n.1. *See also* miscar-
    riage; myth of procreative choice/con-
    trol; pregnancy tests; pregnant identity
pregnancy tests, 54–58, 63; home tests,
    54–55, 56; and mediating role between
    women and their bodies, 56–57; and
    success at "attaining" pregnancy, 58;
    and validation of own feelings, 54
pregnant identity, 63–64, 67; and body im-
    age/weight gain, 73; and changes in
    sense of self at home, 76; and conflict
    with professional/work identity, 73; and
    feeling "different," 67; and joining a
    "maternity," 81; muted, 67–68; as op-
    posed to having a baby, 65–66; partial ac-
    ceptance of, 67
"pregnant persons," and discrimination
    against women, 140, 173–74 n.12
pregnant women as experts on pregnancy,
    146
prenatal baby pictures. *See* ultrasound
"prenatal child abuse," 25–26. *See also*
    mother-blaming
prenatal diagnosis: as choice enhancing,
    3; and control, 138–39; lack of informa-
    tion about, 115–16; and perceptions of

baby, 66; previous research about, 156; and reassurance, 3; and usurpation of women's own bodily sensations, 66. *See also* alphafetoprotein (AFP); ambiguity; amniocentesis; choice of prenatal diagnosis; disability; ultrasound

pressures: to act "not-pregnant" at work, 74–75; to learn fetal sex after amniocentesis, 102–3; to pursue motherhood, 135; and women's choices, 121, 133, 139–40

previous experience and choices about prenatal diagnosis, 106–9

private decisions, 119–20, 139

privilege, and women in study, 40, 157–58

pro-choice, 116, 117, 118

procreative choice: and feeling responsible, 18; versus procreative control, 18–19; social construction of, 18–19. *See also* myth of procreative choice/control

procreative freedom: struggles to maintain, 141; threatened by anti-choice activists, 34

procreative technologies: as choice-enhancing, 3; controversy about, 4–5; as liberating, 1–3; and social control, 3–4. *See also* prenatal diagnosis

production metaphors for women's procreative processes, 82. *See also* Martin, Emily

"products" of procreation, 23

professional socialization of doctors, 41

professional/work identity, incompatibility with pregnant identity, 73, 174 n.13

profitability of reproductive technologies, 22–23

pro-natalism, 134, 144

psychoanalytic feminism, 170 n.62

public dimensions of pregnancy, 79, 139–40

public persona, pregnant woman as, 123

quality control: of children, 22; and eugenics, 24; in pregnancy, 23

"quickening," 65–66

quilting, as a metaphor for women's choices, 143

racism, 48

radical feminism, 16–21, 52, 125, 144; and false consciousness, 17; and illusion of choice, 16–17; and negative and positive essentialism, 20; and procreative control, 18–19; and social construction of choice, 17–18, 48; and social control of women, 7; and technology as liberating, 20

Rapp, Rayna, 159

rational choice model, 13–14, 93, 126, 132, 148; and choice of health provider, 52; and choices regarding prenatal diagnosis, 126–27; consistency with liberal feminism, 13; critiques of, 15–16; decision-analysis as example of, 14; health behavior model as example of, 14

reassurance, ultrasound and, 90–91

reforms in development and distribution of procreative technologies, liberal feminist view, 12–13

Reinharz, Shulamit, viii, 38, 140

relational notion of autonomy, 145

relational decision-making, 120–21, 125, 130

reliability of prenatal tests, 86

relinquishment: of control, 138, 139; of custody of children, 135; as deliberate strategy, 51; of pregnant identity (Louise Frey), 64; of privacy, 119, 122; of sense of self as independent, 76

"reproductive roulette" (Kristin Luker), 6, 31

responsibility: and blame, 120, 136; and choices, 134–40; feelings of, 133

retrospective rationalization regarding choices, 48

rhetoric of choice, 9; as marketing technique, 9; and mother-blaming, 128; and status quo maintenance, 27

Riessman, Catherine Kohler, 145

risk: and choosing prenatal diagnosis, 124; women's versus medical notions of, 94, 106

risk factors in pregnancy, 23, 71, 86, 96, 175–76 n.3; changed view of, following miscarriage, 38; perceptions of, 86–88, 126, 133; and prenatal diagnosis, 113–14, 118, 146. *See also* "high-risk"

risks: of going public, 58–59; of ultrasound, 90; "younger" versus "older" women's perceptions of, 96–99

risks/benefits analysis, 94, 95, 125
role conflict: employee/out-of-home
  worker versus expectant mother/
  mother roles, 73–76
role strain. *See* role conflict
Rothman, Barbara Katz, viii, 66, 80, 84,
  101, 105, 129, 173 n.7
"routine" intervention: medical versus
  women's views, 90; ultrasound as, 108
routinization of use of procreative
  technologies, 3; and assumptions about
  need for testing, 4
Rowland, Robyn, 18

Sanders, Barbara, 4, 51, 59, 65, 69, 95,
  105, 112, 121, 126, 153
Saxton, Marsha, 24, 114
secret amnios, 119–20, 140
sexism, 48, 144, 155
sexist approach of doctors at "Mountain
  Clinic," 46
sex-role stereotyping, prenatal, 101–2
sexuality and pregnant body(ies), 73
"showing," 63, 75. *See also* visible pregnancy
siblings, feelings about in relation to attempting pregnancy, 33
sickle cell anemia, 99
signs of pregnancy, 63
Silent Scream, The, 169 n.55
Simas, Anna, 31, 46, 49, 50, 51, 58, 65,
  69, 81, 88, 97, 117, 119, 127, 153
Simon, Herbert, 13–14
Skaggs, Merrill M., 122
skepticism about test results, 56–58
Smith, Barbara, 2, 37, 42, 49, 51, 64, 69,
  80, 88, 96, 97, 104, 112, 114, 117,
  153–54
Smith, Dorothy E., 155
social category, pregnancy as, 63
social childbirth versus medicalized childbirth, 19
social class and women's differing descriptions of their procreative processes, 83. *See also* Martin, Emily
social construction, 142, 147; of "choice"
  in radical feminism, 17–19, 24, 26, 133;
  of pregnancy, 79
social contexts of choices during pregnancy, 24, 120
social control, 139; in radical feminism,
  17–19, 133, 138; of women, 138, 140,

  144, 169–70 n.58, 179–80 n.9,
  180 n.10
socialist feminism, 21–24, 144; dual versus unified systems theories of,
  167 n.39; and commodification of reproduction, 22–23; and constraints on
  choice, 48, 52; and Marxist feminism,
  21–22
socialization, 134, 142, 179 n.5
social location(s), 79, 130, 159
sonogram. *See* ultrasound
specialists in obstetric care, 49
spina bifida, 86, 112, 127. *See also* neural
  tube defects
standard-of-care, advertising's contribution to, 23
standpoints of women, vii, 156, 158
statistical risks: and choice to have prenatal diagnosis, 114, 116, 137, 138; versus subjective feelings, 113–14
Stewart, Pamela Rae, 26
stigma and body weight, 79
stillbirth, 82
Stone, Deborah A., 164 n.18
subjectivity, and perceptions of high-
  and low-tech medicine, 49–51
support, female, needed in pregnancy
  and birthing, 47
survival strategies, choices as, 143
Swanson, Sara, 33, 47, 57, 65, 67–68, 72,
  81, 89, 98, 102, 110–11, 123, 130, 154

Taylor, Harriet, 12, 162 n.3, 163 n.5. *See
  also* Mill, John Stuart
Tay Sachs, 99
technological "fix," 18
technology: and development of standard
  of care, 17–18; role in patriarchal society, 27
"tentative pregnancy," 66, 129, 173 n.7.
  See also Beeson, Diane; Rothman, Barbara Katz
termination of pregnancy, feelings about,
  in relation to prenatal diagnosis, 112–
  13. *See also* abortion
tests. *See* pregnancy, tests during; pregnancy tests; prenatal diagnosis
Thomas, Roxanne, 32, 42, 45, 46, 55,
  62, 72, 79, 88, 89, 98, 100, 101, 118,
  121, 132, 136, 154
timing of pregnancy, 30
Todd, Alexandra Dundas, 83

Tong, Rosemarie, 170 n.62
"Town Clinic," 45–47; versus "Mountain Clinic," 46–47
trajectory of pregnancy, 78, 85, 86
transformation of constraints into control, 77
trust of health providers, and impact on choice of prenatal diagnosis, 111

ultrasound, 85, 88, 89, 90–93, 103, 106, 107, 109, 115, 118, 125, 126, 132, 158, 161 n.2; as alternative to amniocentesis, 176–77 n.6; and "bonding," 91; as "cheap thrill" (Louise Frey), 91; discomfort during, 90–91, 108; and emphasis on fetus, 25; as empowering experience for women, 91; and feelings about pregnancy, 65, 66; lucrativeness of, 177 n.7; and question about viability of pregnancy (Laura Aston), 37; and reassurance, 90–91; seeing the baby during, 90–93; unknown risks of, 71; as "window on womb," 25; women's desire for, 89–90
uncertainty about choice of prenatal diagnosis, 115
unplanned and "surprise" pregnancies, 35, 118

valorization: of female biology, 20; of women, ix
videotaping baby's image during ultrasound, 90

violations of personal autonomy during pregnancy, 75
visible pregnancy, 122–23. *See also* "showing"
visual information. *See* ultrasound

weight gain during pregnancy, 72–73, 79
Wells, Ida B., viii
Wertz, Dorothy C., 145, 162 n.3, 167–68 n.46
Wilson, Nancy, 2, 3, 36, 60, 65, 69, 80, 89, 95, 96, 109, 115, 121, 130, 154
Wollstonecraft, Mary, 12, 163 n.5
woman doctor, preference for, 41–42, 43–44, 45, 47, 49
"womb envy," 20
women as agents of own lives, ix, 30, 39, 58, 140–41, 142, 143, 144, 147, 159. *See also* agency
women in study, 149–54; as privileged group, 40, 157–58
women's experiences of pregnancy, versus medical model, 78–84
women's health movement, 34, 141, 145, 171 n.5, 180 n.14
women's voices: in feminist research, 155, 156; and social policy, 146, 156
worries about possible teratogens during pregnancy, 63
Worthington, Sarah, 1–2, 3, 6, 13, 21, 26, 29, 38, 41, 45, 62, 65, 75, 88, 97, 105, 112, 114, 117, 119, 123, 133, 141, 154, 158